The Raindrop Connection

The Raindrop Connection

Connecting the Dots of Erosion, Sediment,
and Pollutant Control at Construction Sites

JOHN M. TERAVSKIS,
QSP/QSD, CPESC, CESSWI, QISP, ToR
and WGR Southwest, Inc.

PALMETTO
PUBLISHING
Charleston, SC
www.PalmettoPublishing.com

Copyright © 2025 by WGR Southwest, Inc.

All rights reserved.

This book may not be reproduced, in whole or in part, including illustrations, in any form (beyond that copying permitted by Sections 107 and 108 of the U.S. Copyright Law and except by reviewers for the public press), without written permission from the author.

Hardcover ISBN: 9798990550308
Paperback ISBN: 9798990550315
eBook ISBN: 9798990550322

Acknowledgments

This book is a compilation of the lessons I've learned from many storm water professionals, including David Franklin, John McCullah, Rich Muhl, Bob Shults, Mary Larsen, and Robin Tully. But I also owe much to others connected to our industry, such as construction managers, farmers, landscape specialists, engineers, park rangers, municipal staff, and the regulatory community. All of these individuals and many others have, as David Franklin says, held my "two-wheeler bicycle up" as I learned to steady myself and make the connections of effective storm water management. Of course, I want to also acknowledge my longtime employer and friends at WGR Southwest, Inc. who have believed in many of my unorthodox and somewhat crazy ideas. And then there is also my lovely and devoted wife, Kerry Sue, and our three children, their spouses, and our first grandchild, who are my biggest fan club and source of encouragement. Without their prayers and support, I probably would have given up long ago. I also want to acknowledge my true source of inspiration and strength, my Lord and Savior, Jesus Christ. As Proverbs 3:4-5 says, "Trust in the Lord with all your heart and lean not on your own understanding. In all your ways acknowledge Him, and He will direct your paths." I am sure glad He directed my path into storm water in 1992 by having me read the first issuance of the General NPDES Permit and suggesting I "dabble in it."

Dedication

This book is dedicated to those who not only want to create SWPPPs and install and inspect BMPs but who also want to understand the whys and hows behind what we do on a daily basis. It is also for the person who goes to the Grand Canyon to *gawk and ponder*—not on what they see but on what is missing and how it was removed. It is dedicated to those wanting to connect the dots in their minds and on the jobsite.

Contents

Acknowledgments v
Dedication vii
Foreword xiii

Why It Is Important 1
The Problem 1
The Disconnect 3
Making the Connections 5

Connecting the Dots of Erosion and Sediment Theory 7
Definitions 8
Agents and Accelerators 12
Rain Erosion 14
Wind Erosion 22
Movement Erosion 29

Connecting the Dots of Pollutant Source Assessment 33
Identifying the Construction Activities 33
Identifying Pollutant Sources within Each Activity 42
Associating Pollutants with Sources 48
Determining the Quantity and Physical Characteristics of the Pollutants 57
Identifying Pollutants That May Be Exposed to Storm Water 60
Identify What Is Being Protected 68

Connecting the Dots of Best Management Practices 73
Standards for BMPs 74
Site Management BMPs 82

- Scheduling (SM-1) 82
- Budgeting and Procurement (SM-2) 84
- Pollution and Spill Prevention (Cover, Secure, and Contain) (SM-3) 88
- Wind and Fugitive Dust Controls (SM-4) 92
- Education and Training (SM-5) 103
- Expectations and Enforcement (SM-6) 109

Raindrop BMPs 115
- Scheduling (RD-1) 115
- Maintain Existing Effective Soil Cover (RD-2) 117
- Establish Temporary or Permanent Effective Soil Cover (RD-3) 118
- Maximize Organic Content (RD-4) 134

Slow-the-Flow BMPs 138
- Linear Controls (SF-1) 139
- Speed Bumps (SF-2) 163
- Fat Spots (SF-3) 173
- Flow Spreaders and Energy Dissipators (SF-4) 176

Treatment BMPs 180
- Compost Socks and Berms (T-1) 180
- Treatment of Tires (T-2) 184
- Treatment of Streets (T-3) 189
- Treatment Trains (T-4) 193
- Active Treatment Systems (T-5) 198
- Passive Treatment Measures (T-6) 200
- De-watering (T-7) 204

Corrective Action and Maintenance 207

Connecting the Dots of SWPPP Development 209
- Choose the Right SWPPP Document Format 211

    Make Sure the SWPPP Developer Meets the Requirements of the Regulatory Agency That Has Jurisdiction over the Project 228

    Do Your Homework First by Getting to Know the Project Site 257

    Crunch the Numbers 284

    Develop SWPPP Maps That Tell the Story of the Project from Beginning to End 312

    Identify the Players Involved in the Project 316

    Incorporate the Pollutant Source Assessment and BMP Selection 318

Connecting the Dots of an Effective Monitoring Program 321

    Identify Run-on and Run-off Locations 322

    Inspector Qualifications 328

    Permit-Required Inspection Program 331

    Permit-Required Monitoring Program 338

    Tools of the Trade 350

    Using the Data for Connecting the Dots 352

Connecting the Dots of Final Site Stabilization 355

    Full SWPPP Implementation 355

    Final Stabilization 358

    Post-construction Storm Water Control Measures 361

    Permit Termination 372

Closing Summary 375

List of Acronyms 379

Index 383

The Raindrop Connection Resources 389

LIST OF TABLES

For up-to-date versions of the tables, go to https://wgr-sw.com/theraindropconnection/

Table 1 – Agents and Accelerators of Erosion on Construction Sites	13
Table 2 – Trades, Construction Activities, and Potential Pollutant Sources	34
Table 3 – Water Quality Conditions	49
Table 4 – Inventory of Potential Pollutant Sources	62
Table 5 – Dust Palliatives	96
Table 6 – Methods of Communication	104
Table 7 – Soil Covers	122
Table 8 – Linear Control Cost Comparisons	150
Table 9 – Linear Control Measures	152
Table 10 – DI Protection Scenarios	166
Table 11 – Construction SWPPP Development Requirements by State	230
Table 12 – Runoff Coefficients for Various Surface and Soil Types	286
Table 13 – Runoff Curve Numbers	291
Table 14 – C Factors for Selected Construction-Related Cover Methods	307
Table 15 – P Factors for Construction Sites	309
Table 16 – Storm Water Run-on Locations	324
Table 17 – Storm Water Pre-Grading Discharge Location	325
Table 18 – Storm Water Discharge Locations During Construction	326

LIST OF EQUATIONS

Equation 1 – Wind Erosion Equation	26
Equation 2 – Fluid Flow Rate	176
Equation 3 – Weighted Runoff Coefficient	288
Equation 4 – Runoff Volume	289
Equation 5 – Time of Concentration	290
Equation 6 – Rational Equation	294
Equation 7 – Revised Universal Soil Loss Equation	298

Foreword

Remember back before you could ride a bike? You know, tricycle days. Then one day, you realized you were ready for two wheels, and your dad or another adult spent time, hours, days holding up your bike until that magical moment. You were on your own! And they say that once you learn, you never forget how to ride a bike.

In our world of Storm Water Management, knowing how to ride a bike is referred to as being a "Qualified Person." Becoming a Qualified Person is the result of receiving support from someone who has gone before—someone who knows how to hold up the bike.

The Raindrop Connection is one of many reformations introduced to the world of storm water compliance by author John Teravskis, someone who has truly gone before. His vision over the last decades has provided the storm water world with professionally produced training videos, free and informative monthly newsletters for industrial and construction storm water readers, thousands of hours of free professional development units provided yearly via the creatively conceived Storm Water Awareness Week where subject matter experts provide one-hour workshops that attendees can view live or online later.

There are many avenues to understanding how to control erosion and prevent pollution from construction sites. Notable to the path taken by the Raindrop Connection is the focus and feel. The focus is technical accuracy on topics ranging from calculations to chemistry, principles to practices, regulations to responsibilities, and assessments to assertions that are then delivered in a conversational, easy to understand feel. Whether using your head or using your hands, connecting the dots of storm water management is made approachable.

The Raindrop Connection serves as a guide that allows users to logically assess regulatory compliance as it applies to their unique construction site conditions in a manner that is not overthought. This frees users to apply their own diligence and creativity in the problem-solving process while helping to avoid the pitfalls of canned or habitual prescriptions.

Artwork by Abigail Teravskis

Nowhere in the grand world of construction is the scope of work so egregiously misunderstood and destructively implemented on a regular basis than in that specialty field we call Storm Water Management. Yet, protecting our nation's water resources for today and for the future need not be elusive, expensive, or futile. There are answers; there are tools; there is pride in knowing that you know how to make a difference. Think of the Raindrop Connection as that hand on the back of the seat of your two-wheeler. Are you ready to hop on and never forget?

David Franklin
EnviroTech NPDES Services

CHAPTER 1
Why It Is Important

THE PROBLEM

Figure 1 - Soil loss at a subdivision project. (Photo credit: John Teravskis)

According to a 2009 report published by the United States Environmental Protection Agency (USEPA), at that time, construction was taking place on approximately 853,000 acres in the continental United States.[1] Studies show that the average soil loss rate for an unprotected construction project ranges from 100 to 500 tons/acre/year. So, if we multiply the number of construction acres with an annual soil loss of 100 tons/acre and assume an average soil density of 1 gram/cm^3, it equates to 2.1 trillion cubic feet of soil loss per year. That would be equivalent to excavating

---

1   USEPA Environmental Impact and Benefits Assessment for Final Effluent Guidelines and Standards for the Construction and Development Category, November 2009, EPA-821-R-09-012, https://www.epa.gov/sites/default/files/2015-06/documents/cd_envir-benefits-assessment_2009.pdf.

20 feet of dirt from 2,412 acres every year.[2] That's a lot of dirt being carried off of construction sites by water, wind, and equipment. So, what's the big deal? Why does it matter? The problem lies in where the dirt (or sediment) ends up. When sediment is suspended in a waterbody that supports aquatic life, it can cause fish to suffocate by clogging their gills or by causing dissolved oxygen to plummet. Suspended soils also cause the waterbody to warm, which may have an impact on organisms that are dependent on cooler waters and affect the food chain for that environment.[3] Furthermore, when sediment settles in a waterbody, it can bury habitats, benthic[4] organisms, and fish eggs. Solids that settle out in rivers and dams may have a detrimental effect on navigation and flood control. Both suspended and settleable solids can reduce the usefulness of a waterbody for drinking water, agriculture, and recreation. And, of course, unintended soil loss from a parcel of land can have economic impacts for the land owner, the contractor, and those having to address the sedimentation in municipal drainage systems and receiving waters.

The real problem, though, is that we often do not recognize the erosion and sedimentation problem until it is too late—until the damage has been done or the violation has been issued by the regulatory agency. The owner of the construction project and the contactor are often surprised by how they ended up in trouble with the State or Federal government—they just didn't see it coming. They didn't make the Raindrop Connection.

---

[2] Shirley Morrow, Michael Smolen, Jim Stiegler, and Janet Cole, Ohio State University, Using Vegetation for Erosion Control on Construction Sites, February 2017 https://extension.okstate.edu/fact-sheets/using-vegetation-for-erosion-control-on-construction-sites.html#:~:text=The%20typical%20construction%20site%20can,500%20tons%2Facre%2Fyear

[3] National Oceanic and Atmosphere Administration (NOAA), Nonpoint Source Pollution - Suspended Sediments; https://oceanservice.noaa.gov/education/tutorial_pollution/011sediments.html.

[4] Organisms associated with the bottom of a waterbody.

THE DISCONNECT

Figure 2 - The climbing fence wattle. (Photo credit: Jonah Sonner)

While in California, we have seen many people become certified as Qualified SWPPP Practitioners (QSPs) and Qualified SWPPP Developers (QSDs) since 2010, and there is far more awareness of best management practices, Storm Water Pollution Prevention Plans (SWPPPs), and the storm water regulations; however, there still seems to be a lack of adequate controls at many construction sites as evidenced by poor storm water runoff quality. It is like there is a disconnect between the sound pollution prevention principles contained in NPDES[5] permits, many SWPPPs, and what happens in the field. This is further evidenced by how best management practices (BMPs)[6] are used or installed. For instance, fiber roll (which we often refer to as miracle

---

5 National Pollutant Discharge Elimination System, a permitting mechanism specified by the Clean Water Act; USEPA NPDES Permit Basics; https://www.epa.gov/npdes/npdes-permit-basics.

6 "Best Management Practices (BMPs are management practices and structural controls used to prevent or reduce the discharge of pollutants from runoff, spillage or leaks, sludge or waste disposal, or drainage from raw material storage to waters of the United States. BMPs include scheduling of activities, prohibitions of practices, operation and maintenance procedures, treatment, and vegetated infiltration basins amongst other practices." From the California Construction General Permit Order 2022-0057-DWQ Glossary, Attachment B; https://www.waterboards.ca.gov/water_issues/programs/stormwater/construction/docs/2022-0057-dwq-with-attachments/cgp2022_att_b.pdf.

roll) is flung out on the ground and expected to "do its thing." It is almost as if there is a mystical reliance on this "straw in a sausage casing device" that is laid out around the project's perimeter without staking it down or keying it in. Many project managers expect it to magically control all erosion and sedimentation issues. Lest we place too much blame on the installers, it is not always their fault. They are paid to install the BMPs per the Erosion and Sediment Control Plan. Frequently SWPPP preparers view the Construction General Permit's requirement for establishing and maintaining an effective perimeter sediment control to literally mean that every inch of the project's perimeter must be surrounded with fiber roll or silt fence no matter where the perimeter traverses. As a result, we have seen the ridiculous: fiber rolls going uphill, along the top of the hill, across creeks and other areas of concentrated flow, across paved surfaces and driveways, and even up and over chain link fences! I remember inspecting a site where silt fence was installed up against a four-foot-high concrete retaining wall. During the past decade, we have not been training QSPs and QSDs to install sediment control measures in this way, so what is causing the disconnect? I have had many conversations with Regional Water Quality Control Board staff who have expressed similar concerns based on what they are seeing in the SWPPPs and the BMPs installed (or not installed) in the field. They often lament over, or are even angered by, SWPPPs certified by a QSD but lacking adequate erosion and sediment controls, or by site inspections that the QSP signed off as having no issues, but actual field conditions clearly would indicate otherwise. These state inspectors wonder, "Where is the disconnect?" Was their training inadequate? Is the QSP/QSD program flawed? Is there a loophole that allows individuals who lack fundamental knowledge of erosion and sediment control to become certified QSPs and QSDs? Is it due to lack of quality control, laziness, or human nature? Or is it because QSDs are oftentimes so removed from the field that they miss the obvious and are out of touch with reality at the construction project? Perhaps QSPs are overworked or have taken on or been given more projects to manage than feasible.

Why It Is Important

In the California 2022 renewal of the Construction General Permit (CGP), it is evident that the permit writers at the State Water Resources Control Board have also been receiving similar feedback from the Regional Board inspectors, because new requirements have been incorporated into the renewed permit. In an attempt to get QSDs to become more in touch with the field, they are now required to visit their projects at the beginning of construction, at least twice a year, and when there is a transition to a new QSD. In addition, whenever there has been a numeric action level exceedance for pH or turbidity, both the QSP and QSD will need to inspect the site (presumably together) to identify the cause and to work together to identify appropriate corrective action. The 2022 CGP also includes new language that allows the State Water Board to suspend the certification of a QSP or QSD if, in the course of their duties, they demonstrated a lack of adequate knowledge or training. Once suspended, they cannot be reinstated until they have obtained additional training. The permit also authorizes the Water Board to rescind any QSP or QSD certification if at one or more sites they either willfully or negligently caused or allowed a violation of the CGP; submitted false or misleading information to the Water Board; used fraud or deception; or failed to use reasonable care and good judgment.

MAKING THE CONNECTIONS

The purpose of this book is to help storm water professionals make the necessary connections at construction projects to protect water quality. To what connections are we referring? The connection of theory to practice. The connection of permit compliance to sound best management practices. The computer screen to the subdivision lot. Budget line items to what is actually installed and maintained. The actions we take to the water quality we are protecting and desire to retain.

And the connection of the start of the project to its completion. To that effect, this book is organized in the following way:

- Connecting the dots of erosion and sediment theory
- Connecting the dots of pollutant source assessment
- Connecting the dots of best management practices
- Connecting the dots of SWPPP development
- Connecting the dots of an effective monitoring program
- Connecting the dots of final site stabilization

NOTE TO THE READER:
Because I am from California and have spent my career practicing erosion and sediment control in the Golden State, I tend to be quite California-centric. Therefore, the majority of my regulatory references and illustrations will be based on the California NPDES Construction General Permit, the State Water Resources Control Board, and its nine Regional Water Quality Control Boards. However, the bulk of the information presented in this book is applicable to the Federal Clean Water Act, the USEPA Construction General Permit, and, therefore, to any of the Construction General Permits issued by other States. Table 11 in Chapter 5 contains information and links to the Construction General Permits for all fifty states of the Union.

CHAPTER 2
Connecting the Dots of Erosion and Sediment Theory

If you wanted to compose a symphony for an orchestra, it would be absolutely necessary to know a few things about music theory. Without an adequate understanding of meter, rhythm, key signatures, and notes, the musicians would end up producing a cacophony of random and dissonant notes, resulting in a disastrous end to your budding musical career. In the same way, cooks need to know the science behind cooking, pilots need to know avionics, and medical professionals need to know something about physiology. It is no different in the field of erosion and sediment control. Applying random BMPs on a SWPPP map or on a construction site might not send everyone running out of the concert hall covering their ears, but you will probably not see the type of water quality you were hoping for in your storm water discharges. To correctly specify BMPs, you need to know something about the problem needing to be addressed—namely, erosion and sedimentation. Therefore, it is vital for SWPPP writers and storm water inspectors to be well schooled in erosion and sedimentation theory.

DEFINITIONS

Let's start with defining erosion. According to the State Water Board's glossary in the CGP[7]:

> "Erosion is the process, by which soil particles are detached and transported by the actions of wind, water, or gravity."

The key word in this definition is "detached." When a soil particle becomes detached it has been eroded. In the natural world, erosion is constantly occurring all around us. Even the most durable things like granite, concrete, and asphalt erode over time; albeit perhaps slowly, but they are still losing particles due to external and internal forces. The State Water Board's definition mentions that the particles are transported by wind, water, and gravity. But it does not specify what the agents of erosion are—or those forces that cause particles to become detached. More about that later.

But that's only half of the story. We are talking about erosion *and* sedimentation theory. So, we need to talk about the other side of the coin. Now, I get it. For convenience, oftentimes we just refer to it all as "erosion controls." From time to time, I will receive a phone call from a contractor saying something like, *"Hey, could you giv' me a quote for that SWPPPie thang?"* I have come to learn what the contractor means is for us to develop a site-specific SWPPP, prepare the Notice of Intent on the State Water Board's SMARTS website, perform the QSP inspections and sampling, provide training for the on-site personnel, prepare the annual

---

[7] CGP Order WQ 2022-0057-DWQ, Attachment B; https://www.waterboards.ca.gov/water_issues/programs/stormwater/construction/docs/2022-0057-dwq-with-attachments/cgp2022_att_b.pdf

Connecting the Dots of Erosion and Sediment Theory

reports, and submit the Notice of Termination when the project is complete. But it is much easier to refer to it all as the "SWPPPie thang." In our desire for convenience, it is important to not forget the need to address sedimentation as much as we address erosion, for both are equally important. The State Water Board gives us a definition of sedimentation:

> "Sedimentation is the process of deposition of suspended matter carried by water, wastewater, or other liquids, by gravity. It is usually accomplished by reducing the velocity of the liquid below the point at which it can transport the suspended material."

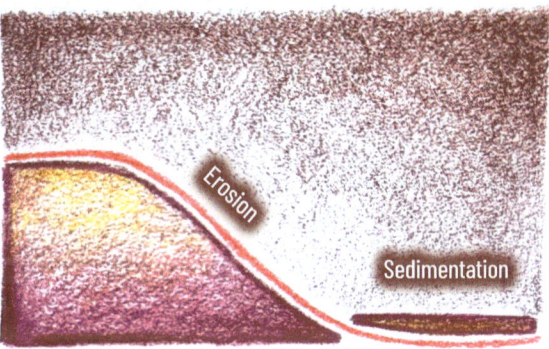

Figure 3 - Erosion occurs where water is moving fast; sedimentation happens where water slows down. (Sketch by Abigail Teravskis)

Erosion is directly proportional to the velocity of runoff. The faster water is moving, the more erosion there will be. But, when we slow water down, eroded particles being transported by the water can settle out when the forces of gravity supersede the forces exerted by water movement. The particles (sediment) are then deposited in these areas of slow flow. Fast water will usually occur where there are slopes. Slower water is found on flatter surfaces. I often will tell contractors that the enemy of erosion control is fast water. So, slow the flow!

Figure 4 - Chain link fence sediment control measure. (Photo credit: John Teravskis)

To illustrate the effectiveness of slowing the flow, take a look at Figure 4—a photo that I took several years ago while performing a site inspection. The erosion and sedimentation observed in the photo were caused by a single storm event.

But look carefully at the sedimentation and note where it is in relation to the chain link fence. You will observe it is on the uphill side of the fence. What is it doing there? What caused it to be deposited there? Did the chain link filter the sediment? Many people believe fiber rolls and silt fence filter storm water. But that is because they do not understand erosion and sedimentation theory. The chain link fence obviously did not filter it. So, what happened? It slowed the flow down just enough to allow sediment particles to deposit at that spot. Of course,

I think these sandy particles were just begging for an excuse to drop out, which the fence provided. Did some get past the fence? You bet they did! But not all of the sediment. Count the links of fence to see how much was deposited—two to two and a half links! How tall is the linkage on a chain link fence? Almost three inches. Therefore, in this single-storm instance, over half a foot of sediment was deposited because the flow was slowed by some galvanized wire. We can only wonder how much more sediment would have been caught if a silt fence had been placed along the uphill side of the chain link fence.

Figure 5 - At least six inches of sediment was "caught" by the chain link fence during a single storm event. (Photo credit: John Teravskis)

When preparing erosion and sediment control plans, it is important to address both concepts—erosion *and* sediment control. Many plans we review for municipalities do not adequately address both. Usually, only sedimentation controls are specified such as fiber rolls, track-out controls, drain inlet protection, and stockpile management. When asking contractors if they plan on installing erosion controls, I will often hear, *"Yeah, it's there!"* while pointing out the fiber roll placed along the perimeter. A good erosion and sedimentation control plan consists of erosion control, which keeps soil particles from becoming detached; and sediment control, which captures on-site any particles that might have become detached. You need both for adequate site control and a fighting chance to protect the water quality of the discharge.

AGENTS AND ACCELERATORS

I was hiking in the Grand Canyon and, if you know anything about me, you will know I was looking at the canyon walls rather than the overall scenery. I'm fascinated by erosion. For me it is an hourglass that is constantly dropping grains of sand to the bottom. While on the Hermit Trail, I ran across an impressive display of erosion as shown in Figure 6.

Figure 6 - Seven forms of erosion visible on the Hermit Trail in the Grand Canyon. (Photo credit: John Teravskis)

There are no fewer than seven separate agents of erosion visible in this one photograph. And that is in a natural setting! On a construction site there are even more. Therefore, erosion can occur much more quickly and dramatically than in a natural setting because of the construction-related erosion accelerators. Table 1 lists significant agents of erosion and erosion accelerators present at construction sites.

Table 1 – Agents and Accelerators of Erosion on Construction Sites

Agents	&	Accelerators
Storm water		Removal of vegetation
Non-storm water		Run-on that comes into contact with areas of soil disturbance
Wind		Removal of topsoils with high organic content exposing underlying soils with low organic content and removal of wind-breaking canopy and duff cover.
Chemicals and salts		Failure to minimize the necessary use and to eliminate the avoidable discharges.
Vehicle traffic		Creating points of concentrated flow (by pumping or channeling water)
Foot traffic		Creating temporary (e.g., plastic sheeting) or permanent (e.g., pavement or roof tops) impervious surfaces which flow onto areas of soil disturbance
Use of heavy equipment		Stockpiles

This list is by no means comprehensive but represents common significant agents and accelerators of erosion. While it may be impracticable—and probably impossible—to prevent the agents of erosion from doing their work to detach soil particles, something can be done to mitigate the effects of the accelerators. We will identify the accelerator mitigation measures in the form of best management practices (BMPs) in **Chapter 4**. But first, let's look at the processes of three particular agents of erosion that are often the focus of construction site SWPPP plans: rain, wind, and movement.

RAIN EROSION

In the 1940s, the United States Department of Agriculture prepared a short cartoon to address soil conservation.[8] It is a clever depiction of the somewhat naughty Junior Raindrop as it chronicles his story from Papa Cloud to Mother Earth where he forms a gang of hooligan raindrops and creates havoc. The cartoon's narrator states that the destruction Junior caused *"isn't Mother Earth's fault. She just isn't getting enough cooperation from the people living in the U.S. of A."* While the message of the cartoon was addressing agricultural related soil conservation issues resulting from the previous decade's Dust Bowl environmental disaster, the message now resonates with a more modern audience—construction sites.

Junior and his gang of delinquent raindrops has switched their attention from overgrazed range land to large subdivision projects, where oftentimes bare soil can be exploited by them. The cartoon actually does a very good job of illustrating the various processes involved in rain erosion. And it all starts with Junior!

---

[8] The Adventures of Junior Raindrop; by U.S. Dept. of Agriculture, Forest Service; 1948; https://www.loc.gov/item/2018601440/

Connecting the Dots of Erosion and Sediment Theory

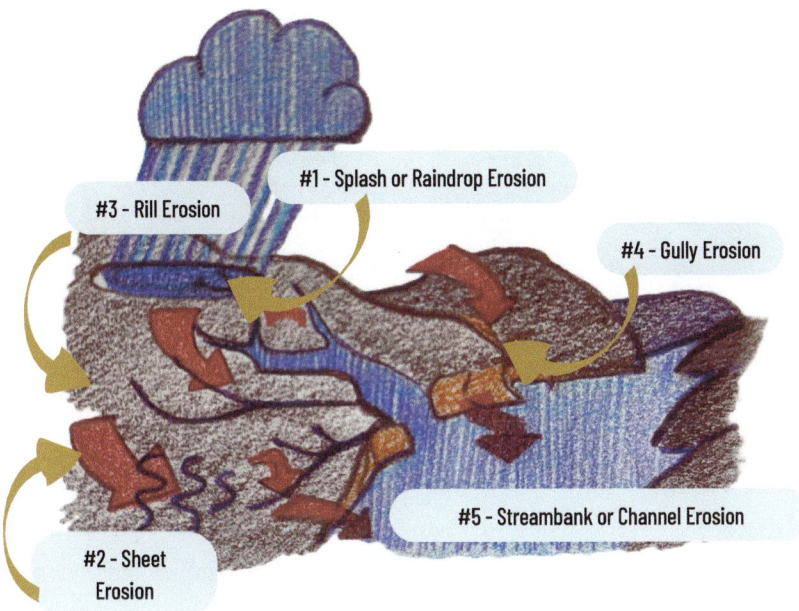

Figure 7 - Five processes of erosion - Source: USDA (Sketch by Abigail Teravskis)

There are five stages to uncontrolled erosion, and we will look at each of them. But erosion starts with the raindrop. Every raindrop that hits the earth is like a miniature bomb. After all, raindrops fall from the sky at a relatively high velocity. Applying physics to a raindrop (assuming a raindrop radius of 0.3 mm), we get a terminal velocity of 10.9 m/s (24.4 mph).[9] What happens when Junior hits the dirt at this speed? He creates a crater—well, a very small one.

---

9   The terminal velocity of a raindrop is 10.9 m/s for a raindrop with a radius 0.3 mm falling through the air of viscosity (η)= 1.8×10^{-5} Ns/m². The density of raindrop (ρ) = 103 kg/m³, acceleration due to gravity (g) = 9.8m/s² and the density of air we will consider negligible. Weight of a raindrop **ρ x volume** (v) of the sphere calculated using the formula **4/3(πr^3 ρg)** is assumed to equal the drag force on the spherical raindrop expressed as **6 π η rv_t**, where v_t is terminal velocity. Solving for v_t, we find that the raindrop is traveling 10.9 m/s when it hits the ground.

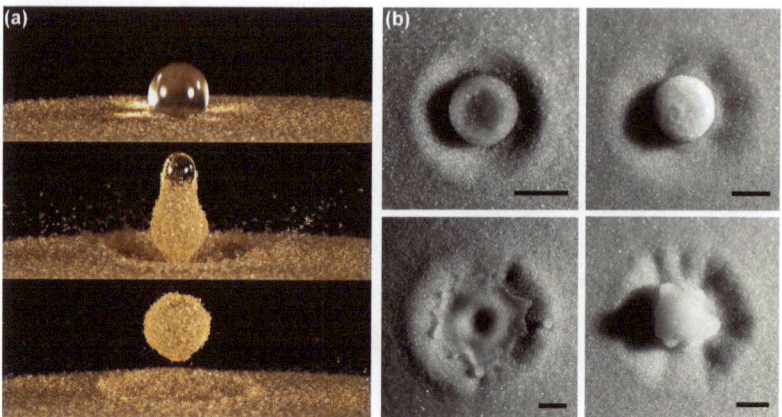

Figure 8 - University of Minnesota study on the impact of a raindrop.

The University of Minnesota studied the impact of a raindrop [10] and found that the crater it produces is, in fact, similar to craters produced by massive asteroid strikes on planetary bodies. The researchers took high resolution rapid photographs of a drop of water falling onto a bed of fine glass beads. Figure 8 shows the results of the impact. The black bars shown in the gray colored photos (b) represent 3 mm. The displaced volume within the raindrop crater in this laboratory demonstration was 880 mm^3, which equates to 0.05 cubic inches. Not much you say? Well, that is only *one* raindrop. But how many raindrops fall on a one-acre project during a storm that produces 0.5 inches of rain? Approximately 1.2 trillion! [11] If each one displaces only a third of the volume of the above photographed laboratory example,

---

10 Runchen Zhao, Qianyun Zhang, Hendro Tjugito, and Xiang Cheng, University of Minnesota Department of Chemical Engineering and Materials Science, *"Raindrop impact on a sandy surface"*, Physics of Fluids 27, 091111 (2015) https://doi.org/10.1063/1.4930917 Dynamics and morphology of granular impact cratering by liquid drops. **(a)** Dynamics showing the impact of a 3.1-mm-diameter water drop on a granular surface composed of 90 μm glass beads. The impact energy $E = 9.5 \times 10^{-6}$ J. The duration of the impact is about 60 ms. **(b)** The resulting impact craters at four different impact energies. From the upper left corner in clockwise order: $E = 1.2 \times 10^{-5}$ J, 3.9×10^{-5} J, 8.2×10^{-5} J, and 2.8×10^{-4} J. Scale bars: 3.0 mm. Source: APS-DFD (http://dx.doi.org/10.1103/APS.DFD.2014.GFM.V0015) and https://aip.scitation.org/doi/abs/10.1063/1.4930917 (for copyright information).

11 The number of raindrops in a gallon of water depends upon the size of the raindrop and can be more than one million, but for this demonstration we will use a conservative value of 90,000 drops/gallon. A 0.5" rainfall on a one-acre jobsite (43,560 ft^2) would result in a precipitation volume of 1,815 ft^3 or 13,576 gallons. Using the conservative drops/gallon figure, approximately 1.2 billion raindrops fell on that one-acre parcel.

approximately 11,458 ft³ (424 cubic yards) of soil would be displaced just from Junior and his gang of hooligans! This is what is called **Raindrop or Splash Erosion**. And that's only the beginning of the site's erosion problems. There are four more processes that may occur on the project.

Figure 9 - Raindrop or Splash Erosion in sandy soil. (Photo credit: Mike Lewis)

As we saw in the video, Junior doesn't stay by himself for very long; he joins with other raindrops. Flowing downgradient in a laminar or sheet flow condition, we might say. In proportion to the slope inclination, this film of water can "push along" or "carry on its back" those particles of sediment displaced by the raindrop bombs. This second process of erosion we call **Sheet Erosion**. This is the sneakiest form of erosion, because it's difficult for our eyes to see the sediment in the laminar flow against the backdrop of the surface from whence they were detached. Only further downgradient will you realize your project has been robbed blind of tons of sediment, oftentimes valuable topsoil! This condition is more visible to the eye as the water becomes increasingly turbid and viewed against different backgrounds. If you ever had the opportunity to observe a soil-exposed slope over the course of the wet season, you might have noticed that it almost appears like someone was dumping aggregate on the surface. Throughout the winter months you start to see more and more coarse sands and gravel on the surface of the slope. Well, guess what? You were robbed and didn't even know it! What you were actually observing was sheet erosion. With this form of erosion there are not the telltale signs like we will see in the next processes. Sheet Erosion removes the fine particles and leaves the coarse ones in place. So, from a distance, it looks like everything is holding up and that you dodged the erosion bullet. You have to get close to the surface to see what is actually happening or go to downgradient sediment control measures and see what has deposited behind them. This form of erosion can account for many tons of soil loss, because while the raindrop detaches the sediments, sheet flow moves them!

Figure 10 - Have you been the victim of a robbery? The coarse aggregate is often the clue the thief left behind. (Photo credit: Jonah Sonner)

Water likes to take the easy road; it tends to move to paths of preferential flow. This is where the next form of erosion occurs: **Rill Erosion**. At these locations of preferential flow, soil loss occurs at a higher rate than the surrounding areas. Therefore, as particles are detached and transported away, a depression in the soil occurs and a rill is formed. The working definition of a rill is something that you can easily step over. We will see bigger forms of erosion later. But it is important to note where the rills are forming, because they will tell you what is happening at the site. A misunderstanding of rills may result in a significant waste of money, time,

Figure 11 - Top-down rill erosion. Hydraulic mulch had been applied to the slope, but it was run-on that caused the problem. (Photo credit: John Teravskis)

and effort for a project that is trying to control erosion. Years ago, we had a project along a stretch of the California Delta levees that was wrapping up its construction activities. The contractor wanted to finish their portion of the work and decided to apply a hydraulic mulch / hydroseed mix to the landside surface of the levee slope. Noting the compacted roadway at the top of the levee, we commented that run-off controls should be installed along the levee road to dissipate and spread out the flow from the roadway onto the slope or to provide slope drains to provide a controlled flow from the roadway to the base of the slope. The contractor did not want to extend the project any longer and chose to, instead, apply a durable hydraulic mulch blend at a greater application rate (not a cheap proposition!). In spite of our warning that it may be a waste of money, the mix was applied. After the next series of storms, our predictions proved to be accurate. Rills extended from the top of the slope to the bottom, much like what is shown in Figure 11. We knew that would be the result because we had been watching rills form at the top of the slope throughout the life of the project.

But sometimes rills do not form at the top of the slope and instead begin to take shape ten to thirty feet down the slope. This is a different problem and therefore needs a different solution. Remember Junior and his gang? After landing on the surface of the slope and traveling ten-plus feet down the slope, the gang finds a path of preferential flow, and that is where the rill begins. This is why the California Construction General Permit requires Risk Level 2 and 3 projects to install linear sediment controls along the face of the slope and at the grade breaks of exposed slopes. The linear sediment controls (typically fiber rolls) are required by the permit to be spaced between ten and thirty-five feet apart depending upon the slope ratio. Essentially, these linear sediment controls stop the sheet flow and "reset the clock" (so to speak) for rills. A properly installed horizontal line of fiber roll will, at least in theory, "buy" another ten to thirty-five feet of sheet flow travel before rills once again become likely to occur. Now make no mistake about it, raindrop and sheet erosion are still occurring, but these linear sediment controls will hopefully keep the erosion processes from progressing beyond them and help capture any particles that became detached.

When rills start to intersect and runoff flows become greater, far more sediment will be removed from the—now combined—paths of preferential flow. More water with greater velocities means greater soil loss, which leads to the next erosion process—**Gully Erosion.** The working definition of a gully is something that you can stand in. Figure 14 shows a gully we could easily put the whole construction crew in. There are many factors that can lead to the formation of gullies, such as the nine back-to-back atmospheric rivers that occurred from late December 2022 through mid-January 2023 in California. They can also result from poor site management and planning. Directing too many drainage management areas into a single flow path will cause gullies to form in erodible soils. The combined flows will result in greater volumes of runoff and higher flow rates and will overwhelm the undersized conveyance. But, to get to this stage of erosion, a project usually fails to regard the three earlier forms of erosion elsewhere on the project and is not applying adequate controls

Figure 12 - Rill beginning partially down the slope. Linear sediment controls would have prevented this occurrence. (Photo credit: John Teravskis)

Figure 13 - An effective use of linear sediment control measures on a slope. (Photo credit: John Teravskis)

to slow and manage the flow. Gullies are typically a symptom of a bigger problem.

The last of the five erosion processes is **Channel Erosion**. Now, as we mentioned before, erosion is natural and is constantly occurring even in the hardest of rock or most stabilized channel. In a stream or a river, channel erosion, sometimes referred to as stream bank erosion, is part of the healthy balance of that waterbody. But it is the erosion accelerators that typically lead to channel erosion that are detrimental to water quality.

Figure 14 - A fifteen- to twenty-foot deep gully that formed during the nine atmospheric rivers that hit California from late December 2022 through mid-January 2023. (Photo credit: Matt Lewis)

Channel erosion will typically not occur on a construction site or would even be attributed to a single construction project. Rather, it is the result of changes in a watershed. Table 1 identifies erosion accelerators for construction sites, but when these accelerators are occurring to a significant level in a watershed, channel erosion may and probably will occur in a downgradient waterbody or conveyance. With new development comes more impervious surfaces. Increase imperviousness results in more frequent discharges, higher peak flow rates, and greater volumes. When this increase of discharge from a watershed flows through a downgradient concrete-lined channel we might not see much change other than higher and more frequent flows. But when the water reaches a portion of the channel that is erodible, guess what gives! The erodible channel is the weak link, and it is where we observe channel erosion. This not only results in

Figure 15 - Natural Channel Erosion in Death Valley off of Artist Drive. (Photo credit: John Teravskis)

significant increases of sediment in the waterbody but will also threaten habitat along and in the channel; cause downstream dams, reservoirs, or lakes to fill up with sediment; threaten properties along the eroding banks of the channel; and potentially cause flooding at the point where the eroded sediment settles out.

Yes, Junior and his gang of delinquent raindrops can cause quite a mess. But they are not the only agent of erosion that typically attacks a construction site. Next, we will address Agent Wind.

WIND EROSION

We often hear contractors exclaim that they do not need erosion controls because it is in the middle of the dry season and there will not be any rain for months. What they fail to realize is that there are other agents of erosion at work even when there are no clouds in the sky. Soil particles can and do become detached even on dry days, especially when the wind is blowing. Wind erosion can occur in three different forms—I like to call them the three S's of wind erosion: saltation, soil creep, and suspension.

Connecting the Dots of Erosion and Sediment Theory   23

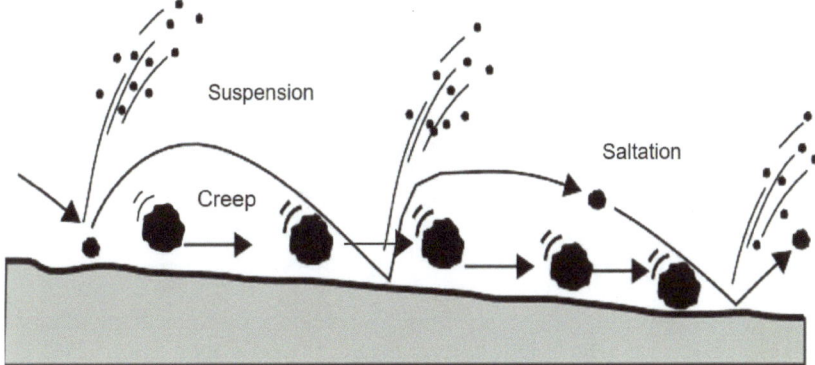

Figure 16 - Three S's of Wind Erosion. Graphic from the USDA Dust Mitigation Handbook.

According to the United States Department of Agriculture (USDA) Dust Mitigation Handbook, these 3 S's are defined as follows: [12]

Saltation: This is when individual particles, typically 0.1 to 0.5 millimeters (mm) in diameter, lift off of the soil surface at a 50- to 90-degree angle. But gravity and air resistance shortly overcome the force of the wind and cause the particles to fall back to the surface at a 6- to 14-degree angle from horizontal. When these particles strike the ground, they very much do the same thing that the raindrop does when it hits the ground—they break loose other particles. You might think of saltation as a self-propagating form of erosion. The impact of these particles can be quite forceful when driven by the wind. The USDA calls them *"abrading bullets that remove the protective soil crusts and clods."* Around 50 to 80 percent of soil transported off-site due to wind erosion is from the saltation process. One way to remember this form of wind erosion is to recall the Spanish verb for *"to jump,"* which is *saltar*—for jumping particles.

---

12   Smarik, S., S. Aney, A. Boes, D. Brown, D., Dubois, B. Edwards, E. Elias, M. Eve, R. Steele, N. Webb, M. Wilson, G. Zwicke,. 2019. Dust mitigation handbook. Las Cruces, NM: U.S. Department of Agriculture. Chapter 2

Figure 17 - The power of saltation can be observed on Death Valley's ventifact ridge (located across from the turnoff for Artist Drive). Specimens of basalt and other hard igneous and metamorphic rocks have been sand blasted and whittled down by the wind-driven particles. Pitting can be observed on both sides of these "ventifacts" because the wind direction changes. In the photos shown above, small piles of sand are located on the southside of the rock, which is the most recent lee side due to the wind coming from the north. (Photo credit: John Teravskis)

Soil Creep: I often joke that this is a geologist. But in the context of wind erosion, it is when sand-sized particles, and sometimes even small aggregates, are set in motion horizontally along the ground surface propelled by the wind. You may remember seeing the ground appear to be moving when you were outside during a very windy day. Like saltation, soil creep is also a self-propagating form of erosion. The friction of particles moving along the ground breaks other particles loose. Soil creep can account for 7 to 25 percent of soil loss from a site due to wind erosion.

Suspension: This is the form of wind erosion that most people think of. It's that dust cloud blowing off your project, which may very well get you in trouble with the local air district. Suspended dust clouds are made of the finer soil particles, less than 0.1 mm in diameter. According to the USDA, some of the suspension particles are present in the soil, but many are created by the other two forms of wind erosion. Depending on the soil texture, 20 to 60 percent of the wind eroded particles that are transported off-site are removed due to suspension.

Figure 18 - Suspension is when small particles become airborne. Sometimes they can stay in the air for hundreds of miles. (Photo credit: John Teravskis)

Wind erosion was the main driver of the Dust Bowl that occurred in the central part of the United States during the 1930s. It is considered to be a human-caused environmental disaster because it was a result of millions of acres of soil exposed for agriculture with little or no soil conservation practices in place. There have been windy days and seasons since the dust bowl, but we have not had a repeat of this disaster since the wide-scale implementation of soil conservation methods in farming. As a result of the Dust Bowl, the USDA developed tools to help farmers be able to understand and predict soil loss due to wind erosion. Using nearly twenty years of field and laboratory studies, scientists at the USDA Agricultural Research Service (ARS) Wind Erosion Research Unit developed an

Figure 19 - Dust Bowl farm near Dalhart, Texas. June 1938 https://www.loc.gov/pictures/item/2017770642/

empirical equation for determining soil loss due to wind erosion[13]. The Wind Erosion Equation (WEQ) is:

Equation 1 – Wind Erosion Equation $E = f(I,K,C,L,V)$

Where:
  E = the average soil loss due to wind (tons/acre/year),

And soil loss "E" is a function of:
  I = the soil erodibility,
  K = the soil ridge roughness,
  C = the climatic factor,
  L = equivalent unsheltered distance across the field along the prevailing wind erosion direction, and
  V = the vegetative factor.

Don't worry, we are not going to make you get your calculators out, but let's look at each of these factors.

---

13 Smarik, S., S. Aney, A. Boes, D. Brown, D., Dubois, B. Edwards, E. Elias, M. Eve, R. Steele, N. Webb, M. Wilson, G. Zwicke,. 2019. Dust mitigation handbook. Las Cruces, NM: U.S. Department of Agriculture. Chapter 3

Connecting the Dots of Erosion and Sediment Theory

Soil erodibility "I" is defined by the USDA[14] as the susceptibility of soil to erode. There are three basic soil textures: sand, clay, and silt. Sandy soils generally have larger particle sizes. Clays are made of the smallest soil particles. Soils with low erodibility include fine textured soils high in clay that are resistant to detachment because they tend to be cohesive and coarse textured soils that are high in sand content because the heavier particles do not move as easily away from the soil matrix or they settle out immediately. Soils that have a high silt content are highly susceptible to erosion because silts are small particles but, unlike clays, they are "footloose and fancy free"—ready to travel. Silty soils are going to present the biggest problem for controlling wind erosion.

"K" represents the soil ridge roughness factor. Did you know a very effective way to control erosion is to break up the soil by disking or scarifying it? Seems counterintuitive, doesn't it? How can breaking up the soil surface possibly help with wind erosion? Remember the 3 S's? What happens when the jumping saltation particle jumps into a low spot or depression? Game over! It is out of play. Same with the surface-scooting soil creep particle—when it passes over a void, it too drops out. Two of the wind erosion processes are now knocked out, what about the third one? Soil loss due to suspension is a function of surface area. When we scarify a surface and create mounds and depressions, only the wind-facing mounds are susceptible to wind loss. The lee side of the mounds and the depressions are relatively wind protected, and, therefore, are not as likely sources for suspended particles. This is why on a windy, dry day in the country you can go by a freshly plowed field and see very little visible dust coming off of it. But you can drive by a mature vineyard, which you would think is relatively wind protected, and see large dust plumes rising out of it. For some phases of a construction project, scarifying the soil can be more effective than running a water truck all day.

---

14   Ibid. Glossary

Climate "C" is a factor for some locations because some places are just windier than others. I have had the opportunity to work for many years in Hawaii, and I have spent considerable time on most of the major islands. I don't know why, but everyone always wants to go to Maui. I tell them, "Don't go to Maui, go to the Big Island." It's too windy in Maui; I don't like becoming a ventifact while I lay on the beach (remember saltation?). Some construction projects also tend to be located in places that are almost constantly windy.

Which leads me to the "L" factor. This factor represents the equivalent unsheltered distance across the project along the prevailing wind direction. When I do visit Maui, I tend to go places that most tourists don't have on their "must-see" list. My attention is usually drawn to construction sites. On Maui, you will find construction sites surrounded by what appears to be a ten-foot-tall silt fence. Actually, it is a wind fence. (Did I mention it is windy in Maui?) Furthermore, much of Maui's soil is red due to the high iron content. For years, enterprising businesses

Figure 20 - Did you miss this tourist spot the last time you were in Maui? (Photo credit: John Teravskis)

have sold T-shirts to tourists dyed with Maui's red soil. Although your mainland family members may love the T-shirts you bought for them, the owner of a white building or car situated next to a construction site, will probably not be as excited about the new coral tint it received as a result of the neighboring construction activities. That is why dust screens or wind fences are required to be installed around construction projects to control fugitive dust.[15] According to the USDA[16],

---

15 Hawaii Administrative Rules, Section 11-60.1-33, Fugitive Dust; https://health.hawaii.gov/cab/files/2015/09/Hawaii-Fugitive-Dust-Fact-Sheet-Oct-2014-.pdf.
16 USDA Natural Resources Conservation Service Agriculture Information Bulletin 339, Windbreaks for Conservation, https://www.fs.usda.gov/nac/assets/documents/morepublications/windbreaksforconservation.pdf.

soil particles do not ordinarily become airborne until wind velocity is about thirteen miles per hour at one foot above ground level. This is known as the threshold velocity, above which the capacity of winds to carry soil is proportional to the wind velocity (V_w) raised to the third power (V_w^3). This means the windier it gets, the amount of dust leaving the site will increase exponentially. But it also means that small reductions in wind velocity can cause a greater proportionate reduction in the rate of soil loss due to wind. Windbreaks (such as trees, buildings, or wind fence) can provide protection to a downwind stretch of the project ten times the height of the break. So, a ten-foot-tall wind fence placed perpendicular to the wind direction would give downwind protection to approximately one hundred feet of the project.

As with rain erosion, the ultimate protection for wind erosion is to establish an effective soil cover, whether that be a temporary or permanent control measure. This brings us to the last factor in the Wind Erosion Equation—the "V" vegetative factor. Many of the erosion control measures used for rain erosion will also be effective for wind erosion control. This was the lesson learned from the Dust Bowl. The key to soil conservation is keeping it covered as much as possible.

MOVEMENT EROSION

So far, we have looked at rain and wind—two common agents of erosion at construction sites. But there is one more. Movement! Whether we are moving big Cat dozers or a wheelbarrow, soil particles become detached. Movement is not just limited to things with wheels; soil can also erode by foot traffic, the movement of equipment and supplies, and non-storm water running through a project.

Movement of construction equipment and supplies does not only disturb the soil, but it will oftentimes relocate erodible soil to places where it is vulnerable to further dispersion by wind and rain. Heavy equipment and site activities can also cause normally cohesive clay soils to become pulverized and lose their cohesiveness, making them susceptible to forming a colloidal clay suspension when exposed to storm water.

Figure 21 - Deep ripping is certainly detaching particles but is also providing post-construction water quality benefits by promoting infiltration. (Photo credit: John Teravskis)

Heavy Equipment: Obviously, the purpose of heavy equipment on a construction site is to move soil. It can be done in a way that is beneficial to erosion control, such as terracing, track walking, scarifying the surface, or creating a sediment basin or trap. Heavy equipment can also be the source of erosion control problems, such as opening an excessive amount of soil at one time, placing stockpiles in locations near receiving waters or drain inlets, creating instable slopes, performing dirt work during the rainy season, and damaging impervious or vegetated areas. In controlling erosion caused by heavy equipment it is important to pay attention to the grading plan, the SWPPP plan, and the construction schedule. These three documents will allow a knowledgeable and experienced operator to know when and where dirt should be disturbed and when it should be left alone.

These documents will also identify mitigation measures to control the effects of using and moving the equipment.

Track-Out: Vehicles and equipment not only disturb soil and detach particles, but they also can track them out onto paved surfaces. The deposition of sediment on roadways then becomes subject to secondary erosion, in which these particles will be further eroded and transported away by the movement of other vehicles, rain, and wind. Regulatory agencies give much attention to track-out. If a contractor is not controlling track-out, it is very likely other areas of the site are also lacking appropriate erosion control measures.

Figure 22 – Track-out from a subdivision lot onto a paved roadway.
(Photo credit: John Teravskis)

Non-Storm Water Flows: As we saw with rain erosion, water can be a powerful agent of erosion. The movement of non-storm water flows, if not controlled, can result in rills and gullies. Dry weather discharges can be intentional, such as saw cutting water, or unintended, such as from a water line break. The best control measure is to eliminate or reduce the flow. When it is not possible to stop the flow, it is best to attempt to divert the flow or control the discharge so that it does not pass through erodible soil. Until the flow can be stopped, sediment control measures need to be in place to slow the flow and to help mitigate the effects of erosion caused by non-storm water flows.

Figure 23 - Non-storm water flowing through utility repair work has eroded soils and is carrying them to the drain inlet. (Photo credit: John Teravskis)

Now that we have connected the dots of erosion agents and accelerators, let's move onto making a connection between other activities and pollutant sources present at a construction site.

CHAPTER 3
Connecting the Dots of Pollutant Source Assessment

In this chapter, we encounter a significant disconnect for many SWPPP writers. These writers may even have a good handle on erosion and sediment theory, but when it comes to what happens on a construction site, they are clueless. Their ignorance about construction activities and sources is primarily because they have never worked at a construction site, other than possibly performing a quick storm water inspection. In this chapter, we hope to provide some links between the dots of the various trades involved in the construction industry, what they do, and the materials they use on the jobsite. This will then provide insight into the pollutant sources associated with each of these trades. With this information, we should be able to connect to the next dot, which is to associate specific pollutants to the activities and trades.

IDENTIFYING THE CONSTRUCTION ACTIVITIES

Unless the project is owner-built (e.g., some public works projects, or projects that are owned by a builder), a general contractor will be in charge of the project. The general contractor is the entity who has contracted with the project's owner to perform the construction project. In some instances, the contractor is capable of and willing to perform all of the activities associated with the project.

However, oftentimes other contractors who specialize in certain types of construction will be hired, or subcontracted, by the general contractor to perform these services. These specialized areas are referred to as trades. Some trades can be very specific and specialized. Table 2 presents a list of trades common to the construction industry.

Table 2 – Trades, Construction Activities, and Potential Pollutant Sources[17]

Trades	Activities	Potential Pollutant Sources
Asphalt Pavers	Deliver and install asphalt products, hot and cold mixes, for roadways, parking lots, and other paved surfaces.	• Heavy petroleum oils used in asphalt • Diesel for cleaning and fuel • Lubricating oils for equipment • Solvents and detergents for cleaning • Sand and gravel • Vehicle / equipment fuel; coolant; and hydraulic, brake, and transmission fluids • Solid waste / trash
Boilermakers	Assemble, install, maintain, and repair boilers, closed vats, and other large vessels or containers that hold liquids and gases.	• Metal dust and filings • Welding slag • Solvents and detergents • Lubricating oils • Sand or other media from sand blasting • Solid waste / trash

---

17   List of trades and activities partially derived from the U.S. Bureau of Labor Statistics Occupational Outlook Handbook, https://www.bls.gov/ooh/home.htm.

Connecting the Dots of Pollutant Source Assessment

Trades	Activities	Potential Pollutant Sources
Carpenters	Construct, repair, and install building frameworks and structures made from wood and other materials.	• Wood dust and particles • Semi-volatile compounds (SVOCs) from treated or manufactured wood or wood-replacement building materials • Metal dust and filings from steel or aluminum posts and studs • Solid waste / trash
Concrete Workers	Deliver and pump concrete; pour, finish, and cure concrete surfaces. Stain, stamp, and perform other concrete treatments for specialty finishes and textures. This area includes concrete tilt-up construction, stucco, shotcrete, gunite, and concrete slurry work.	• pH altering concrete and cementitious substances • Metals, SVOCs, and polymers from colorants • Ammonia, calcium, metals, phosphates, salts, and acids from admixtures • Oils for forms and sealing concrete • Solid waste / trash
Construction Equipment Operators, Mechanics, and Fuelers	Drive, maneuver, or control the heavy machinery used for grading and excavation and constructing roads, buildings, and other structures. Mechanics repair and maintain heavy equipment. Fuelers, typically mobile fuelers, deliver and dispense fuel and lubricants.	• Lubricating oils for equipment • Solvents and detergents for cleaning • Sediment and solids from earthwork • Vehicle / equipment fuel, coolant, hydraulic, brake, and transmission fluids • Solid waste / trash

Trades	Activities	Potential Pollutant Sources
Coring, Drilling, Grinding, and Saw-Cutting Workers	Cut, core, and grind asphalt and concrete surfaces.	• Water and slurry from cutting, coring, and grinding • Solids and pH altering substances from slurries and waste piles • Lead and other hazardous wastes from grinding operations • Fuel and lubricants
Demolition Workers	Deconstruct and remove buildings, roadways, and other structures. Sort, transport, and dispose of/recycle demolition waste.	• Dust and particles from asphalt, concrete, wood, metal, and other building materials • Hazardous waste, including, but not limited to, asbestos, leaded paint, and PCBs • Solid waste / trash • Sediment and solids from disturbed soils
Drywall Installers, Ceiling Tile Installers, Tapers, and Plasterers	Hang wallboard and install ceiling tile inside buildings. Tapers prepare the wallboard for painting.	• Dry wall, gypsum, or plaster dust and particles • pH altering substances in mud and wallboard • Solid waste / trash
Electricians and Telecommunications Installer	Install, maintain, and repair electrical power, communications, lighting, and control systems.	• Metal dust, filings, and particles • Solvents and glues for conduit • Cable and wire pulling lubricants • Sediment and solids from trenching • Treated wood for poles • Solid waste / trash

Connecting the Dots of Pollutant Source Assessment

Trades	Activities	Potential Pollutant Sources
Elevator and Escalator Installers	Install, maintain, and fix elevators, escalators, moving walkways, and other lifts.	• Metal dust and filings • Welding slag • Solvents and detergents • Lubricating oils • Paints and surface coatings • Solid waste / trash
Fencer	Construct wood, metal, and chain-link fences.	• Wood dust and particles • Semi-volatile compounds (SVOCs) from treated or manufactured wood or wood-replacement building materials • Metal dust and filings from steel, galvanized, or aluminum posts and studs • Solid waste / trash
Flooring Installers and Tile and Stone Setters	Lay and install carpet, wood, vinyl, tile, and other flooring materials.	• Dust and particulates from installation, removal, and/or resurfacing of flooring. • Glues and adhesives • Leveling compounds (pH altering) • Solvents and detergents • Solid waste / trash
Glaziers	Install glass in windows, skylights, and other fixtures in buildings.	• Dust, filings, and particulates from window installation • Glues and adhesives • Cleaning compounds • Solid waste / trash
Hazardous Materials Removal Workers	Identify and dispose of harmful substances such as asbestos, lead, mold, toxic, and radioactive waste.	• Hazardous waste • Solid waste / trash

Trades	Activities	Potential Pollutant Sources
HVAC Technicians	Install, maintain, and repair heating, ventilation, and air conditioning systems.	• Metal dust, filings, and particles • Solvents and glues for conduit • Cable and wire pulling lubricants • Solid waste / trash
Insulation Workers	Install and replace the materials used to insulate buildings or mechanical systems.	• Dust and particulate matter • Solvents and glues • Solid waste / trash
Ironworkers	Install structural and reinforcing iron and steel to form and support buildings, bridges, and roads.	• Metal and wood dust, filings, and particles • Welding slag • Solvents, oils, and lubricants • Surface coatings
Landscapers	Shape and install outdoor features including turf, plants, trees, compost, mulch, walkways, water features, and irrigation systems. Maintain vegetation including the application of fertilizers and pesticides.	• Sediment and solids from earthwork, trenching, and stockpiles • Organic material from compost, wood mulch, and soil amendments • pH altering substances for soil treatment • Fertilizers and pesticides • Glues and solvents for PVC irrigation piping • Dust and particles from treated wood • Concrete and cement containing substances

Trades	Activities	Potential Pollutant Sources
Masonry Workers	Use bricks, concrete and concrete blocks, and natural and manmade stones to build structures, walls, and road and walkway pavers.	• Sediment and solids from earthwork, trenching, and stockpiles • pH altering cementitious substances • Metals, SVOCs, and polymers from colorants • Ammonia, calcium, metals, phosphates, salts, and acids from admixtures. • Oils for sealing concrete • Solid waste / trash
Millwright	Install, maintain, and repair industrial machinery and equipment.	• Metal and wood dust, filings, and particles • Welding slag • Solvents, oils, and lubricants • Surface coatings
Painters	Apply paint, stain, and coatings to walls and ceilings, buildings, large machinery and equipment, and bridges and other structures.	• Paint, primer, stains, and surface coatings • Solvents • Cleansers and detergents • Sand or other media for sand blasting • Metal, oxide, and paint particles from sand blasting activities (spent sand blast grit) • Solid waste / trash

Trades	Activities	Potential Pollutant Sources
Pile Driver and Drillers	Drill holes and drive posts in soil for structural supports. Install coffer dams and other subgrade structural supports.	• Lubricating oils for equipment • Solvents and detergents for cleaning • Sediment and solids from drill cuttings • Bore hole mud and clay • Cementitious materials • Vehicle / equipment fuel; coolant; and hydraulic, brake, and transmission fluids • Solid waste / trash
Plumbers, Pipefitters, and Steamfitters	Install and repair piping fixtures and systems.	• Metal and PVC dust, filings, and particles • Solvents, glues, and sealers for piping • Pipe threading oils • Pipe solder • Sediment and solids from trenching • Sanitary waste from sewer work • Hyper-chlorinated water from hydrostatic testing or system disinfecting • Solid waste / trash
Roofers	Replace, repair, and install the roofs of buildings.	• Metal, shingle, and wood dust, filings, and particles • Sediment from composite and tile shingles • Solvents and glues • Asphalt and tar • Solid waste / trash

Connecting the Dots of Pollutant Source Assessment

Trades	Activities	Potential Pollutant Sources
Scaffolding, Rigging, and Crane Workers	Install scaffolding. Use and maintain cranes to support construction activities. Prepare loads to be hoisted by a crane.	• Lubricating oils for equipment • Solvents and detergents for cleaning • Sediment and solids from soil disturbance by crane tracks and equipment • Vehicle/equipment fuel; coolant; and hydraulic, brake, and transmission fluids • Solid waste / trash
Sheet Metal Workers	Fabricate or install products made from thin metal sheets.	• Metal dust, filings, and particles • Solvents and glues • Surface coatings and galvanized materials • Cleansers and detergents • Solid waste / trash
Sign Installers	Install, maintain, and repair signs and related lighting/electronics.	• Metal dust, filings, and particles • Solvents and glues for conduit • Cable and wire pulling lubricants • Sediment and solids from trenching and post holes • Concrete for post holes • Treated wood for poles • Solid waste / trash
Soil Chemical Treatment Contractors	Installation and placement of subgrade chemical treatment for stabilization of soils.	• pH altering materials such as lime, cement, and fly ash

Trades	Activities	Potential Pollutant Sources
Solar Photovoltaic Installers	Assemble, set up, and maintain rooftop or other systems that convert sunlight into energy.	• Metal dust, filings, and particles • Solvents and glues for conduit • Cable and wire pulling lubricants • Sediment and solids from trenching and post holes • Concrete for post holes • Cleaning agents • Solid waste / trash
Welder	Welding by various means of metal and pipe surfaces, joints, and connections. Involves grinding, cutting, and preparation work.	• Metal dust, filings, and particles • Welding pipe dope and solder • Welding slag • Lubricants and solvents • Solid waste / trash

IDENTIFYING POLLUTANT SOURCES WITHIN EACH ACTIVITY

From [Table 2](), it is evident there can be many different trades people associated with a project. For example, a housing subdivision project would involve heavy equipment operators, concrete workers, plumbers, carpenters, electricians, drywall installers, HVAC installers, roofers, glaziers, stucco installers, painters, flooring installers, masons, cabinetry installers, landscapers, and probably quite a few more not listed. A roadway project could include demolition contractors, heavy equipment operators, carpenters, steel workers, welders, crane operators, concrete workers, electricians, painters, and landscapers. Each of these trades come with their own set of pollutant sources and challenges to maintaining good water quality for construction site runoff.

Connecting the Dots of Pollutant Source Assessment

By reviewing the Potential Pollutant Source column on Table 2, you may notice that certain pollutants commonly reoccur for the various trades. Not surprisingly, solid waste (or trash) is one of the most reoccurring pollutant sources listed. This is because every trade has a waste product of some sort, whether it is the wrapping around a pallet of material, the bag containing a powdery substance such as concrete, debris generated from demolition, the spent absorbent used to clean up an oil spill, or just the wrapper from the breakfast burrito that was consumed that morning. While Table 2 has listed potential pollutant sources, these are not necessarily construction site pollutants. But it can get a bit confusing. Is trash a pollutant or a pollutant source? It is both. Trash itself is a pollutant. Like most States, the State of California has established prohibitions for trash in storm water runoff. However, trash is also a pollutant source. The decomposition of paper trash can increase the Biological Oxygen Demand (BOD) in runoff water and lower dissolved oxygen content in the receiving water. Plastic waste will degrade into microplastics that threaten wildlife and even human health.[18] But trash is a carrier for just about any pollutant found on a construction site, because solid waste comes into contact with most of the materials that are used or wastes that are generated at a project site. A residue of the previously stored material will remain on the packaging or items that came into contact with the pollutant. Whether trash is deposited on the ground or is placed in an uncovered

Figure 24 - Is trash a pollutant or a pollutant source? It can be both! That is why trash bins should be covered when it is raining. (Photo credit: John Teravskis)

---

18 Campanale C, Massarelli C, Savino I, Locaputo V, Uricchio VF. A Detailed Review Study on Potential Effects of Microplastics and Additives of Concern on Human Health. Int J Environ Res Public Health. 2020 Feb 13;17(4):1212. doi: 10.3390/ijerph17041212. PMID: 32069998; PMCID: PMC7068600. https://www.ncbi.nlm.nih.gov/pmc/articles/PMC7068600/.

waste bin, if exposed to storm water, the pollutant residue will be mobilized from the discarded items. While the generation of trash and solid waste cannot be eliminated from a construction project, in Chapter 4, we will look at actions that can be taken to minimize the impact of solid waste on water quality.

Many of the trades' work involve materials or activities that may alter the pH of the storm water discharge. Some of these cause pH to be lowered by exposure to acids or materials that have a low pH.

Acids are oftentimes utilized in concrete and masonry work to clean or prepare surfaces. Acid can also be used as a retarder in a concrete mixture to slow down the concrete hardening process. However, more often than not, pH is altered upward with the use of caustic materials on the project. Most cementitious materials will have a high pH or caustic properties. Obviously, concrete work has the potential to raise the pH of storm water runoff, but so does work involving stucco, tiling, masonry, and lime treating soils. Not only do new concrete materials cause pH to be altered, but old materials may also influence storm water pH levels when they are cut, ground, or demolished. This includes slurry and water runoff from concrete cutting and grinding operations.

Figure 25 - Concrete cutting, coring, and grinding can result in slurries and non-storm water discharges that are high in pH. (Photo credit: Jesse Allen)

When it comes to erosion accelerators and sources of sedimentation, the finger of blame often gets pointed to the heavy equipment operators. While it is true that nothing can disturb soil like the giant wheeled scrapers or a tracked excavator, there are many other culpable parties present at a construction site when it comes to sedimentation issues. Every pickup truck or pair of work boots that crosses from an area of soil disturbance to a paved surface is a potential source of sediment track-out, which obviously involves all of the trades listed on Table 2. This is especially true during the wet season when soils are muddy. But, as we saw in Chapter 2, erosion and sedimentation can and does occur during the dry season when sediment particles are transported by wind. Just because a project is past the grading phase and is in the dry season does not mean we can get rid of the sediment control devices. There is potential for erosion and sediment transport until the last trade is gone and the project is completed.

For the various trades, Table 2 identifies metals, solvents, cleaners, detergents, paints, adhesives, welding compounds, lubricants, and a host of other things contractors might use in the performance of their jobs. If you want to get a better idea of what these materials might include, go visit your local hardware store and peruse the stocked shelves by department. There is a myriad of chemicals and products that are used for construction that you probably have never considered being present on a jobsite—and that is just in the plumbing section of the store! The degree to which these materials might be a pollutant source depends largely on their exposure to storm water: when and how they are stored, used, or discarded. An adhesive which arrives to the jobsite in the back of a van, contained in a tube, and used exclusively for interior construction may only be a concern as a solid waste when the empty tube is discarded. But a concrete colorant admixture contained in totes or buckets and stored and used outside will, therefore, have a much greater exposure to storm water. In Chapter 4, we will discuss site management practices to reduce overall exposure of such materials.

However, even with the most diligent site management, accidents do happen. Small and large spills of materials brought to the jobsite will occur. Spills might be a liquid material that leaks from or escapes a container such as from an overturned or leaking drum. Liquid hazardous materials may also be lost from construction equipment such as from a burst hydraulic line, a piece of equipment that needs repair, or during fueling operations. But spills are not limited to liquids; powders can be spilled or blown from their storage or usage locations. While many spills are accidental, some are due to negligence, others to ignorance, and some are even

Figure 26 - While spills can be accidental, many are due to negligence, ignorance, or are intentional. (Photo credit: John Teravskis)

intentional. Take concrete washout as an example. A concrete washout device that overflows during a rain event is likely due to negligence. It was negligence that allowed the device to not be monitored and the waste liquid to reach a level that did not have sufficient freeboard for rainfall. Negligently, the storm forecast was also not being watched so that the concrete waste was not pumped and hauled off in time or the washout device covered before the rain began. Spilled concrete washout can also be due to ignorance. It is possible that the contractor didn't know there was a concrete washout device located about 200 feet away. I suppose it is

Figure 27 - Was the washout due to ignorance or was it intentional? (Photo credit: John Teravskis)

possible that this was also the concrete worker's first day on the job and didn't know waste concrete and washout are not allowed to be placed on the ground. That is why good site management practices must have an active educational element to it. But, more likely than not, spilled concrete waste material or washout was intentionally placed there because of time and convenience (or possibly laziness). After preaching proper concrete washout practices for nearly two decades, it is hard for me to believe that ignorance about it still exists.

There is another potential pollutant source that has little to do with the construction activities or trades present. This site-specific source is from previous activities and, sometimes, natural causes. It may be the project is part of an environmental cleanup or a brownfield restoration project. I once was on a project near the Port of Oakland that was formerly a creosote wood treatment facility. For decades, the soils had been impacted with creosote. Therefore, additional mitigation measures and monitoring were needed to prevent the creosote-contaminated soil from coming into contact with storm water runoff. Not far away from that project, I worked on another Bay-area project where naturally occurring asbestos was present in the soils. In this case, extra care and mitigation measures were necessary not just for water quality reasons but also for the protection of on-site workers and public health. As with soil erosion, construction activities can act as accelerators to worsen the exposure of these pre-construction pollutant sources to storm water runoff from the construction project.

Hopefully, you are starting to connect the dots from the raindrop to the construction project, to the trades present on the site, and to the pollutant sources associated with those trades. Now, let's connect the next dot—associating specific pollutants to their sources.

ASSOCIATING POLLUTANTS WITH SOURCES

As we discussed about trash, sometimes the pollutant is obvious and is one and the same as the pollutant source. But other times, we know we have a source of storm water pollution, but we are not quite sure what the actual pollutant is. In fact, there might be many pollutants that are associated with a single pollutant source. Take, for example, a leak or spill of gasoline. While it is quite easy to point to the source (spilled gasoline) and see the results on the surface of the storm water runoff (an oily sheen), it is not a simple matter to identify that actual pollutants, which are many and varied. Gasoline has at least 150, and for some blends up to 1,000, volatile organic hydrocarbon compounds (VOCs) and semi-volatile organic compounds (SVOCs).[19] Similarly, if we are concerned about metals affecting water quality, we need to know which ones and in what form. There are more than twenty different metals (e.g., aluminum, antimony, barium, cobalt, copper, iron, mercury, silver, zinc, etc.) that can be present in water either in a dissolved state or as particulate matter. So, before we start the somewhat arduous process of identifying pollutants, let's categorize the pollutants by what they do to water quality. This will help us determine if the potentially present pollutants are a threat to the water quality of the site's runoff and the nearby receiving waters.

The first thing to understand is that not all "pollutants" are actually pollutants but are conditions caused by other pollutants. This would include the analytical tests shown in Table 3.

---

[19] Agency for Toxic Substances and Disease Registry (ATSDR). 1995. Toxicological profile for automotive gasoline. Atlanta, GA: U.S. Department of Health and Human Services, Public Health Service. https://www.atsdr.cdc.gov/ToxProfiles/tp72-c3.pdf.

Connecting the Dots of Pollutant Source Assessment

Table 3 – Water Quality Conditions

Condition	Measurement Method	Pollutant Sources that Cause the Condition	Effects on Water Quality
Turbidity	Field instrument	Suspended sediment Suspended particulate matter	Causes impairment to receiving waters including damage to benthic organisms and habitats, lowering of dissolved oxygen or the ability of fish to receive oxygen through their gills, and warming of water.
pH	Field instrument	Acids Bases (Caustics) Cementitious materials	Low and high pH is harmful to immature fish and insects; it also threatens beneficial uses of surface water and groundwater used as a source of drinking water and for crop irrigation.
Low Dissolved Oxygen (DO)	Field instrument	Organic material Excessive algae growth Nutrients Elevated temperature	Fish need dissolved oxygen to breath. Low DO can cause fish kills and keep fish from spawning.
Biological Oxygen Demand (BOD)	Laboratory test	Sugars Organic material Nutrients which prompt population growth of organisms that consume oxygen	Elevated BOD is usually associated with low DO.

Condition	Measurement Method	Pollutant Sources that Cause the Condition	Effects on Water Quality
Chemical Oxygen Demand (COD)	Laboratory test	Includes the same causes as for elevated BOD Chemical oxidizers	Elevated COD is usually associated with low DO.
Specific Conductance (SC)	Field test	Dissolved solids / salts	Elevated SC can make a waterbody inhabitable for certain species of organisms and plants. It can also make it unusable for drinking water and for agriculture. It can cause groundwater to become more saline.

The following are several categories of pollutants common to construction projects. There are certainly other categories, such as radioactive, but they would be more typical of an industrial or cleanup project than an average construction site.

Sediment: It can come in two forms: settleable and suspended. As we observed in Chapter 2, heavier particles will settle out when the flow of water slows. As water velocity decreases, the heavier and coarser materials will fall out first, then as water continues to slow, smaller and smaller particles will drop out. If you inspect a construction site after runoff has occurred, you will notice this phenomenon in the sediment control measures that have been installed. At the top of the slope, oftentimes we will observe the larger aggregates and coarser sands, but as we move further away onto more level terrain, we will see accumulation of finer particles at subsequent sediment control measures. But not all sediment can or will be captured from traditional sediment control devices such as fiber roll or silt fence. Very fine particles, such as clays and silts, can stay in suspension for long periods of time. Settling times for colloidal clay suspensions can be extremely long (over 200 years[20]). Many people erroneously assume that this is because the suspended particles are extremely small and cannot readily settle out by gravity.

Figure 28 - Suspended sediment in storm water. (Photo credit: John Teravskis)

While it is true that suspended particles are very small, the actual reason they stay in suspension is because they tend to have a negative electric charge. Like charges repel each other. So, if we have a pond of highly turbid water, what we really have is billions, if not trillions, of suspended particles trying to get away from each other. The electromagnetic forces are actually agitating the pond—essentially the pond has a magnetic stirrer keeping the particles in suspension.

---

20   CONFERENCE ON ADVANCED TREATMENT FOR CONSTRUCTION SITES CalEPA – October 21, 2004. https://www.waterboards.ca.gov/water_issues/programs/stormwater/docs/advtreat/clearwatercompliance.pdf

For situations other than colloidal clay suspension, eventually, the sediment will settle out somewhere. As we will discuss in Chapter 4, the trick is to get the sedimentation to occur where we want it to happen.

pH altering: As we observed in Table 3, pH is a condition caused by pollutants that are either acidic or basic (caustic). To control this condition, we need to observe for sources of acids and bases. Acids may be present naturally in some soil types and organic materials. According to University of California, Davis, *"acidification of soil occurs due to: 1) weathering of soil silicate minerals, leaching of base cations, and formation of iron and aluminum oxides 2) oxidation of native and applied carbon, sulfur, and nitrogen, 3) release of plant root exudates that include protons, organic acids and CO_2, and 4) alternating wet-dry conditions that lead to proton generation by ferrolysis.*[21]*"*

Figure 29 - Stucco activities and waste are caustic pollutants that elevate pH in storm water. (Photo credit: John Teravskis)

---

21 University of California, Davis; Soil Health website; https://soilhealth.ucdavis.edu/soil-challenges/acidity

In certain regions, acid rains resulting from natural or environmental factors may also contribute to low pH of storm water runoff causing aluminum to leach from soil clay particles and having a negative effect on fish and wildlife[22]. Bases may originate from natural sources, such as groundwater or springs, and certain soil types. While there is not too much that can be done to prevent these natural or regional pH altering sources from impacting the construction site, we do need to pay attention to construction-related sources of acids and bases. Acids may be used in cleaning surfaces (particularly concrete and masonry surfaces) and as a retarder for concrete hardening, and, of course, acids are present in vehicle and equipment batteries. Bases (also referred to as caustics) are far more commonly found on construction projects and come in the form of cements, stucco, grout, and other cementitious materials. Many cleansers and detergents are caustics that elevate pH. Soil conditioning amendments such as lime can also cause elevated pH.

Oxygen consumers: These are pollutants that directly or indirectly cause low dissolved oxygen (DO) or elevated BOD or COD. This may come from oxidizer chemicals, such as peroxides, bleach, and chlorine, used on-site to sanitize drinking water systems or in cleaning products. Oxidizers will increase COD. Decomposing organic debris, compost, and paper trash can cause increased BOD. Fertilizers and other sources of ammonia, nitrates, and phosphates (nutrients) can promote algae growth that will consume more and more dissolved oxygen as its population increases. Another oxygen consumer many people fail to consider is temperature. If water is allowed to flow across warm surfaces or be warmed in a shallow holding pond, its ability to contain dissolved oxygen will be reduced. While this is, technically, not an oxygen consumer, it will exasperate the effects of other potential oxygen consumers.

---

22   Effects of Acid Rain, United States Environmental Protection Agency (USEPA) https://www.epa.gov/acidrain/effects-acid-rain

Dissolved Solids: These are solids that will go into solution when added to water. They are typically dry and liquid forms of salts. On a construction site, salts may be found in concrete admixtures, fertilizers, some dust suppressants (such as magnesium chloride), and, in colder environments, deicing agents. Dissolved solids are typically colorless and odorless. Their presence can be detected with a field instrument that measures specific conductance or by a laboratory test for total dissolved solids or salinity.

Metals: Metals come from a myriad of different sources at a construction site. They can be natural occurring or in the pre-construction soils present at the site. For example, clays tend to be high in aluminum and iron concentrations. But there are plenty of construction-related sources as well, including: grinding, drilling, cutting, pounding, sand blasting, and welding of metal surfaces and structures; wear and tear of brakes, tires, tracks, and other moving parts on heavy equipment; and the cutting and sanding of treated wood. Metals are also present in most new and used lubricants, surface coatings, roofing materials, cementitious materials, and concrete admixtures. They are literally everywhere on a construction site! Metals can occur in two different phases: dissolved and particulate. Although there most certainly will be an amount of dissolved metals present, particulate metals are far more abundant. For the most part, if you can control the particulate form, you will be able to effectively manage the dissolved form. Because metals primarily occur in the particulate form, sedimentation devices are useful in helping to control them. Typically, where we see high turbidity and total settable or suspended sediment concentrations, we also see elevated metal concentrations.[23]

---

23   Herngren, Lars & Goonetilleke, Ashantha & Ayoko, Godwin. (2005). Understanding Heavy Metal and Suspended Solids Relationships in Urban Storm-Water Using Simulated Rainfall. Journal of environmental management. 76. 149-58. 10.1016/j.jenvman.2005.01.013.

Oils: When the United States Environmental Protection Agency (USEPA) references oil it *"means oil of any kind or in any form, including, but not limited to: fats, oils, or greases of animal, fish, or marine mammal origin; vegetable oils, including oils from seeds, nuts, fruits, or kernels; and, other oils and greases, including petroleum, fuel oil, sludge, synthetic oils, mineral oils, oil refuse, or oil mixed with wastes other than dredged spoil."*[24] For the most part, that is the same definition we use for this pollutant category. Sources of oil at a construction site include fuels, oils, and lubricants used for vehicles and equipment; oils used in paving; pipe cutting oils; form oil for concrete work; surface sealers; and lubricants, rust-inhibitors, and oil-containing chemicals used by the various trades. Oil will be manifested as a pollutant by a visible rainbow sheen. A certain amount of it can also go into solution, which may be detected by a variety of laboratory analyses including total oil and grease (or Hexane Extractable Material), total petroleum hydrocarbons (specifying the targeted carbon chain lengths, such as gasoline, diesel, or motor oil ranges), and as VOCs or SVOCs.

*Figure 30 - Oil sheen from leaking equipment is an obvious sign of a problem.
(Photo credit: Danny Aspiras)*

---

24 Code of Federal Regulation 40 CFR Part 112.2

Toxics: This broad group of pollutants can include materials that are part the oil pollutant category but also include other chemicals that are typically found in solvents, admixtures, surface coatings, cleansers, detergents, antifreeze/coolant, pesticides, and other chemicals present on a construction site. Included in the toxics category are legacy pollutants such as DDT, asbestos, lead paint, or polychlorinated biphenyls (PCBs) that may be exposed to storm water via grading of contaminated soils or demolition of structures or surfaces that contain them.

Figure 31 - Toxic chemicals that are not stored within secondary containment and under a rainproof cover may be exposed to and mobilized by storm water. (Photo credit: Mike Lewis)

Pathogens: This group includes bacteria and viruses that may come into contact with storm water from on-site sources, such as sewage and sanitary sewer lines, portable sanitation facilities, and contaminated soil and surfaces (including solid waste), as well as natural sources.

Figure 32 - Port-a-potties can be sources of bacteria and pathogens when not properly maintained, contained, or secured from tipping over. (Photo credit: Matt Lewis)

DETERMINING THE QUANTITY AND PHYSICAL CHARACTERISTICS OF THE POLLUTANTS

3. COMPOSITION/INFORMATION ON INGREDIENTS

Mixtures

Chemical name	CAS number	%
Calcium Sulfoaluminate Cement	960375-09-1	20-60
Silica, quartz	14808-60-7	40-80
Smectite Clay	12199-37-0	0-2

Figure 33 - List of ingredients in rapid set stucco mix. Important thing to note about this material is the amount of cement present (a pH altering material).

In order to determine to what extent a pollutant may be mobilized by storm water, it is important to understand its physical characteristics. For example, is the pollutant a solid or liquid? Does it dissolve in water? Is it a dust that can be dispersed by the wind? To obtain this information, there are two basic practices. First, make some general observations about the packaging. Does it come in a bucket, drum, or tote, or is it in a bag or sack? Is it delivered by bulk or in discrete packaging? Look for a label on the packaging to learn more about the properties of the product and any warnings associated with it. Second, obtain and review a safety data sheet (SDS) for the material. Hopefully, the SDS is already physically present at the site. But many times, the easiest way is to use a Web browser to search for it online. When reviewing the SDS, you will want to look for the chemical constituents. For example, a rapid set stucco mix might have the following listed for composition:

Scrolling down the SDS, we will find the physical and chemical properties listed. From Figure 34, we can see that rapid set stucco is a powder with a high pH when wet. Based on this information, we would expect this product to be contained in a sack. We would want to make sure the rapid set stucco mix does not come into contact with storm water, otherwise we may have an elevated pH problem. Therefore, it should be stored in a dry and covered location.

9. Physical and chemical properties
Appearance

Physical state	Solid.
Form	Powder.
Color	Tan.
Odor	Low.
Odor threshold	Not available.
pH	11 – 12 when wet
Melting point/freezing point	Not applicable.
Initial boiling point and boiling range	Not applicable.

Figure 34 - Physical and chemical properties of rapid set stucco.

Let's suppose that we had a spill of antifreeze on the jobsite and we need to know what pollutants may be present or mobilized by storm water. In the downloaded the SDS, we find the following:

3. COMPOSITION/INFORMATION ON INGREDIENTS

Synonyms   Ethylene Glycol; 1,2-Ethanediol; Ethylene Alcohol

Chemical name	CAS number	Weight-%
Ethylene glycol	107-21-1	42-98
Proprietary inhibitors	Proprietary	Proprietary
Potassium hydroxide	1310-58-3	0.2

If Chemical Name/CAS No is "proprietary" and/or Weight-% is listed as range, the specific chemical identity and/or percentage of composition has been withheld as a trade secret.

Figure 35 - List of antifreeze ingredients (at least the ones they are telling us about—some are trade secrets). Notice that up to 98% of it is ethylene glycol.

Connecting the Dots of Pollutant Source Assessment

Moving down to Section 9 in the antifreeze SDS, we find the physical and chemical properties listed.

9. PHYSICAL AND CHEMICAL PROPERTIES			
Information on basic physical and chemical properties			
Physical State	Liquid		
Appearance	Gold, Red or Green liquid	Odor	Mild
Color	Gold, Red or Green	Odor Threshold	Not determined
Property	Values	Remarks • Method	
pH	Not determined		
Melting Point/Freezing Point	Not available		
Boiling Point/Boiling Range	163-171 °C / 325-340 °F		
Flash Point	121-123 °C / 250-254 °F	TOC	
Evaporation Rate	Not determined		
Flammability (Solid, Gas)	n/a-liquid		
Upper Flammability Limits	15.3		
Lower Flammability Limit	3.2		
Vapor Pressure	Not available		
Vapor Density	Not available		
Specific Gravity	1.115-1.133		
Water Solubility	Completely soluble		
Solubility in other solvents	Not determined		
Partition Coefficient	Not determined		
Auto-ignition Temperature	398 °C / 748 °F		
Decomposition Temperature	Not determined		
Kinematic Viscosity	Not available		
Dynamic Viscosity	Not available		
Explosive Properties	Not determined		
Oxidizing Properties	Not determined		

Figure 36 - Physical and chemical properties of antifreeze

From this section, we learn more about what to expect from the spill of antifreeze when it comes into contact with storm water. Because of its specific gravity being greater than 1.0, it will initially sink in water. But, according to this SDS, it will readily go into solution with water. Regarding pH the SDS states "not determined." This is not because they don't know the pH, but it is most likely variable or they are just not wanting to disclose it for some reason. However, the main concern about the spilled antifreeze would be its ethylene glycol content. Glycols are polar organic compounds within the alcohol classification, which makes them soluble. Ethylene glycol is toxic to fish and wildlife (which is why if you are a pet owner, you don't want to have a spilled puddle of antifreeze in your garage). It also will cause an increase in BOD and COD which can result in a decrease in the dissolved oxygen content of the receiving water.[25] Therefore, the best course of action is to clean up the spilled antifreeze so that it does not come into contact with and dissolve in storm water. It would also be a good idea to store it in a contained area and under a stormproof covering.

Quantity is another important piece of information needed to connect the dots of pollutant sources. In other words, how big of a dot are we dealing with? If a gallon container of antifreeze is kept within the storage container, that is certainly not as big of a potential pollutant source as a 275-gallon poly tote stored outside. In connecting the dots of pollutant sources, we need to determine which dots are significant and which ones are less important. So, in order to determine significance, in the next section, we are going to evaluate not only the volume stored but especially the degree of exposure to storm water while stored, used, or discarded on the project site, and direct and indirect routes to which the potential pollutant could be mobilized by storm water.

IDENTIFYING POLLUTANTS THAT MAY BE EXPOSED TO STORM WATER

As previously mentioned, just because a chemical or material is on-site does not mean that it is a potential pollutant. Well, OK, it may be a potential pollutant just because it is on location. After all, something weird could happen; while walking from the truck to the new building, the one 250 ml bottle of counter top cleaner could fall out of the bag, shatter, and lose its contents upon hitting a storm drain grate during a qualifying rain event. But that is not what we are talking about. We don't necessarily want to identify every chemical and material that is brought onto the jobsite. What we need to do is to identify the likely potential pollutant sources

---

25   Switzenbaum, M. et al., University of Massachusetts Amherst Water Resources Research Center, (1999) Best Management Practices for Airport Deicing Stormwater, https://downloads.regulations.gov/EPA-HQ-OW-2004-0038-0233/content.pdf.

connecting the dots of where and when they are used and how they might come into contact with storm water. To do so we will create an inventory of significant pollutant sources which will be included in the SWPPP document.

Table 4 provides an example of a partial potential pollutant source inventory for a residential subdivision project. Notice that it helps to connect the dots discussed in this chapter. In identifying the potential pollutant, we have also linked to it the phase of construction during which it will be utilized. By doing so, we will know approximately when that particular pollutant source might be present at the project and have a pretty good idea of the trades that may be using it. The phases of construction, by convention, are typically:

1. Demolition
2. Grading
3. Roadway
4. Utility (or sometimes referred to as Underground)
5. Vertical
6. Landscaping (or sometimes referred to as final stabilization)

However, not every project has all of these phases, or will necessarily progress through them in that specified order. Some projects will have multiple phases (different sense of the word) in which a section of the project may be graded this year and move into roadway, utility, and vertical phases later in the year, while another section will have grading start next year. So, we could have one project with a section in the grading phase, while another section is in the vertical phase, and a third is nearing completion with the landscaping phase. It is possible that some of the potential pollutant sources listed on Table 4 may be initially present, go away, but come back for a later phase or a different section of the project that is now at a point needing that material.

Table 4 – Inventory of Potential Pollutant Sources

Potential Pollutant	Predominate Phases of Construction when Utilized	Interior or Exterior Use	Physical Properties
Concrete, ready mix	Roadway, utility, vertical	Exterior	Solid/slurry, caustic
Concrete, 90 lb. bags	Roadway, utility, landscaping	Exterior	Solid/powder, caustic
Admixtures for concrete	Roadway, utility, vertical	Exterior	Powders and liquids
PVC glues and primer	Utility, vertical, landscaping	Exterior and interior	Liquids
Sand	Utility, vertical	Exterior	Solids, bulk
Diesel, red-dye diesel, gasoline, motor and hydraulic oils, coolant	Grading	Exterior	Liquid

Connecting the Dots of Pollutant Source Assessment

Pollutants of Concern	Method of Contact with Storm Water	Anticipated Storage Location	Expected Quantity to Be Stored
pH altering	Direct	Not stored on-site	N/A
pH altering	Direct and indirect from windblown powder or discarded bags	South storage unit	One pallet
Metals, dissolved solids, COD	Direct, and Indirect from discarded containers or wind dispersion of dust	Tote under plastic sheeting; buckets in the south storage unit	One tote and six 5-gallon buckets
VOC	Direct from use or spills	On electrician, plumber, HVAC, and landscaper vehicles	Varies, estimated at a dozen half-quart cans at any one time.
Settable solids	Direct and indirect from wind and stockpile migration	Small stockpiles in front of the home lots	Approximately twenty stockpiles of one cubic yard each
Oil & Grease, VOC, SVOC, BOD/COD, metals	Indirect by spills or leaks	Only in vehicles; fuel delivered by mobile refueler	N/A

Potential Pollutant	Predominate Phases of Construction when Utilized	Interior or Exterior Use	Physical Properties
Gasoline	Utility, vertical, landscaping	Exterior	Liquid
Stucco mix	Vertical	Exterior	Solid/powder, caustic
Form oil	Vertical	Exterior	Liquid

Connecting the Dots of Pollutant Source Assessment

Pollutants of Concern	Method of Contact with Storm Water	Anticipated Storage Location	Expected Quantity to Be Stored
Oil & Grease, VOC, SVOC	Indirect by spills or leaks	In 5-gallon fuel cans stored in covered secondary containment outside of south storage unit	Four 5-gallon cans
pH altering	Direct and indirect from windblown powder or discarded bags	Brought to the project when needed by the contractor, staged at each work area, covered with plastic	One to two pallets on site at any one time
Oil & Grease	Direct by rain contact with treated forms; indirect by spills or leaks	Brought to the project when needed by the contractor in 5-gallon buckets or smaller containers, staged at each work area or on work trucks, when not in use put in containment and covered with plastic.	Up to two 5-gallon (or smaller) containers.

By identifying the phase of construction in Table 4 for each potential pollutant source, we will have a pretty good idea of the trades which may be using that material. Concrete, obviously, is used by concrete workers, and stucco by stucco installers. Others may be used by multiple trades, such as the example shown on Table 4 of PVC glues and primer, which are used by electricians, plumbers, HVAC installers, and landscapers. Table 4 connects the dots from pollutant to pollutant source by listing the physical properties and the pollutants of concern. So, for the mobile refueler used during grading operations, we know the pollutant sources are the fuels, lubricants, and coolant dispensed by the refueler to the heavy equipment. Associated with those vehicle-related fluids are pollutants that include oil and grease, volatile organic compounds (VOCs), semi-volatile organic compounds (SVOCs), and oxygen demanding substances that elevate BOD and COD. Table 4 then provides information about how these pollutants might be exposed to storm water. There is a column where it is noted if the material is used outside, inside, or both. Another column identifies the methods of contact the pollutant may have with storm water—namely, direct and indirect. Direct is where rain is falling on or across the stored or applied material. Indirect is where the material may be carried or exposed to storm water in another way, such as windblown particles or discarded containers that are placed in a waste bin. Another clue provided in this inventory concerning potential exposure to storm water is the column that provides information on where and how the material is stored. Materials stored outside are going to have more potential exposure than those items stored in the South Storage Unit. Finally, the last column on Table 4 provides some information to determine the magnitude of the potential pollutant source—the size of the dot we are connecting! This last column provides an estimate of the amount of material stored on-site. For example, we probably would consider pallets or a tote of material to be a bigger dot than a dozen half-quart cans. But it really depends upon the information in the other columns. When we look at the phase of the project (which we can associate to a time of year), whether the material is used inside or outside, who is using it, how much is present, and where it is stored,

Connecting the Dots of Pollutant Source Assessment   **67**

we can then make a reasonably informed evaluation about the potential for this pollutant source to come into contact with storm water runoff.

In creating these inventories, it is important to note a few key points:

- The inventories should first be developed before the project starts as a part of the SWPPP development that we will cover in Chapter 5. To prepare a SWPPP, it is necessary to understand the scope of the work planned for the project. Therefore, an experienced SWPPP writer using the information presented in Tables 2 and 3 of this chapter should be able to do a fairly decent job of populating Table 4 with at least the more significant potential pollutants.
- A key rule with SWPPPs is that they need to be "evergreen;" meaning, they need to change and be updated as site conditions change and additional information becomes available. The storm water inspector will need to provide information to update Table 4 periodically throughout the duration of the project.
- Don't get overly detailed! To have an effective inventory of pollutant sources, you do not need to record every container of cleanser, type or color of paint, or whatever a contractor might bring onto the project site. In connecting the dots of construction activities to trades, to what trades use, and to the pollutants, we are only concerned about pollutant sources that present a significant risk to affecting the water quality of storm water runoff from the project—the bigger dots! Some of the materials at the project site, because of their quantity or where and how they are used or stored, do not present a credible threat to water quality. These "dots" are minuscule and do not need to be included on the inventory. It is also acceptable to list general categories of potential pollutants such as adhesives, solvents, or paint. This inventory is not

meant to be a comprehensive list for Cal/OSHA[26] but a tool to help you identify and evaluate the potential threats to water quality so that you can prepare and implement an effective SWPPP.

IDENTIFY WHAT IS BEING PROTECTED

In connecting the dots of pollutant source evaluation, there is one more connection point we need to make, and that is to identify what is to be protected. To where is the storm water runoff flowing? Is storm water impounded in a large retention basin where it mostly infiltrates into the ground and evaporates? Does it enter a municipal separate storm water sewer system (MS4)? Does it flow directly into a creek, river, or the ocean? This connection step could be referred to as the analysis of the **fate and transport**[27] of storm water pollutants. In many cases, unless we know what we are protecting, we won't know if the pollutants we identified are actually potential threats to the environment. Case in point, if our construction project discharges to a large retention basin with no outlet, water with elevated suspended solids or high turbidity will not be a significant problem. Another example would be a project that discharges to a saline or brackish waterbody. In such a case, dissolved solids would certainly not be as much of a concern as if the project were discharging the same water to a fresh water stream.

First let's consider "transport." As we will see in Chapter 5, to write an effective SWPPP, it is absolutely necessary to understand how surface water moves across

---

26 The State of California Division of Occupational Safety and Health (DOSH), better known as Cal/OSHA; or the worker safety agency in your region.

27 The United States Center for Disease Control defines "fate and transport" as how the nature of contaminants might change (chemically, physically, or biologically) and where they go as they move through the environment. https://www.atsdr.cdc.gov/pha-guidance/conducting_scientific_evaluations/exposure_pathways/environmental_fate_and_transport.html#:~:text=%E2%80%9CFate%20and%20transport%E2%80%9D%20refers%20to,they%20move%20through%20the%20environment.

and off of the project site. How much infiltrates into the ground? How is it conveyed across the site? Is there on-site storm water impoundment? If so, how much? And where does the water leave the project boundary? All of these are important questions that must be answered. But, for pollutant source assessment, it is also important to understand where water is travelling on and off the site. If we have areas of infiltration, we are going to want to be aware of construction related pollutants that might harm groundwater quality such as pH, nutrients, dissolved solids, and toxics. All of these can be transported through the soil to groundwater. If the construction site is discharging storm water to a municipality, most likely there will be restrictions regarding the quality of the discharge. Many MS4s have now implemented measures requiring full trash capture for construction site discharges into their systems.

Storm water "fate" is, in our context, where the water finally ends up. Now, I know "all drains lead to the ocean," and in most places in California that may be true. But, more important to know is what water will runoff from the construction project first encounter. Knowing this information is not just some good trivia, but it provides you with information about other potential pollutants of concern to address at the construction project. To do this you need to know in what watershed the project is located. Typically, in California, storm water professionals like to look at the HUC-12 watersheds.[28] The California State Water Resources Control Board has developed some HUC-12 mapping tools to help identify in which HUC-12 watershed a project is located.[29]

---

28   Hydrologic Unit Codes (HUCs) are watersheds delineated by USGS using a nationwide system based on surface hydrologic features. This system divides the country into 21 regions (2-digit), 222 subregions (4-digit), 370 basins (6-digit), 2,270 subbasins (8-digit), ~20,000 watersheds (10-digit), and ~100,000 sub-watersheds (12-digit). A hierarchical hydrologic unit code (HUC) consisting of 2 additional digits for each level in the hydrologic unit system is used to identify any hydrologic area. A complete list of Hydrologic Unit codes, descriptions, names, and drainage areas can be found in the United States Geological Survey Water-Supply Paper 2294, entitled "Hydrologic Unit Maps". https://nas.er.usgs.gov/hucs.aspx.

29   California Water Boards Industrial General Map Tool https://gispublic.waterboards.ca.gov/portal/apps/webappviewer/index.html?id=d2e422cdf19148cfa36f40e075b9889e

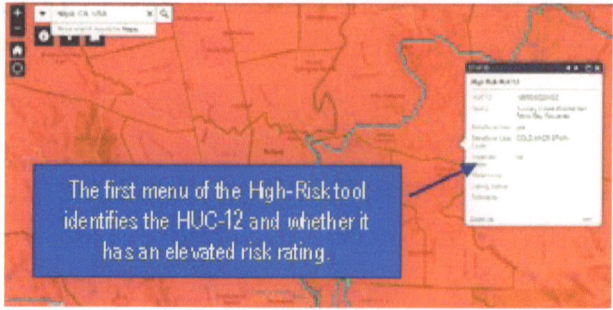

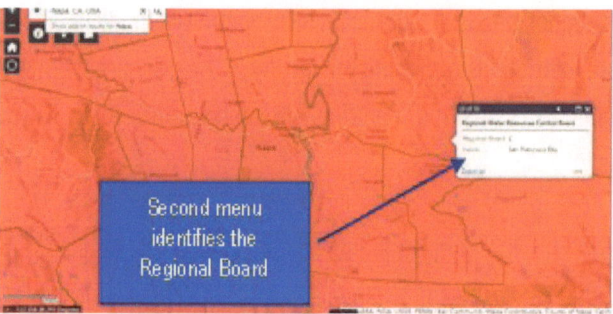

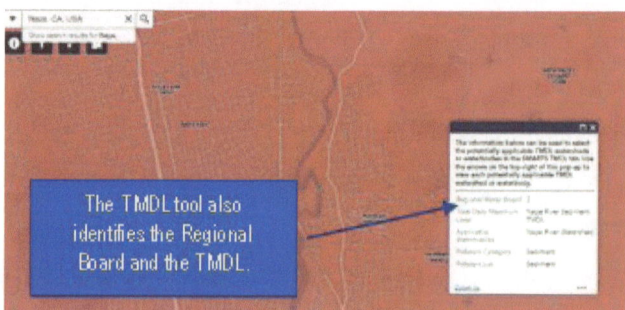

Figure 37 - The State Water Board's online Construction Storm Water General Permit TMDL and High-Risk Receiving Water mapping tools provide an easy way to identify the HUC-12 and Regional Water Board where a project is located and to identify construction-related TMDLs associated with the watershed. Both mapping tools can be accessed on the Water Board's Construction General Permit website. https://www.waterboards.ca.gov/water_issues/programs/stormwater/construction/general_permit_reissuance.html

For projects in California, knowing the HUC-12 watershed along and the Regional Water Quality Control Board where the project is situated will make it possible to identify any impairments or Total Maximum Daily Loads (TMDLs) that are associated with that location. These are for pollutants associated with the waterbody to which your storm water runoff is discharging. They are a result of the Federal Clean Water Act[30] which requires States to implement the following steps:

1. Identify all of the Waters of the United States (WOTUS).[31] Determine the beneficial uses of each identified waterbody (e.g., drinking water, agricultural, recreation, and a variety of ecological uses such as spawn, cold, and migratory).
2. Set water quality standards for each waterbody or type of waterbody.
3. Determine the impairments in or affecting the waterbody that might keep it from fully realizing its beneficial uses (incidentally, these impairments are put on a list called the 303d list, which refers to Section 303, paragraph d of the Clean Water Act).
4. Determine the maximum amount of the impairment that the waterbody can assimilate without jeopardizing any of the beneficial uses. This is called the Total Maximum Daily Load (TMDL).
5. Taking into account the number and types of dischargers to the waterbody, divide up the TMDL among all of the "stakeholders." Each stakeholder/discharger gets a slice of the TMDL pie. The slice is called a Waste Load Allocation (WLA) and is typically in the form of a concentration limit for the pollutant of concern. However, it is not always possible to identify a concentration or to accurately detect down to the specified level. Therefore, in lieu of concentration limits, some TMDLs consist of best management practices required to be implemented on the construction project to satisfy the TMDL requirements.

---

30 USEPA's summary of the Clean Water Act can be found at https://www.epa.gov/laws-regulations/summary-clean-water-act.
31 Waters of the United States definition: https://www.federalregister.gov/d/2022-28595.

The California Construction General Permit provides an attachment[32] which lists the applicable construction-related TMDLs for various locations around the state. Part of the connecting of dots for the pollutant source assessment is to identify in which waterbody the project is located, determine if it has any TMDLs associated with construction activity, and compare this with the Potential Pollutant Source Inventory you previously created. If you find that materials on your inventory may be a source of a TMDL, you will want to include them in the monitoring program described in Chapter 6 and make sure that you have adequate control measures in place to keep them from contacting storm water, as we will discuss in the next chapter.

---

32 California Construction General Permit Order 2022-0057-DWQ, Attachment H https://www.water-boards.ca.gov/water_issues/programs/stormwater/construction/docs/2022-0057-dwq-with-attachments/cgp2022_att_h.pdf.

CHAPTER 4
Connecting the Dots of Best Management Practices

Let's review the dots we have connected thus far. In Chapter 1, we took a look at the environmental problems associated with construction activities and the disconnect in addressing these problems. In Chapter 2, we defined the dots of erosion and sedimentation and connected them with the agents and accelerators present at construction sites. In the previous Chapter, we conducted a pollutant source assessment by connecting the dots of construction activities, trades present on the project, sources of pollutants, and the pollutants themselves. The purpose of this chapter, Chapter 4, is not to present another library of best management practice (BMP) specifications. There are good collections of specifications by organizations like the California Stormwater Quality Association (CASQA), California Department of Transportation (Caltrans), and others that can be used to assist with specifying control measures in a SWPPP and to provide inspectors, installers, and maintenance crews with ample information on how to properly install, maintain, and inspect these BMPs. The purpose of this chapter is to help the reader connect the dots between the pollutant source assessment and preparing an effective SWPPP. As such, we present a different perspective on categorizing BMPs in the hopes that it will assist in the understanding of how different BMPs complement and interact with each other. But, first let's review the standards that have been developed for BMPs.

STANDARDS FOR BMPS

When selecting and specifying BMPs, it is vital to understand what is being required either by a regulatory agency, the owner of the project, or the SWPPP developer. The selection of erosion, sediment, and pollutant control measures is not always left completely to the discretion of the SWPPP developer. In most cases, there will be one or more regulatory agencies who have specific requirements that need to be met. When it comes to governmental compliance, there are layers of laws and regulations applicable to a project. The first layer is federal. For storm water runoff from construction projects, the Clean Water Act (CWA) is the highest authority. This overarching law was enacted to protect the quality of Waters of the United States (WOTUS). By end of the twentieth century, the quality of rivers, lakes, and other water bodies in the United States had been significantly degraded by urban and agricultural discharges. The CWA established a nationwide goal of making WOTUS drinkable, fishable, and swimmable. To accomplish this, it required each state to take an inventory of all of its water bodies and watersheds. Once identified, the CWA required states to determine the beneficial uses for each waterbody. In other words, how is the waterbody used? What benefits to humans or the ecosystem does the waterbody provide? Potential beneficial uses include drinking water, recreation, navigation, industrial supply, agricultural use, groundwater recharge, as well as ecological beneficial uses

Figure 38 - Clean Water Act's goals include making Waters of the United States drinkable, fishable, swimmable and to protect their beneficial uses. (Photo credit: John Teravskis)

such as cold, spawn, migratory, estuarine, and wildlife habitat. The CWA contains mechanisms to make sure the beneficial uses of each waterbody are protected. These mechanisms include establishing water quality standards and identifying what types of discharges and dischargers should be regulated. The CWA sets up the framework for regulating these entities and their discharges by establishing the National Pollutant Discharge Elimination System (NPDES) permitting structure and by "setting the bar" for the level of effort needed in protecting water quality. This "bar" or standard for water quality control is not only a high standard but also an upwardly moving one. It is defined as Best Available Technology Economically Achievable (BAT) and Best Conventional Pollutant Control Technology (BCT).

Best Available Technology Economically Achievable (BAT) [33]

As defined by USEPA, BAT is a technology-based standard established by the Clean Water Act (CWA) § 304(b)(2) as the most appropriate means available on a national basis for controlling the direct discharge of **toxic**[34] **and nonconventional**[35] **pollutants** to navigable waters. The BAT effluent limitations guidelines, in general, represent the best existing performance of treatment technologies that are econ**omically achievable within an industrial point source category or subcategory.**

Best Conventional Pollutant Control Technology (BCT)[32]

As defined by U.S. EPA, BCT is a technology-based standard established by the Clean Water Act (CWA) § 304(b)(4) for the discharge from existing industrial point sources of *conventional pollutants including biochemical oxygen demand (BOD), total suspended sediment (TSS), fecal coliform, pH, and oil and grease.*

---

33 Definitions from the California Construction General Permit Order 2022-0057-DWQ, Attachment B.
34 Toxic pollutants include the sixty-five chemicals / groups of chemicals listed in 40 CFR § 401.15.
35 Nonconventional pollutants are those that are not conventional or listed in 40 CFR § 401.15 as toxic and include parameters such as chlorine, ammonia, nitrogen, phosphorus, chemical oxygen demand (COD), and whole effluent toxicity (WET).

It is a moving standard because technology is always changing; therefore, to comply with this CWA requirement, you have to stay up with the times and utilize the best existing treatment technologies currently available. But, if you are like most people, you have probably already spotted a potential loophole—"*economically achievable.*" But let me caution you. What you and I consider economically achievable is not necessarily what the USEPA or the state storm water agency consider to be economically achievable. Case in point, active treatment systems tend to be fairly expensive and probably outside of most people's budget. But if they were not considered to be economically achievable, the USEPA and the State of California would not have included a section in their respective Construction General Permits to address the use and control of them.

When it comes to implementing the CWA, the USEPA relies largely on delegating the responsibilities to the state storm water agencies. In California, the State Water Resources Control Board (Water Board) has the responsibility for issuing and enforcing its own NPDES permits. Which brings us to the next layer of regulatory control. In the regulatory world, as the oversight agency becomes more local, each lower agency can add more regulations or make the existing requirements more stringent; but a lower-level agency cannot remove or lessen the regulations of a higher-level agency. For example, the California Construction General Permit embodies the federal requirements but it also contains many permit requirements that are not a part of the Federal Construction General Permit (CGP). You might be wondering, if the states have their own NPDES permits for construction, why is there a Federal Construction General Permit? This is because:

Figure 39 - Layers of government; State regulations need to be at least as stringent as the Federal regulations, and local municipal regulations as stringent as those of the State (Sketch by Abigail Teravskis)

Connecting the Dots of Best Management Practices

1. Not all states have accepted the USEPA's delegated authority—Massachusetts, New Hampshire, and New Mexico do not have their own NPDES permits and, therefore, construction projects must apply for coverage under the Federal CGP.
2. Some states have issued their own permit by wholly or partially adopting the USEPA version. But remember, the state permit must be as stringent as the federal one.
3. Tribal lands, U.S. territories, and the District of Columbia are under federal regulatory jurisdiction. Even in states that have their own CGP, a construction project occurring on tribal lands will need to apply for coverage under the federal permit. Interestingly, it does not apply to federal facilities such as military bases, prisons, and national parks. Construction projects occurring at these federal facilities are required to file for coverage under the state's CGP.

The third layer of governmental control is at the local level, which includes cities and counties. Typically, these municipalities are subject to another type of storm water NPDES permit called a Municipal Separate Storm Sewer System (MS4) NPDES Permit. These permits require the municipality to implement a construction management program in which construction projects are conditioned and inspected for compliance with the erosion, sediment, and pollutant control requirements in the municipal code. The exact requirements will vary from one MS4 to another. For example, while some municipalities allow the placement of gravel bags in the curb and gutter to be used as drain inlet protection devices, other municipalities prohibit anything placed in the street and require the use of a flush-mounted drain inlet sediment control measure. It is important to know what the local municipal code requires for each project site.

As you can see, there are many authorities who have a say about BMP selection, sizing, and implementation. In addition to the agencies mentioned above, there are other governmental agencies that may condition a construction project with water quality-related BMPs or control measures. They include the United States Army Corps of Engineers (USACE), Federal and State Fish and Wildlife agencies, Air Pollution Control Districts, CEQA/NEPA[36] lead agencies, and other governmental entities who may include BMP requirements in their permits or conditions of approval.

Governmental agencies are not the only entities who condition projects with specific BMPs; often the owners will have specific requirements for the selection and installation of control measures on their projects. The owner can be a large governmental organization such as Caltrans or Departments of Transportation in other states.

Figure 40 - Caltrans-approved biodegradable fiber roll wrapped with jute mesh. (Photo credit: John Teravskis)

In California, Caltrans has created its own culture of storm water compliance programs with BMP fact sheets specific to highway projects, extensive storm water-related contract specifications, designated bid line items for BMPs that may be used on a project, training requirements, inspection and reporting form templates, and a SWPPP template. For example, on Caltrans projects, only biodegradable jute-covered fiber rolls may be used. Fiber rolls with monofilament netting are prohibited because they can photodegrade

---

36 California Environmental Quality Act / National Environmental Policy Act.

and contribute microplastics in storm water runoff and they can also entrap snakes and other wildlife. If you are preparing a SWPPP for a Caltrans project it will be absolutely necessary to familiarize yourself with the requirements in their specifications, standards, and BMP fact sheets.

It is always important for the SWPPP developer to check the owner's specifications for project or site-specific BMP requirements. These requirements are typically a part of the bid specifications. Sometimes they just state, *"comply with the Construction General Permit,"* but other times they get very specific. Oftentimes the owner will call out a certain specification for BMPs, as shown in Figure 41.

SECTION 02270

EROSION AND SEDIMENT CONTROL

PART 1   GENERAL

1.1   SECTION INCLUDES

    A.   Implement and install erosion and sediment control measures as required by the Stormwater Pollution Prevention Plan (SWPPP) and as shown on the Construction Drawings.

1.2   RELATED SECTIONS

    A.   Section 02200 — Site Earthwork

1.3   SEQUENCING AND SCHEDULING

    A.   All erosion control features must be approved by the Engineer before beginning site earthwork. Submit erosion control plan in accordance with SWPPP.

    B.   Route runoff from cleared or disturbed areas. Route through temporary sediment traps, straw bale barriers, and/or silt fences. Place erosion control facilities prior to any earthwork, clearing, and grubbing. It is preferable for construction to progress in an upstream direction starting with downstream erosion control facilities as the first items of construction.

    C.   Stabilize disturbed ground at the end of each work day. Perform surface roughening immediately upon reaching final grade of non-lined areas by uniformly track-walking up and down slopes with a crawler tractor or sheepsfoot roller, leaving a pattern of growsers or cleat imprints that parallel the slope contours. Implement permanent soil stabilization and erosion/sedimentation controls upon reaching final grade.

Figure 41- Owner's specification. Note the specificity of the stabilization and track-walking requirements.

Another part of the same owner's specification calls out hydroseeding details, as shown in Figure 42.

A. Approved native low profile grass seed mix that has been used previously within the local area or at the site that is certified free of noxious seed and consisting of the following:

1. California Brome (Bromus Carinatus): 16 lbs/acre
2. California Meadow Barley (Hordeum Californicum): 12 lbs/acre
3. Small Fescue (Vulpia Microstachys): 4 lbs/acre
4. Arroyo Lupin (Lupinus Succulentus): 4 lbs/acre
5. Purple Needlegrass (Nasella Pulchra): 4 lbs/acre
6. Rose Clover (Trifolium Hirtum): 3 lbs/acre
7. Golden Yarrow (Eriophyllum Confertiflorum: 0.5 lb/acre

All seed shall be in conformance with the California State Seed Law of the Department of Food and Argiculture. Each bag shall be delivered sealed and marked with the species, purity, percent, germination, dealer's guarantee and dates of test.

B. Rice straw mulch that is applied at 4,000 lbs/acre or other approved combination of rice straw and degradable green-dyed wood cellulose fiber specifically blended for hydromulching.

C. Tackifier that is derived natural organic plant sources containing no growth or germination inhibiting material, hydrates in water, readily blends with other slurry materials. Stabilizing emulsion shall meet or exceed the requirements of Caltrans Standard Specification 21-1.02.

D. Fertilizer as recommended by the seed mix supplier. Fertilizer shall conform to requirements of the California Food and Agriculture code.

Figure 42 - Owner's specification for hydroseeding.

In this case, the owner has specified a mix of grass and wild flowers for their project. Also note how the owner is referencing other specifications, such as the California State Seed Law of the Department of Food and Agriculture and a Caltrans standard specification.

Connecting the Dots of Best Management Practices

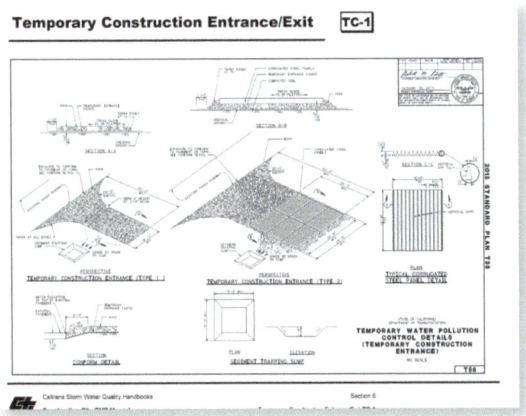

Figure 43 - Caltrans TC-1 Specification for track-out control measures

Many times, a SWPPP developer will incorporate BMP specifications into their SWPPP that were developed by a third party, such as the Erosion Control Technology Council (ECTC)[37], California Stormwater Quality Association (CASQA)[38], Caltrans[39], a university, or by another state or agency. Once included with the SWPPP, the NPDES permits require the BMP or control measure to be implemented and maintained as described in the specification. For example, Caltrans has a specification for track-out control called "TC-1." It requires that a minimum of twelve inches of crushed aggregate (ranging in size from three to six inches) be placed on a filter fabric. The length of the track-out control must be as long as four times the circumference of the largest construction vehicle tire and the width needs to be able to accommodate anticipated traffic. None of this specificity is in the regulatory requirements, but when the SWPPP developer includes this TC-1 specification in the SWPPP, it is now required to be implemented for this project. Of course, the SWPPP developer can change the specifications as needed, as long as the altered BMP complies with the permit requirements.

37 https://www.ectc.org/
38 https://www.casqa.org/
39 https://dot.ca.gov/programs/construction/storm-water-and-water-pollution-control

Most construction projects will have some level of regulatory or owner-driven BMP requirements, but let's now turn our attention to selecting BMPs based on the activities and dynamics of the project. To do so, in order to provide enhanced insight into the purpose and functionality of the BMPs, I have created a new way of defining and categorizing the standard and essential erosion, sediment, and management BMPs. The four refined BMP categories we will explore include: Site Management BMPs, Raindrop BMPs, Slow-the-Flow BMPs, and Treatment BMPs.

SITE MANAGEMENT BMPS

When it comes to BMPs, most sites do a pretty decent job of installing fiber roll, track-out control measures, and drain inlet protection. Some projects will even have erosion controls in place such as erosion control blankets or hydraulic mulch. But many project managers fail to realize that having an effective erosion, sediment, and pollutant control program involves much more than installing a few BMPs. The projects that are truly successful in controlling these pollutants have implemented procedures, systems, and management practices that allow them to have adequate control of what happens at the site. This type of BMP is something that needs to be incorporated into the project planning process and the jobsite culture. **Most projects fail at adequate pollutant control because they failed to connect the dots of proper site management.**

Scheduling (SM-1)
When doing a group exercise to create a SWPPP map, I often joke in my classes that we should have the project start when most projects start—October (which is the start of the rainy season in California). All joking aside, it does seem that many project managers do not take into account the rainy season when planning the project's scheduling and sequencing. California tends to be a land of extremes, especially when it comes to rainfall. It is either drought or flooding. As a result, during the dry years builders tend to think it will always be dry and plan

their projects accordingly. But, when a wet season occurs, like in 2023 when twelve significant atmospheric rivers sweep through the state, these same builders are caught completely unprepared for the impact to their projects. **The schedule is the most important site management BMP to utilize.** Delaying the start of the project to coincide with the dry season will not only significantly assist erosion and sediment control but can also greatly improve the efficiency of the project and, thereby, reduce the cost of construction. During the 2017 wet season, we observed two projects, in particular, that experienced huge inefficiencies by not paying attention to the rainy season in their scheduling and sequencing. Both projects (one an industrial facility and the other a commercial development) failed to install asphalt roadways when they had ample opportunity to do so during the dry season. As a result, during that very wet season, dirt roadways used by construction traffic became muddy bogs. So much so, that the contractors had to excavate two to three feet of mud to be able to access the project. Without doubt, that activity was not in the project's budget or schedule. You may have noticed that, when the site is muddy, work is either greatly hampered or is not occurring at all. So, why was it so important to start the project in October rather than waiting until May? By the time the site dries out and work can resume, it will be May.

Figure 44 - The 2022/2023 rainy season caught many construction projects unprepared for the amount of runoff generated by the twelve atmospheric river events. (Photo credit: John Teravskis)

SM-1 Scheduling:

Good site management allows for both the storm season and imminent or short-term storm forecast to dictate when activities occur that present a high risk of exposing pollutants to storm water. The grading phase and other construction activities that disturb a significant amount of soil should be scheduled to occur during a time when precipitation is unlikely to occur. Construction activities that include pollutants that can be mobilized by storm water and cannot be protected with a stormproof cover during storm events should be discontinued until dry weather returns. Good site management also utilizes scheduling to phase activities, BMP installation, and project milestones so that the construction site will have maximum protection in place before the storm season begins. This can include:

- Installing temporary or permanent effective soil covers (Raindrop BMPs);
- Installing impervious surfaces (e.g., installing a first lift of asphalt in the parking lot or roadway to use as a stabilized work area or construction roadway during the wet season);
- Backfilling and covering utility trenches;
- Establishing settling basins and sediment traps; and
- Stabilizing storm water conveyances, such as drainage swales, drain inlets, and concentrated flow discharge locations.

Budgeting and Procurement (SM-2)

This is another area where many erosion and sediment control programs go awry. Even in cases where a fully compliant and well-thought-out SWPPP may have been prepared, some projects get into trouble because they failed to connect the dots from the BMPs called out on the SWPPP map to the BMPs included in the project budget. Good site management entails having a realistic understanding of the BMPs required for a project, when they are needed, and how they will impact the budget and project costs. There are several places where the financial disconnects can happen:

- ☑ ***The project was bid without consideration of the SWPPP.*** This might happen because there was no SWPPP in place when the project was bid. Or it may be that those bidding the project were not aware of the SWPPP. It may also be that, to cut costs and be more competitive, the dollars allocated for BMPs were reduced or altogether eliminated.

- ☑ ***Only certain bid items are reimbursable by the project owner.*** This can often be a problem if the bid item restrictions were not communicated to the SWPPP developer. For example, the bid items might only include fiber rolls and applying bonded fiber matrix (BFM) at a certain specification. The SWPPP writer, unaware of this restriction in reimbursable charges, might have called out compost socks and a flexible growth media hydraulic mulch in the SWPPP. The contractor is then faced with trying to fit a square peg into a round hole. They need to either get the owner to allow the alternative BMPs or the SWPPP developer to agree to changing the plan. However, in so many cases, there is no communication between the parties, and the contractor procures and installs what seems best to him or her.

- ☑ ***A misunderstanding about when the BMPs are needed.*** The prevailing school of thought among contractors seems to be that 1) fiber roll gets installed at the start of the project and 2) hydroseeding is done at the end of the project. Although it is somewhat understandable how they arrived at this idea, it is also a misconception that can lead to inadequate funding for the project's BMPs. True, linear sediment controls (such as fiber roll) are oftentimes installed at the very beginning of the project.

But that is not the only time they will need to be installed. Additional installations will certainly be needed as the project progresses. Same with the application of sprayed-on erosion control products. So many times, the contractor delays having it done because not all areas have been finalized and are ready to be sprayed. The budget only included one mobilization of the hydroseeding subcontractor, and the project manager does not want to call them out until the very end when everything is ready to be sprayed. By doing so, the project manager allows large portions of the project to be out of compliance with the Construction General Permit. Over the years, we have seen many epic erosion control failures for this very reason. In their race to get everything done by the start of the rainy season and not wanting to call out the erosion control provider until everything is ready, when the first rain of the season does come, the project is not prepared for it. When asked about it, the contractor will often state, "*We called the hydroseeder, but they are booked up and cannot come for another two weeks*" or "*We were caught by surprise by this first rain event.*" In reality, much of the site could have been sprayed weeks, if not months, before. The real reason is that the contractor did not budget adequately for multiple mobilizations of the erosion control provider.

- ☑ **Not understanding the life expectancy of BMPs.** Even in cases where BMPs called out in the SWPPP were taken into account by the bidder, we observe a financial disconnect in failing to realize most BMPs will wear out and need to be replaced. Perhaps the bidder did a good job of identifying the linear feet of silt fence needed on the project. But, if the project duration is three years, the linear feet figure should probably be multiplied by a minimum of two or three times, and in harsher climates, perhaps five or six times. This is because silt fence has a life expectancy of not much more than a year. Winds and sun rays will cause the fence fabric to tear and break down and, therefore, no longer be an effective sediment control. The same can be said of installation of hydraulic mulches or other sprayed-on products. Depending on the type and amount used and the amount of runoff and abuse it gets from foot and equipment traffic, the erosion control product will very likely need to be reapplied for longer projects until final stabilization can be achieved.

- ☑ **Not allowing enough time for procurement.** We have seen that the supply chain is not always reliable and timely. Even for projects whose BMP budgets are adequate, a financial disconnect can happen because of delays in procurement. This can be due to supply chain problems. In recent years, there have been times when it was nearly impossible to obtain certain types of BMPs, such as burlap-wrapped fiber rolls or the Caltrans-approved black felt gravel bags. In these cases, usually a work-around can be found and approved by the project's owner. Typically, procurement problems result because of a delay in initiating the process. As was previously mentioned, at the start of the rainy season everyone and their brother is calling the hydroseeding contractor and running to the local construction material supplier for a pallet of fiber rolls. It should not be surprising when there is a waiting time for the hydroseeder or the supplier is out of stock. We have also observed last-minute applications of hydraulic mulch or other sprayed-on products rendered ineffective because they were installed with not enough time to allow them to fully cure before the rain event started. I have literally seen freshly installed hydraulic mulch washed off of a site. This is often a colossal waste of money, especially if the project had budgeted for only one application of the product. Having good site management means scheduling and procuring early, as well as stockpiling erosion and sediment control supplies on site.

SM-2 Budgeting and Procurement:
Good site management includes budgeting adequately for BMPs and procuring them in time to be in place and effective when they are needed. To assist with this, practices that should be implemented include:

- Making sure the bidder or project cost estimator is aware of the BMPs specified in the SWPPP (if a SWPPP has not yet been developed, they should be aware of the BMP expectations of the state, local municipality, and the owner);
- Communicating bid line restrictions to the SWPPP developer;
- Understanding the project's duration and harshness of the climate to estimate the life-expectancy of the BMPs and how often they will need to be replaced;
- Identifying the number of mobilizations needed of erosion control providers and BMP installers;
- Ordering products and services early enough to have them in place when needed and/or required; and
- Stockpiling an adequate supply of BMPs on site to allow for timely repairs or maintenance.

Pollution and Spill Prevention (Cover, Secure, and Contain) (SM-3)

Proper site management for construction materials, supplies, equipment, and waste is to cover, secure, and contain them. The bottom line is to keep pollutant sources and storm water separated. The best way to do this is to give some thought about where and how materials, supplies, equipment, and wastes are stored. **Powders,** such as stockpiles of sand, soil, soil amendments, fly ash, and other construction materials, should be stored in a way so that they are protected from being dispersed and carried away by wind or rain. They can be stored in bags (such as bags of concrete), in covered and bermed stockpiles, and in covered drums, totes, and bins. The uses of powders should be done in such a way that excess fugitive dust will not be generated and any powders deposited on the ground or surface of structures can be cleaned up before the next rain event. Likewise, non-storm water **liquids** (hazardous and non-hazardous) should be kept from coming into contact with storm water. Liquids at a construction site can include wash waters, concrete slurries, sanitary waste, contaminated groundwater, water treatment chemicals, and non-hazardous and hazardous liquids used in construction or for fueling and maintaining vehicles. Liquids are typically exposed to storm water when they have been spilled or are leaking from their container. Therefore, a spill prevention and control program is a vital part of good site management. Spill prevention can be achieved through the establishment of Standard Operating Procedures (SOPs), training of site personnel on the SOPs, and putting systems into place to prevent spills from occurring.

Prevention SOPs should include:

- ☑ How and where to store liquids on site;
- ☑ How to load/unload buckets, drums, and totes to/from a delivery vehicle;
- ☑ How to receive a bulk liquid delivery;
- ☑ How to pump off liquid to a transport tanker; and
- ☑ How and where to fuel vehicles and equipment.

Systems for spill prevention should include the following:

- ☑ Secondary containment for where liquids are being stored or transferred;
- ☑ Designation of a specific location to fuel vehicles and equipment and to perform bulk transfers of liquids;
- ☑ Providing a covering to prevent the accumulation of storm water within the secondary containment;
- ☑ Equipping storage containers with a mechanism to determine available capacity;

- ☑ Providing locks and security measures to prevent vandalism or tampering of storage containers;
- ☑ Providing protection to storage containers from vehicles and equipment; and
- ☑ Providing accessible valves and/or switches to immediately terminate a transfer if needed.

Control SOPs should include:

- ☑ How to respond to a spill including information and instructions on initial control, cleanup, and notifications;
- ☑ How to manage waste generated from spill cleanup; and
- ☑ How to follow up on a spill to assure it will have no lingering effects on storm water quality.

Systems for spill control should include the following:

- ☑ Providing adequately sized and equipped spill kits, supplies, and tools to be able to control, contain, and clean up a spill for the types of liquids present on site;
- ☑ Adequate lighting to be able to detect a spill and perform spill response activities after dark; and
- ☑ Providing waste drums, bins, labels, and supplies for disposing of cleanup materials.

Solids also need to be managed on site. Solid waste may consist of trash, demolition debris, concrete waste, asphalt grindings, contaminated soil, sawdust, cuttings and grindings, and spent sandblast grit. Solids also include aggregates, structural materials, and landscaping materials. Some solids / building materials are meant to be utilized outside and do not present a threat to storm water quality and, therefore, do not require special handling. But other materials can be mobilized by wind or water or can leach pollutants into the ground. These materials should be secured within a bin or a contained and covered stockpile. Any materials that could leach pollutants into the soil should be placed within an enclosed, lined or leakproof covered bin; or on plastic and covered with plastic. Trash should always be placed within a bin that is covered during rain events and windy conditions.

Figure 45 - Solid waste and trash should be stored in a bin and covered during rain events and windy conditions. (Photo credit: John Teravskis)

SM-3 Pollution and spill prevention (cover, secure, and contain):
- Good site management includes keeping materials and their pollutants that can be mobilized by rain or wind covered, secured, and contained. This includes properly managing powders, liquids, and solids. To assist with this, practices that should be implemented include:
- Covering and berming stockpiles so that the stored materials are not dispersed by water or wind (instead of berming, stockpiles can be located in a depressed area where migration of materials will not occur);
- Storing liquids within secondary containment and covered so that storm water does not accumulate in the containment;
- Implementing Standard Operating Procedures (SOPs) and systems to prevent and control spills of liquids;

- Cleaning up spills upon discovery and properly disposing of clean-up-related wastes;
- Storing and using powdered substances in a way to minimize dispersal and transport by water and wind;
- Covering and protecting solid construction materials (that are not meant to remain outdoors) from contact with rain and wind; and
- Placing solid waste in a bin or other weather-resistant container and covering the bins/containers during rain events and windy conditions.

Wind and Fugitive Dust Controls (SM-4)

Maintaining good site management includes keeping particles from blowing off site. Typically referred to as "dust control," these are management practices that prevent wind erosion and dispersal of sediment and other particulate matter. As we covered in Chapter 3, the Wind Erosion Equation (Equation 1) can be helpful in identifying dust control measures.

Recall that the Wind Erosion Equation (WEQ) is:

$$E = f(I,K,C,L,V)$$

Where:

E = the average soil loss due to wind (tons/acre/year),

And soil loss "E" is a function of:

I = the soil erodibility,

K = the soil ridge roughness,

C = the climatic factor,

L = equivalent unsheltered distance across the field along the prevailing wind erosion direction, and

V = the vegetative factor.

Connecting the Dots of Best Management Practices

We can use each of the factors in the equation to identify clues and tips for potential dust control measures.

The **soil erodibility (I) factor** can be adjusted, even when we have highly erodible soils, by adding a substance that will lessen the erodibility or make it less likely for the fine particles to become airborne. Dust palliatives are substances applied to soil surfaces to reduce airborne dust and its health impacts. The most common substance to add is water, but it is by no means the only substance for dust suppression. Table 5 contains a list of dust palliatives (or suppressants) that may be used on a construction site. Construction roadways can be stabilized with the use of crushed rock or one of the dust palliatives shown in Table 5.

> **Dust Control Terminology**
>
> **Agglomerate:** to gather smaller particles into a larger mass.
>
> **Anionic:** an ion having a negative electrical charge.
>
> **Cationic:** an ion having a positive electrical charge.
>
> **Deliquescent:** a substance that absorbs moisture from the air and dissolves in it or becomes itself a liquid.
>
> **Hygroscopic:** a substance that tends to absorb moisture from the air but remains a solid.
>
> **Palliative:** a substance which reduces airborne dust.
>
> **Suppressant:** a substance used to minimize fugitive dust and control erosion.

The **soil ridge roughness (K) factor** was demonstrated in Chapter 2, where scarifying the soil was shown how it can capture and trap saltation and soil creep particles and how it also reduces the wind exposed surface area to effectively reduce suspension.

The obvious lesson from the **climate (C) factor** is to suspend work when conditions become windy. Air pollution control districts will often require outdoor construction activities to cease operations whenever visible dust emissions cannot be effectively controlled. Other site management controls, such as maintaining vehicles speeds less than fifteen mph and covering stockpiles, can help prevent the generation of excessive fugitive dust.

The **wind shelter (L) factor** is where a wind screen is installed on the prevailing wind upgradient side of the project. As described in Chapter 3, with each vertical foot of wind screen, approximately ten horizontal feet of the project is wind protected. As such, a ten-foot-tall wind fence should provide a wind block for approximately one hundred feet of the project.

The **vegetative (V) factor** applies to both the beginning and the end of the project. To prevent wind erosion, vegetation should not be removed until it is absolutely necessary. Disturbing large areas of soil and leaving them uncovered will become a source for fugitive dust. (Remember the Dust Bowl?) After soils have been disturbed, it is equally important that they be covered with a temporary erosion control measure or with permanent vegetation as soon as possible.

Table 5 - Dust Palliatives[40] - see next page

---

40 Adapted from the United States Department of Agriculture Forest Service Dust Palliative Selection and Application Guide, Bolander, Peter, ed. 1999, https://www.fs.usda.gov/t-d/pubs/pdf/99771207.pdf.

Table 5 – Dust Palliatives

Dust Suppressant Category	Attributes
Water	• Agglomerates the surface particles. • For many projects, readily available. • Helps with compaction.
Water Absorbing: Calcium Chloride (deliquescent)	• Ability to absorb water from the air is a function of temperature and relative humidity; requires a minimum relative humidity of 25%. • Significantly increases surface tension of water film between particles, helping to slow evaporation and further tighten compacted soil as drying progresses. • Treated roads can be regraded and recompacted with less concern for losing moisture and density.
Water Absorbing: Magnesium Chloride (deliquescent)	• To absorb water from the air requires a minimum 32% relative humidity independent of temperature. • More effective than calcium chloride solutions for increasing surface tension, resulting in a very hard dirt surface when dry. • Treated surfaces can be regraded and recompacted with less concern for losing moisture and density.

Limitations	Application	Environmental Considerations
• Evaporates readily. • Short-term dust control. • Needs to be reapplied throughout the day.	• Frequency depends on temperature and humidity; typically needs to be applied every two to eight hours.	• Drought-related limitations or water conservation restrictions.
• Does not perform as well in dry climates. • Does not perform as well as MgCl in long dry periods and better than MgCl when high humidity is present. • Slightly corrosive to metal, but highly corrosive to aluminum and its alloys; attracts moisture, thereby prolonging the active period for corrosion. • Storm water tends to leach out highly soluble chlorides. • If the treated material has a high percentage of fines, the surface may become slippery when wet.	• Generally, one to two treatments per season.	• Runoff water quality impact: generally negligible if the proper buffer zone exists between treated area and water. • Fresh receiving water impact: may elevate chloride concentrations and harm freshwater aquatic fish and organisms. • Plant impact: some species susceptible, such as pine, hemlock, poplar, ash, spruce, and maple, as well as some agriculture crops. • Potential concerns with spills of liquid concentrate.
• Not suitable in drier climates • In concentrated solutions, very corrosive to steel (note: some products may contain a corrosive-inhibiting additive); attracts moisture, thereby prolonging the active period for corrosion. • Storm water tends to leach out highly soluble chlorides. • If the treated material has a high percentage of fines, the surface may become slippery when wet.	• Generally, one to two treatments per season.	• Runoff water quality impact: generally negligible if the proper buffer zone exists between treated area and water. • Fresh receiving water impact: may elevate chloride concentrations and harm freshwater aquatic fish and organisms. • Plant impact: some species susceptible, such as pine, hemlock, poplar, ash, spruce, and maple, as well as some agriculture crops. • Potential concerns with spills of liquid concentrate.

Dust Suppressant Category	Attributes
Water Absorbing: Sodium Chloride / Common Salt (hygroscopic)	• To absorb water from the air requires a minimum 79% relative humidity independent of temperature. • Increases surface tension slightly less than calcium chloride.
Organic Petroleum Products (Soil Binder)	• Binds and/or agglomerates surface particles because of asphalt adhesive properties. • Serves to waterproof construction roadways.
Organic Nonpetroleum: Lignin Derivatives (Soil Binder)	• Plant-based lignin binds surface particles together. • Greatly increases dry strength of material under dry conditions. • Works well in low humidity and dry soils making it a better wind erosion control than a water erosion control. • On soils having a high clay content, it tends to remain slightly plastic, permitting reshaping and additional traffic compaction.

Connecting the Dots of Best Management Practices

Limitations	Application	Environmental Considerations
• Not suitable in drier climates. • Moderately corrosive to steel in dilute solutions. • Tends to not hold up well as a surface application.	• Generally, one to two treatments per season • Higher dosages than calcium treatment.	• Runoff water quality impact: generally negligible if the proper buffer zone exists between treated area and water. • Fresh receiving water impact: may elevate chloride concentrations and harm freshwater aquatic fish and organisms. • Plant impact: some species susceptible, such as pine, hemlock, poplar, ash, spruce, and maple, as well as some agriculture crops. • Potential concerns with spills of liquid concentrate.
• Under dry conditions some products may not maintain resilience • If there are too many fines in surface soils and high in asphaltenes, it can form a crust and fragment under traffic and in wet weather. • Some products are difficult to maintain.	• Generally, one to two treatments per season depending on surface condition, dilution, and product.	• There are a wide variety of volatile and semi-volatile hydrocarbon ingredients in these products. • May produce an oil sheen. • "Used" products can be toxic. • Oil in products might be toxic. • Potential concerns with spills and leaching of toxic pollutants prior to the product curing.
• May cause corrosion of aluminum and its alloys. • Surface binding action may be reduced or completely destroyed by heavy rain due to solubility of the product in water. • It becomes slippery when wet, brittle when dry. • It is difficult to maintain as a hard surface, but it can be done under adequate moisture conditions.	• Generally, one to two treatments per season.	• May elevate Biological Oxygen Demand (BOD) of discharges and the receiving water.

Dust Suppressant Category	Attributes
Organic Nonpetroleum: Molasses/Sugar Beet Extract (Soil Binder)	• Provides temporary binding of the surface particles using a plant-based byproduct of sugar bweet processing.
Organic Nonpetroleum: Tall-Oil Derivatives (Soil Binder)	• Adheres surface particles together. • Greatly increases dry strength of material under dry conditions.
Organic Nonpetroleum: Vegetable oils	• Agglomerates the surface particles
Electrochemical Derivatives	• Changes the electric charge and characteristics of clay-sized particles. • Generally effective regardless of climatic conditions.
Polymers (Soil Binder)	• Binds surface particles because of polymer's anionic or cationic adhesive properties.
Clay Additives	• Agglomerates with fine dust particles. • Generally, increases dry strength of material under dry conditions.

Limitations	Application	Environmental Considerations
• Limited commercial and geographic availability.	• There is no extensive supporting research or field experience to dictate an application rate. It will be product and conditions dependent.	• May cause elevated BOD of the discharge and receiving water.
• Surface binding action may be reduced or completely destroyed by long-term exposure to heavy rain due to solubility of the product in water. • Difficult to maintain as a hard surface.	• Generally, one treatment every few years.	• May produce an oil sheen.
• Limited commercial and geographic availability. • Oxidizes rapidly, then becomes brittle.	• Generally, one treatment per season.	• May produce an oil sheen.
• Performance dependent on fine-clay mineralogy. • Needs time to "set up," (i.e., react with the clay fraction). • Limited life span.	• Generally, one treatment every few years.	• Cationic (positively charged) products may be prohibited in some states because they are lethal for fish. • Some products are highly acidic in their undiluted form.
• Difficult to maintain as a hard surface. • Cationic products may be prohibited in some states. • May be slippery when wet.	• Product dependent, but most likely one to two treatments per year.	• Cationic polymers can bind with fish gills causing suffocation and fish kills. • May increase BOD.
• May become slippery when wet.	• Generally, one treatment every five years.	• When crushed and exposed to storm water runoff, it can cause a colloidal clay suspension, which raises the turbidity of the runoff.

SM-4 Wind and fugitive dust controls:

Good site management includes preventing wind erosion and fugitive dust from leaving the construction boundary. This can be accomplished by implementing one or more of the following:

- Applying a dust palliative to the surface of the exposed soil.
- Covering stockpiles and haul truckloads.
- Scarifying the soil.
- Disturbing only as much soil as needed.
- Installing wind barriers or fences upgradient of the project on the prevailing wind side.
- Enforcing on-site speed limits of fifteen mph or less.
- Providing stabilized construction roadways (covered with rock or a dust palliative).
- Ceasing soil disturbing activities during windy conditions when other mitigation measures are not successfully controlling fugitive dust from leaving the project boundary.
- Reestablishing vegetation or other erosion-resistant coverings as soon as possible.

Education and Training (SM-5)

Site management is not just about BMPs. It is equally about the people who work with and around the BMPs. This is an area that is often overlooked or undervalued. We can have the best SWPPP developed, specify an effective suite of BMPs, have qualified inspectors, and the best intentions of compliance with the Construction General Permit, but if we do not communicate our plans and intentions to the on-site managers and field personnel, we will be crippling our efforts and, most likely, will render them ineffective. An effective storm water compliance program takes teamwork. Everyone has to be on board and pulling the same direction. This is why the education and training of managers, contractors, subcontractors, inspectors, and consultants is so important. Expectations, responsibilities, prohibitions, and requirements need to be clearly communicated to all personnel. This communication can be accomplished through a variety of methods. The more forms of communication, the better the message will be heard and understood. Communication of storm water expectations, responsibilities, prohibitions, and requirements can be accomplished by the methods described in Table 6 - *See next page.*

Table 6 – Methods of Communication

Type of Communication	Audience	Delivery and Purpose
Job/task kickoff meeting	Everyone present on the first day of construction or the first day of a new phase or major task.	**Thirty to sixty minutes** – The project manager should introduce the topic and emphasize its importance, a qualified inspector or SWPPP developer can provide the details; it should cover the location of the SWPPP, the BMPs required for the initial phase of the project, location and use of spill cleanup materials and equipment, and location of erosion and sediment control materials; good housekeeping expectations; non-storm water prohibitions; and other storm water-related expectations and prohibitions. A longer version of this type of training would include Foundational Training.
Tailgate meetings	Everyone present on that day of work.	**Five to ten minutes** – Best if performed at the beginning of the day in conjunction with the daily safety and project coordination meeting; cover one or more BMPs associated with that day's work; identify any BMP failures, needed corrective action, or maintenance items from the previous day.

Connecting the Dots of Best Management Practices

Type of Communication	Audience	Delivery and Purpose
Texts and email	Either to all project-related personnel or to specific trades, subcontractors, or delegated inspectors.	**Brief and targeted** – This can be used to communicate a quick message to everyone like, "The south concrete washout is full, please utilize the north washout system;" emails can be used to welcome new subcontractors to the project or to disseminate SOPs, flyers, updated SWPPP maps, etc.
Signage	To all project-related personnel or to specific trades.	**Wherever needed** – Posted in conspicuous and strategic locations with messages such as COVER WASTE BIN AFTER EACH USE, NO CONSTRUCTION VEHICLE EXITING, SPILL KIT, NO WASHING ALLOWED, CONCRETE WASHOUT LOCATION, etc.
Printed handouts / PDF flyers	Either to all project-related personnel or to specific trades, subcontractors, or delegated inspectors.	**Brief and targeted** – These handouts/flyers can be distributed by hand during a tailgate meeting or attached to an email. They can be used to summarize jobsite storm water expectations to all personnel, or they can be used to communicate task-specific BMP and good housekeeping requirements to specific trades/subcontractors.

Type of Communication	Audience	Delivery and Purpose
Standard Operating Procedures (SOPs)	For personnel performing a specific task such as concrete washout, washing of equipment, fueling of equipment, installing fiber roll, etc.	**Task specific** – Create a written step-by-step procedure that personnel can use as guidance when performing specific tasks. Require trained personnel to sign an acknowledgment form that they received, read, and understood the SOP.
Videos	For everyone on the jobsite, new personnel or subcontractors, or for specific trades.	Record an earlier presentation or create a new training – Videos can be used to provide training to new personnel or subcontractors when they start work on the project. The original job kickoff meeting can be recorded and then shared with any new workers. Videos can also be made to supplement the SOPs or to provide specific instruction on BMP implementation and maintenance. The videos can be uploaded to YouTube or Vimeo and a link shared via email or text to the applicable personnel.
One-on-one	Directed to individuals who have specific roles, such as delegated inspectors, samplers, or installers.	**Very targeted** – These one-to-one or small group meetings are good for training about specific roles and jobs. This type of meeting is appropriate for storm water inspectors, samplers, or those overseeing the implementation and documentation of BMPs. Site-specific training would be included in this type of communication.

Regardless of which type of communication is utilized, training can be separated into two main categories: foundational and site-specific. Foundational training covers the prohibitions and requirements of the Construction General Permit. It reviews the general requirements for BMPs, inspections, monitoring, and reporting, but not, to a great extent, what is required for a particular site. Too often, this part of the training program is omitted or overly abbreviated, which results in site managers and personnel lacking the background on why certain activities are allowed or not allowed. Without this fundamental knowledge, these individuals are often operating blindly and not able to understand the big picture of what is required by the permit. A symptomatic result of this lack of knowledge is that they tend to rotely implement BMPs without understanding the purpose and function of them. Foundational training answers the "why" questions. When they understand the permit's requirements, they will be able to comprehend the purpose for the specified BMPs and the rationale for the inspection and monitoring program. Foundational training is best performed in a literal or virtual classroom where specific permit language can be explored and reviewed. At least two to

Figure 46 - Foundational training reviews the Construction General Permit requirements, answers the "why" questions, and helps connect the dots from the permit to the construction site. (Photo credit: John Teravskis)

four hours should be scheduled to thoroughly cover these topics. Although most everyone would gain some value from this type of training, it is best suited for site managers, supervisors, inspectors, and those overseeing BMP installation, maintenance, and repair. This training could be recorded and shown to any new personnel or subcontractors that are joining the project at a later date. Other forms of communication shown on Table 6 can be used to reinforce foundational training.[41]

Site-specific training is essential for those performing inspections and monitoring or installing BMPs. These individuals need to understand where and how these activities are to occur. Site-specific training is the application of the foundational training to a specific location. All of the *"what, when, where, and how"* questions should be answered with the site-specific training. Of course, the best place to hold this training is on the jobsite by walking around and discussing the SWPPP map and discharge locations. The length of the training will depend upon the size and complexity of the project but typically should last about two hours. It is not a bad idea to repeat this training annually (for longer projects) or when new phases of the project commence. If done annually, an ideal time to hold this training is just prior to the start of the storm season (in California, that is typically September-October).

---

41   The California Construction General Permit requires that any inspectors working under the delegation of a Qualified SWPPP Practitioner (QSP receive foundational training as specified by the Construction General Permit Training Team (CGPTT). The CGPTT developed a guidance document that identifies the required foundational and site-specific training required for delegated inspectors. Approximately two hours of foundational training and two and a half hours of site-specific training is required: https://www.casqa.org/wp-content/uploads/2024/02/FINAL-QSP-Delegate-Training-Guidelines-02-12-2024.pdf.

SM-5 Education and Training:

Without educating and training on-site personnel about the storm water permit and SWPPP requirements, it is not possible to effectively manage a site. The following education and training elements should be included in a properly managed project:

- Foundational training on the storm water permit and SWPPP requirements and prohibitions;
- Site-specific training on how to implement the SWPPP and monitoring program at a specific jobsite;
- Job/task kickoff training;
- Frequent tailgate training sessions on storm water BMPs and control measures for the work currently being performed on-site;
- The use of Standard Operating Procedures (SOPs) for specific tasks that involve potential pollutants or for controlling erosion and sedimentation;
- Methods for quickly notifying on-site personnel of storm water related issues or instructions such as texting, emails, flyers, videos, etc.;
- Training new personnel or subcontractors who are starting work on the project; and
- The use of signage to provide direction and reminders to on-site personnel.

Expectations and Enforcement (SM-6)

Whether it is parenting young children, running a successful corporation, coaching a professional sports team, overseeing a military operation, or many other aspects of life, management depends on discipline, and discipline depends on communicating expectations and enforcing those expectations. Without communicating expectations, no one will know what is required of them. Without enforcing expectations, no one will think you are serious about it. Sadly, this is what is missing at most construction projects regarding storm water permit compliance and SWPPP implementation. Many contractors will respond to those statements by replying, *"That's not my job, it is the storm water agency's job to enforce regulations."* Well, that is kind of like a parent stating it is the job of the public school to discipline their kids. If the parent is not actively involved in the process, it just won't work! **This site management BMP is the most important BMP that a contractor needs to implement.** Without it, none of the dots of an effective storm water compliance program will be connected. Surprisingly, many other storm water BMP references make little or no mention of it. All the other BMPs are dependent on the site manager setting the expectations for compliance and SWPPP implementation and enforcing that it happens at his or her project. If the manager is lackadaisical or ambivalent about the SWPPP and permit compliance, that attitude will be observed and caught by on-site personnel, and the site conditions will reflect it. Not implementing this BMP will undo or undermine all of the rest of the BMPs.

So how can expectations be communicated? First, the communication needs to come from the top management and needs to be sincere, consistent, and clear. A good start is to include a SWPPP compliance policy in the contract documents that clearly states the owner's and/or the general contractor's expectations for SWPPP compliance by all subcontractors and site personnel. This written document, signed by each subcontractor, should include specific expectations such as:

- ☑ No unauthorized washing of equipment or vehicles may occur without the project manager's consent;
- ☑ All liquid hazardous materials must be stored within secondary containment when not actively being used;
- ☑ All fueling must be performed within the designated fueling location and a spill kit must be present at all times while fueling;
- ☑ No wash out of concrete materials can occur outside of an approved washout device;

- ☑ All construction materials not intended for permanent outdoor use must be covered with a rainproof covering;
- ☑ All equipment and vehicles found to be leaking fluids must be immediately placed on plastic sheeting and repaired or removed from the project as soon as possible;
- ☑ All vehicles must not exceed fifteen mph while on site;
- ☑ All solid waste must be picked up by the end of each business day and placed in a covered bin or a covered and bermed stockpile;
- ☑ All construction and employee vehicles must exit the jobsite at a stabilized construction exit;
- ☑ Subcontractor personnel must attend weekly storm water training sessions and attend or later view a recording of the kickoff training; and
- ☑ Any erosion and sediment or pollution prevention BMPs damaged by a subcontractor must be repaired or replaced immediately by the subcontractor unless exempted by the project manager in writing.

Other ways for clearly communicating expectations about the project's storm water compliance program is for the project manager to hold a mandatory project or task kickoff meeting during which all personnel and subcontractors are instructed about the SWPPP requirements and what will be expected of them.

Some contractors or builders will place a large sign at the main site entrances stating that personnel are entering a SWPPP compliance zone and informing them that the SWPPP requirements will be strictly enforced.

Figure 47 - Placing signage at the site entrances notifying entrants that a SWPPP compliance program is in place will help set the tone for what is expected on site. (Photo credit: Steve Teravskis)

In the same way, routinely discussing safety topics shows the management's commitment to safety; including a few minutes for a "storm water talk" in daily or weekly tailgate meetings also communicates to everyone that SWPPP implementation and storm water permit compliance is a priority.

Another very visual way of demonstrating to all on-site personnel a commitment to the storm water program is for the project manager to frequently accompany the storm water inspector during site inspections.

Figure 48 - Internal compliance audits are another way in which management can show that compliance is a priority. (Photo credit: John Teravskis)

Of course, people know when it is just lip service. When infractions of communicated expectations go unchecked or have no apparent consequences, the on-site personnel will quickly surmise that storm water BMPs are not all that important and will relax their attitude toward compliance.

This is why enforcement is essential. Enforcement should also be educational and progressive. Many contractors and builders have a similar enforcement program for their safety policies that could be emulated for the storm water compliance program. An effective enforcement program should contain the following elements:

- ☑ Review the weekly and storm event inspection reports, identify needed corrective action, and place the needed actions on a corrective action log. Add to the log your own observations of compliance issues you observed while walking around the site. Assign each corrective action item to a person and set a due date for completion. Regularly follow up on unresolved items.
- ☑ Develop and distribute to all site personnel and subcontractors a progressive enforcement plan that specifies how warnings and punitive action will be carried out for infractions of the SWPPP compliance policy. You may be able to amend or adapt a similar enforcement plan used for the safety program.
- ☑ When an individual or a subcontractor is observed to be conducting an activity or allowing a condition to exist that is not in accordance with the SWPPP compliance policy, notify that individual or subcontractor and require them to cease and desist the activity and/or to rectify the condition. *Don't just be a storm water cop; take time to coach them on the proper way of performing the activity or implementing the BMPs.* Identify the situation on the corrective action log and set a date for completion. If not completed within the time specified, provide a warning and set a new date for completion. If still not completed within the time specified, take the next steps identified in the progressive enforcement plan toward punitive action.
- ☑ Be consistent and equitable. Don't start off with a bang and then fizzle out once the grading phase is completed. The general contractor should make sure they are holding their own crews accountable and not just those of the subcontractors.

SM-6 Expectations and Enforcement:

Clear communication and enforcement of compliance expectations is the most important BMP to implement. Without communicating expectations, no one will know what is required of them. Without enforcing expectations, no one will think you are serious about it. If the manager is lackadaisical or ambivalent about the SWPPP and permit compliance, that attitude will be observed and caught by on-site personnel, and the site conditions will reflect it. Not implementing this BMP will undo or undermine all of the rest of the BMPs. The following should be done to clearly communicate and enforce expectations:

- Develop and disseminate a SWPPP Compliance Policy to all on-site personnel and subcontractors. Require all personnel and subcontractors to sign the policy.
- Develop and disseminate a progressive enforcement plan that identifies how policy infractions will be addressed.
- Post signage at main project entrances that declare the project to be a SWPPP compliance zone and that adherence to the SWPPP is mandatory.
- Hold a project or task kickoff meeting that covers the SWPPP requirements.
- Include storm water compliance information in tailgate meetings.
- Consistently review weekly and storm event inspection reports and place items needing corrective action on a corrective action log. Assign corrective actions to a specific person and set a due date for completion. Follow-up on pending corrective action items.
- Don't just be a storm water cop; take time to coach personnel on the proper way of performing the activity or implementing the BMPs.
- Be consistent and equitable in implementing the SWPPP program.

RAINDROP BMPS

You are probably familiar with the old adage, *"An ounce of prevention is worth a pound of cure."* That certainly is applicable when it comes to controlling erosion and sedimentation at a construction project. Remember, we learned in Chapter 3 that erosion is when soil particles become detached. Once particles become detached, the much more difficult processes of sediment control and water treatment are needed to remove the freed particles from the runoff. Our job in protecting water quality can be made much easier if we are successful in erosion control and prevent soil particles from breaking loose and floating away in the first place—an ounce of prevention. When we reviewed erosion theory in Chapter 3, we saw that of the five erosion processes, raindrop erosion was the first one to occur.

> **Erosion Riddle**
>
> Question: How do you stop a raindrop from hitting bare soil?
>
> Answer 1: Keep the raindrop from falling.
> Answer 2: Put a protective cover over the bare soil.

Both answers to our riddle provide insight into how to effectively stop the first form of erosion. But we will also look at another method of keeping soil particles in place, which is to make it so it is harder for them to break loose. I call this suite of control measures "Raindrop BMPs," which is to remind us of the objective of these control measures—to mitigate the effects of the falling raindrop.

Scheduling (RD-1)

The first answer to the Erosion Riddle was *"keep the raindrop from falling,"* and although we do not have much experience at doing an anti-rain dance or influencing precipitation when there is a drought, we can keep the raindrop from falling on our project by performing construction activities when it is not raining. This is very similar to site management BMP SM-1, so we will keep our comments here brief. The importance of doing the bulk of soil disturbing activities during the dry season cannot be understated. If the raindrop is not falling, storm water erosion will not begin. If raindrops are not falling, it is not as necessary to have a protective cover in place.[42] If you are looking for a way to economize on your BMP expenses, scheduling is usually the least expensive erosion control measure.

RD-1 Scheduling:
If the raindrop is not falling, storm water erosion will not begin. The grading phase and other construction activities that disturb a significant amount of soil should be scheduled to occur during a time when precipitation is unlikely to occur. Construction activities that use or create pollutants that can be mobilized by storm water and that cannot be protected with a stormproof cover during storm events should be discontinued until dry weather returns. Scheduling should be done to phase activities, BMP installation, and project milestones so that the construction site will have maximum protection in place before the storm season begins. This can include:
- Installation of temporary or permanent effective soil covers (Raindrop BMPs);
- Installing impervious surfaces (e.g., a first lift of asphalt in the parking lot or roadway to use as a stabilized work area or roadway during the wet season);
- Backfilling and covering utility trenches;
- Establishing settling basins and sediment traps; and
- Stabilizing storm water conveyances such as drainage swales, drain inlets, and concentrated flow discharge locations.

---

42 Although, keep in mind that many storm water agencies require an effective soil cover to be in place year-round, and they do help control wind erosion.

Maintain Existing Effective Soil Cover (RD-2)

This raindrop BMP goes hand-in-hand with scheduling. To the extent possible, existing vegetation or other non-vegetative cover should not be removed until necessary. The more soil that is exposed to the elements, the more likely it is to have erosion. Over the years, we have seen many projects do mass grading on dozens of acres and then let these areas sit idle for months, if not a year or more, until the next phase of work begins. Obviously, there comes a time when you do need to disturb soil and we are not suggesting that grading be performed only an acre at a time. The project manager will need to make a judgment call as to the economics of multiple mobilizations of the grading operations versus the economics of installing temporary effective soil cover (RD-3). Most storm water permits do not allow large areas of soil disturbance to remain uncovered and unprotected, and there is a real cost to applying temporary erosion control measures. As we saw with RD-1, scheduling and, in this case, leaving existing cover in place for as long as possible may be the more economical option.

Many projects also have vegetated areas that are outside of the development plans or are environmentally sensitive areas (ESAs) within the project that need to be protected. The vegetative cover in these areas should definitely not be disturbed. It is best to delineate these areas with bright orange ESA fencing or with staking and flags. Unintentional or unauthorized soil disturbance in these areas may not only worsen the site's erosion potential but may also be in violation of other environmental permits and regulations.

Figure 49 - ESA fencing should be installed to delineate the soil disturbance boundary and to protect existing vegetation. (Photo credit: John Teravskis)

RD-2 Maintain Existing Effective Soil Cover:

Limit the removal of existing effective soil cover by phasing work and protecting areas that are to be left undisturbed. The more exposed soil, the more opportunities there are for raindrop and wind erosion. Consider the following when planning for removal of existing soil covers, vegetative or otherwise:

- Evaluate the economics of multiple mobilizations of grading operations and the cost of applying temporary soil cover.
- Install ESA fencing, stakes, and/or flagging to delineate disturbance boundaries, and educate the on-site crews on the location of the boundaries.
- Minimize, to the extent possible, the footprint of staging areas, haul roads, stockpiles, grubbing activities, and other open space associated with the construction activities.
- Sequence the work so that existing impervious surfaces can remain during the rainy season and be utilized as stabilized work areas.

Establish Temporary or Permanent Effective Soil Cover (RD-3)

The essence of erosion control is to place a protective "blanket" between the falling raindrops and the disturbed soil. It is not overly important what the blanket is—just so it is effective in keeping raindrops from making contact with bare soil. The erosion control blankets or soil covers can consist of many different types of materials and substances; each of which have their advantages and disadvantages. The soil cover can be temporary for a short or long term and be replaced by a permanent cover later. [Table 7](#) presents a list of soil covers that may be applied to a site as effective temporary or permanent erosion control measures.

Figure 50 - Installing a temporary or permanent soil cover will stop raindrop erosion in its tracks by keeping the raindrop and soil separated. (Photo credit: Mike Lewis)

RD-3 Establish Temporary or Permanent Soil Cover:

Since the erosion process begins with the raindrop, the key to controlling erosion is to keep raindrops and bare soil separated from each other. Once soils have been disturbed and vegetation or other covers removed, it is necessary to cover the bare soil as soon as possible to effectively control erosion. Often it is necessary to utilize an intermediate or temporary cover because the construction activity is not yet completed in that area of the project or is not yet ready for final stabilization methods such as landscaping. Other times, it is possible to have permanent, long-term erosion control measures installed. Use the following considerations and Table 7 to identify the best soil cover option for a particular situation:

- Are soils in the specified location scheduled to be disturbed or reworked again? If so, how long will it be until the soil is again disturbed?
- Will there be vehicle or equipment traffic or extensive foot traffic in the area?
- Is it necessary to keep the area relatively dry to facilitate ongoing construction activities?
- Is it undesirable to have excess organic material on the soil surface because of compaction or development plans for that location?
- Will the area be landscaped?
- Will seed be added to the erosion control mix?
- Are soils infertile and needing amendments?
- Does the site have clayey or silty soils?
- What type of slopes are needing protection?
- For how long are soils needing to have a protective cover?
- Is vegetation undesirable in this location?
- Are there places of concentrated flows within this area?
- Is it undesirable to allow water to infiltrate into the soil?
- Is the specified location ready for final stabilization, such as landscaping or asphalt paving?

Table 7 – Soil Covers - see next page

Table 7 – Soil Covers[43]

Cover Type	Description	Variations
Rolled Erosion Control Products (RECPs)		
Mulch control nets	A net that is applied over a loose wood or straw mulch to secure it in place. If natural biodegradable fibers are used, it can be a permanent installation.	Nets made of natural fibers or synthetic materials.
Open weave textiles	A woven or processed mesh that is made of natural or synthetic yarns such as jute or coir (coconut fibers). If natural, biodegradable yarns are used, it can be a permanent installation.	Mesh made of natural or synthetic yarns. They come in different strengths and can be classified as short-term or long-term.
Erosion control blankets	A blanket comprised of natural or synthetic materials that is stitched together with natural or synthetic thread or is chemically bonded together. If natural biodegradable materials are used for the blanket construction, it can be a permanent installation.	There are many different variations and durabilities. Common materials used in the blankets include coir, excelsior (soft wood shavings), straw, cotton, or polypropylene. Some have netting and others are chemically or physically pressed together.

---

43 Adapted from the Erosion Control Technology Council erosion toolbox. For additional information about erosion control products and specifications, go to https://www.ectc.org/erosion-toolbox, the State of Washington Department of Ecology 2019 Stormwater Management Manual for Western Washington https://fortress.wa.gov/ecy/ezshare/wq/Permits/Flare/2019SWMMWW/2019SWMMWW.htm, and Profile ® Products resources for erosion control professionals https://www.profileevs.com/products/hydraulic-erosion-control.

Connecting the Dots of Best Management Practices

Application	Advantages	Disadvantages
Rolled Erosion Control Products (RECPs)		
Netting is installed above an area that has been covered with loose mulch. The netting is stapled in place.	✓ Secure mulch from blowing or flowing away. ✓ Allows the use of locally derived mulches. ✓ Allows vegetation to grow through the netting and helps to lock in new vegetation.	✗ Synthetic materials may degrade into microplastic trash. ✗ Synthetic materials may cause entrapment of animals. ✗ Not suitable for slopes greater than 5:1.
Rolled mesh is applied either directly to prepared soils or onto seeded mulch or compost. The mesh is stapled in place.	✓ Secures mulch from blowing or flowing away. ✓ Good for stabilization of moderate (3:1) to steep (1:1) slopes when used in conjunction with other erosion controls, such as hydraulic mulch or a compost blanket. ✓ Allows vegetation to grow through the netting and helps to lock in new vegetation.	✗ Synthetic materials may degrade into microplastic trash. ✗ Synthetic materials may cause entrapment of animals.
Blankets are applied either directly to prepared soils or onto seeded mulch or compost. More durable blankets may also be placed in drainage swales or other concentrated flow locations. The blanket is stapled in place.	✓ The blanket contains the "mulch" material. ✓ Good for stabilization of moderate (3:1) to steep (1:1) slopes. ✓ Relatively quick to install. Ideal for smaller areas of soil disturbance or specific slopes.	✗ Synthetic materials may degrade into microplastic trash. ✗ Synthetic materials may cause entrapment of animals. ✗ Not suitable for uneven surfaces.

Cover Type	Description	Variations
Plastic sheeting	Rolled plastic sheeting for temporary cover of areas of soil disturbance or stockpiles.	Black or clear polyethylene sheeting, with a thickness of 6 to 20 mil.
Geotextiles	Geotextiles are typically synthetic materials used to temporarily or permanently strengthen or protect erodible surfaces.	Geotextiles are manufactured of synthetic materials including polypropylene, polyester, polyethylene, nylon, polyvinyl chloride, glass, and other materials. They can be woven or non-woven fabrics. They come in a variety of thicknesses and durabilities.
Turf reinforcement mats	A three-dimensional matrix-like product composed of non-degradable synthetic materials placed permanently over erodible surfaces for slope stabilization, scour prevention, or vegetation support.	Manufactured of synthetic fibers, filaments, nets, wire mesh, and/or other durable materials.

---

44   Leadership in Energy and Environmental Design, U.S. Green Building Council, https://www.usgbc.org/leed.

Connecting the Dots of Best Management Practices

Application	Advantages	Disadvantages
Plastic sheeting is appropriate for temporary short-term covering of erodible surfaces. It is applied directly onto the soil and weighted down with gravel bags or sandbags.	✓ Relatively quick to install. ✓ Impermeable and will keep underlying soil relatively dry. Particularly useful for protecting water-saturated slopes or for keeping work areas dry. ✓ Can be removed quickly, saved, and reinstalled for the next rain event.	✗ Plastic will photodegrade and turn into trash and microplastics. ✗ Plastic increases the velocity of runoff and can cause downgradient erosion. ✗ Prone to being disturbed by wind. ✗ The plastic sheeting may not be recyclable and will add to landfill waste. This may cause problems for LEED[64] projects.
They are often installed as a separator between exposed soil and riprap in sediment traps, post-construction storm water measures, and stone-lined storm water conveyances.	✓ Durable and long-lasting. ✓ Permeable. ✓ Helps to strengthen slopes or conveyances.	✗ Synthetic material will photodegrade over time and turn into solid waste and microplastics. ✗ Relatively expensive.
Installed for long term protection of steep slopes, highly erodible surfaces, and conveyances of concentrated flow.	✓ Durable and long-lasting. ✓ Permeable. ✓ Allows vegetation to grow through it. ✓ Helps to strengthen slopes or conveyances.	✗ Relatively expensive. ✗ Relatively difficult to install.

Cover Type	Description	Variations
Hydraulic (Spray Applied) Erosion Control Products (HECPs)		
Blown straw with a tackifier	Dry straw is either hand or machine scattered and then sprayed with a liquid tackifier.	There are a variety of types of straw and tackifiers. Ideally, a dry straw free of undesirable seed should be used. A tackifier containing plant-based glues is usually preferred.
Cellulose mulch	Cellulose (typically from wood) is mixed with a liquid tackifier and sprayed onto areas of soil disturbance. Cellulose is a polymer that can crystallize to form very strong fibers.	Fiber is typically cellulose derived from wood, paper, or cotton. A plant-based glue/tackifier should be used.
Soil binders/polymers	Although these materials are not a true soil cover, when applied to bare soil, they bind soil particles together making the soil less erodible. Chemical binders are particularly useful with soils having high clay and silt content.	Binders can be all-natural, plant-based adhesives, cementitious materials like quicklime, resin emulsions, or polymers. A very common polymer used for soil stabilization is polyacrylamide (PAM), which is an anionic polymer.

Hydraulic (Spray Applied) Erosion Control Products (HECPs)

Application	Advantages	Disadvantages
Straw should be applied in a soil covering layer that is ideally 2 to 3 inches thick (approximately 2-3 tons/acre). It is best to have varied straw lengths or to include wood or paper cellulose (fiber) mulch to help the tackifier join the pieces together. Requires 48 to 72 hours of dry weather for curing.	✓ Usually this is the most cost effective and durable soil cover, many times lasting up to two seasons. ✓ Straw obtained from feed stores will often contain wheat or oat seed, which will germinate for added erosion control.	✗ Should not be used on slopes greater than 2:1. ✗ Blowing straw can cause excessive dust. ✗ Straw can contain undesirable seed. ✗ Straw may need to be removed for subsequent phases of work.
It can be applied to gently sloped areas (less than 4:1) for very short-term protection. Requires 48 to 72 hours of dry weather for curing. This product is best used in conjunction with blown straw.	✓ Economical ✓ Two-dimensional structure allows it to not interfere with compaction or other surface preparations.	✗ The two-dimensional structure causes it to lie flat on the ground and, therefore, does not hold moisture well and does not provide as much protection from raindrop erosion. ✗ When the cellulose mulch dries, at times and for various reasons, it can form a paper mâché-like layer which is hard for seedlings to penetrate.
Application will be based on the type of soil binder selected. Generally, soil binders are applied directly to bare soil. PAM is often included with a cellulose mulch or other HECPs.	✓ Helps to make soils less erodible. ✓ Can be quickly applied directly to bare soil and, in the case of PAM, requires little curing time. ✓ Can be used in conjunction with other HECPs for improved erosion control.	✗ Depending on the product selected, it can result in the introduction of other pollutants in storm water runoff (e.g., high pH from quicklime, excess polymer, etc.)

Cover Type	Description	Variations
Bonded fiber matrix (BFM)	A wood or straw mulch with a tackifier that is mixed and sprayed onto areas of soil disturbance.	Manufacturers will utilize a variety of fibers and tackifiers to create their own blend of BFM. Additives can include fertilizers, mycorrhizal fungi, organic compost, PAM, and seed.
Flexible growth media (FGM)	A wood or straw mulch with a combination of tackifiers and polymers that provide both chemical and mechanical bonding.	Manufacturers will utilize a variety of fibers and tackifiers to create their own blend of FGM. Additives can include fertilizers, mycorrhizal fungi, organic compost, PAM, and seed.
Mulches & Compost		
Straw	A bed of straw placed on the soil.	There are different types of straw. Some are certified weed-free. Others, like oat straw obtained from feed stores, will often contain seed that will germinate and enhance erosion control.

Connecting the Dots of Best Management Practices

Application	Advantages	Disadvantages
BFMs are ideal for moderate to steep slopes (less than 2:1) on which it should be applied at 4,000 lbs./acre. On flatter surfaces, it can be applied at 2,500 lbs./acre. The soil should be dry and no rain forecasted for 48 hours.	✓ The three-dimensional structure provided by the wood or straw media allows for greater interlocking of fibers and provides more water retention and a better environment for seed germination. ✓ Soil protection for 12 months or less.	✗ Requires dry soil for application and a 48-hour or longer period of dry conditions for curing.
FGMs are ideal for moderate to steep slopes (less than 2:1) on which it should be applied at 4,000 lbs./acre. On flatter surfaces, it can be applied at 2,500 lbs./acre. The soil should be dry and no rain forecasted for 48 hours.	✓ Can be applied when soil is damp or rain is expected within 24 hours. ✓ The three-dimensional structure with the blend of tackifiers and polymers allows for a flexible environment that facilitates seed germination. ✓ Soil protection for 12 to 18 months.	✗ Tends to be the most expensive of the HECPs.
Mulches & Compost		
Hand applied at 2"–3" thick, which should equate to approximately 2–3 bales/1,000 ft^2 or 2–3 tons/acre; or equipment applied straw with a tackifier. A typical bale is 80 pounds x 50 bales = 2 tons which when machine applied to one acre will provide an approximate 1" thick cover. Thickness and number of bales needed will depend on the type of straw utilized.	✓ Hand application for small areas or equipment applied (blown) to large flat areas can be very economical. ✓ Durable.	✗ Should not be used on slopes greater than 2:1. ✗ Straw can contain undesirable seed. ✗ Straw may need to be removed for subsequent phases of work. ✗ Can result in excessive tannin or lignin in storm water runoff.

Cover Type	Description	Variations
Wood	A bed of wood mulch placed on the soil.	Wood mulch comes in a variety of types and coarseness. It can be from chipped green waste or from specific types of wood such as redwood or cedar trees.
Pine duff	A bed of natural pine duff placed on the soil. Pine duff is partly decaying organic matter that includes pine needles, leaves, bark, decaying wood matter, seeds, pine cones, and fungi.	It is usually locally derived and sourced. It will differ from one location to another as the ecosystems change.
Compost	A bed of composted material that is applied on bare soil as a soil cover and to provide a growing media.	There are a variety of compost feedstocks and coarseness of the compost product.

Connecting the Dots of Best Management Practices

Application	Advantages	Disadvantages
Applied at 2" thick, which should equate to approximately 270 cubic yards/acre. Can be applied by a blower truck.	✓ May be used as a permanent measure notably when derived from on-site or locally sourced chipped native vegetation that will contain, attract, or support restorative conditions (i.e., viable seeds, roots, etc.) by design. ✓ May be used around container plants during the landscaping phase when derived from "sterile" sources (i.e., void of viable plant parts). ✓ Some wood mulches, such as redwood or cedar, may help reduce pH. ✓ At times can be economically obtained.	✗ Should not be used on slopes greater than 2:1. ✗ Depending upon the source, it can contain undesirable seed or trash. ✗ Wood mulch may need to be removed for subsequent phases of work. ✗ Can result in excessive tannin or lignin in storm water runoff. ✗ May not be allowed as a ground cover by local fire prevention regulations.
Applied at 2"-3" thick. Usually, pine duff is scraped off the project at the beginning and stockpiled for later use.	✓ Natural ground cover endemic to that location. ✓ May remain in place as a permanent stabilization measure or used with landscaping. ✓ Contains nutrients, fungi, and a seed bank needed for a healthy ecosystem. ✓ Economical to obtain.	✗ Should not be used on slopes greater than 2:1. ✗ Depending upon the source, it can contain undesirable seed or trash. ✗ May not be allowed as a ground cover by local fire prevention regulations. ✗ Can result in excessive tannin or lignin in storm water runoff.
When used as a soil cover, utilizing a 2- to 3-inch layer of a mix of fine (3/8" to 1/2") screened material and course (2"-3") screened materials will provide optimal water retention and protection from raindrop erosion. Can be applied by a blower truck.	✓ Not only provides an effective soil cover, but also retention of storm water and filtering of the storm water that does run off. ✓ May remain in place as a permanent stabilization measure or be used with landscaping. ✓ Provides a growing media on soils that are infertile. ✓ Utilizes recycled materials and can help with meeting green building certification requirements.	✗ Should not be used on slopes greater than 2:1. ✗ Depending upon the source, it can contain trash.

Cover Type	Description	Variations
Other		
Crushed rock	Covering bare soil with a layer of crushed aggregate.	Will vary based on local supply. Typically, 3/4" to 2" rock free of fine material (larger than a #200 mesh sieve).
Paving	Covering soil with a permanent asphalt-concrete (AC) pavement.	This will vary with the engineering design for a particular development or project. It can consist of asphalt, concrete, pavers, or other durable structural pavements.
Sod/landscaping	Covering soil with grass or other vegetation as part of permanent landscaping.	There are multiple variations of sod, seed, and ground-covering plants that may be incorporated into the landscaping design.

Connecting the Dots of Best Management Practices 133

Application	Advantages	Disadvantages
Other		
It should be a 2" thick layer on soil. In areas of high traffic, it may be best to place a permeable geotextile below the rock layer. When installed on low to moderate slopes, having a roughened soil surface and keying in the base will help prevent sloughing of the rock. Rock should have jagged edges, not rounded.	✓ Provides durable and permanent stabilization. ✓ Ideal for areas where vegetation is undesirable, such as road shoulders, or for fire prevention. ✓ Ideal for areas that will have vehicle and equipment traffic.	✗ Expensive and labor intensive. ✗ Can be unsightly. ✗ Can cause increased runoff. ✗ Can contain fines that can cause turbidity increases or have pH altering minerals present. ✗ Aggregate may become "contaminated" with sediment and not be useful as a base layer for paving.
Typically, contractors do not want to install exterior pavement until the end of the project to avoid having it scuffed up or damaged during construction. However, especially with asphalt, paving can be installed in multiple lifts. Installing a first lift of asphalt in a parking lot can provide a stabilized work environment during the rainy season.	✓ Planned site improvements can double as erosion control measures. ✓ Pavement provides a stabilized work area and can allow work to continue during the rainy season. ✓ Pavement is relatively easy to clean and can help with spill control.	✗ Can be damaged during ongoing construction activities. ✗ Can cause short-term issues with elevated pH or oil & grease. ✗ An additional lift will cost more because of additional mobilization of paving crews (but may be offset by the savings on temporary erosion control measures).
Use landscaping design to provide permanent vegetation of erosion control. The design should include not only ground-covering vegetation but also trees and shrubs to act as rain interceptors and to lock in soils.	✓ Effective long-term soil cover. ✓ Uptake and filtering of storm water reducing runoff and improving water quality. ✓ Soil stabilization with roots. ✓ Trees and shrubs provide a rain canopy to lessen effects of raindrop erosion.	✗ Requires maintenance and upkeep. ✗ May require supplemental irrigation. ✗ Will have an establishment period when erosion control is less because of immature plants.

Maximize Organic Content (RD-4)

In the Revised Universal Soil Loss Equation (RUSLE)—Equation 7, the "C" factor stands for cover. The smaller the "C" factor, the more soil loss is reduced. A type of cover used extensively in the agriculture community is crop residue, which consists of leaving in place vegetative residue from the previous crop (e.g., leaves, stalks, root masses). Organic residue will absorb energy from falling raindrops and prevent soil particles from detaching. The organic material helps to provide the soil with structure and natural glues that bind particles in place. On the surface, it will also create miniature "dams" that will impede runoff and encourage infiltration of water into the soil. Although a construction project occasionally may occur on a field that was previously planted and now has crop residue present, organic content can also be maximized at other construction locations by protecting topsoils that are rich in organic material.

Figure 51 - Construction Sandbox test slope. One side is protected with a HECP, and the other has no protection. Or does it have a hidden protection? (Photo credit: Danny Aspiras)

Unintentionally, we discovered the effectiveness of residual organic material in preventing erosion at our Construction Sandbox, which is a simulated construction site we use to test and teach about BMPs. In the sandbox, we have a slope used to test different configurations of erosion and sediment control measures. In order to set up for the next testing scenario, it was necessary to remove the applied hydraulic mulch and disturb the soil. This section of the slope was going to be used as an unprotected comparison to the other section of the slope that had an erosion control measure applied. Therefore, we decided to rototill the surface of the area to be unprotected. However, when we ran the next testing scenario, the unprotected side of the slope did not fail as we had anticipated. When we evaluated the cause for the lack of erosion, we discovered that in rototilling the hydraulic mulch-covered soil, the mulch material was incorporated into the soil. We concluded that the presence of organic matter in the soil was enough to impede erosion and foul our test results.

It is important for contractors and developers to see the value in the conservation of topsoils and organic materials present on the surface. Water quality can be greatly protected when healthy, organic-rich soils are present. Sites that have a bed of organic material, such as pine duff (refer to [Table 7](#)), or topsoils rich in organic material should have those materials either protected in place or carefully scraped off and stockpiled for later use. Soils that are lean in organic content can be enhanced by adding a compost blanket (refer to [Table 7](#)) or by incorporating compost into the top layer of soil, especially where vegetation will be established.

RD-4 Maximize Organic Content:

Wherever possible, soils with high organic content should be either protected in place, or removed, stockpiled, and reapplied where vegetation will be reestablished. Where vegetation is to be established, infertile soils, or those having low organic content, should be amended or at least covered with organic compost. These practices will make the soil less erodible and more capable of retaining and infiltrating water, thus reducing runoff. Consider the following when planning for topsoil conservation or maximizing organic content:

- If the existing topsoil contains noxious weed seeds or contaminants that are undesirable in the new development, import new topsoil or amendments for creating organically rich soils.
- If existing soils lack organic material or structure, amend soils with compost and sandy loam to create a structured soil that allows for infiltration of water and support of healthy plants.
- Order and sequence the excavation of soils so that topsoil is not buried by infertile soil and becomes itself infertile.
- Do not allow topsoil to remain for an extensive period of time under plastic covers or in dry and hot environments where organic material will desiccate and microbes, seed, and fungi may be killed off and, thereby, render the soil infertile. Topsoil should be allowed to "breathe" and be kept moist.

Bind Soil Particles Together (RD-5)

If erosion is when particles become detached, an effective erosion control measure could be to make it harder for them to detach from one another. This can be accomplished by applying a soil binder directly to the soil. Some of the same products used as tackifiers or glues in HECPs can be applied directly to the soil. Although it does not provide as much protection against raindrop erosion as an effective soil cover, the adhesives or chemical binders will help prevent soil particles from detaching from one another, which will help to reduce soil loss from water and wind. Soil binders may be particularly useful when the jobsite is active, during the dry season for wind erosion control, and when attempting to meet the soil compaction requirements that could be hindered by a layer of hydraulically applied mulch. Soil binders are listed in [Tables 5](#) and [7](#).

RD-5 Soil Binders:

Soil binders are products applied directly to the soil that will bind soil particles to one another and prevent them from becoming detached. These products may be used for temporary soil stabilization during dry windy conditions, periods of active soil disturbance, and when an effective soil cover may impede obtaining soil compaction or the progression of the project. Consider the following when using a soil binder:

- Are you following the manufacturer's instructions, which should be designed to prevent an excess of the binder chemicals to flow off-site and/or into a receiving water or municipal storm drainage system?
- Will the binder impede the later establishment of landscaping or vegetation (e.g., the use of magnesium chloride)?
- Will the selected product hold up to construction activities or traffic occurring in the area of application?
- The durability of the product and need to reapply it.

SLOW-THE-FLOW BMPS

Figure 52 - Check dams or runoff "speed bumps" that have captured sediment. "Slow-the-Flow" BMPs require regular maintenance to keep them effective and to make sure they have enough capacity for sedimentation to occur. (Photo credit: John Teravskis)

In [Chapter 3](), we saw an example of how even slightly slowing flow down can have a significant impact on removing soil particles from runoff. In that particular case, the chain link fence was a sufficient enough obstacle to slow the flow just enough to provide the soil particles the opportunity to deposit, resulting in approximately six inches of sediment deposition in a single rain event. When you think about it, that is exactly how sediment control is accomplished at construction sites.

We place obstacles in the flow path to reduce the velocity of the runoff. This not only facilitates sedimentation, but it will also have erosion control benefits. Sediment control devices do not prevent raindrop erosion, but they can have a positive effect on sheet and rill erosion. Fewer soil particles will detach in slower moving water, and slower moving water cannot carry (transport) particles previously detached. Therefore, we categorize this group of control measures as Slow-the-Flow BMPs, which provide both erosion and sediment control. Included in this group of BMPs are:

- Linear controls,
- Speed bumps,
- Fat spots, and
- Flow spreaders and dissipators.

Linear Controls (SF-1)

Oftentimes for effective sediment control, it is necessary to establish a line of defense. This line can be placed at different locations throughout the construction site but is generally placed downgradient of a source of sediment. Typically, linear measures used for sediment control are placed at the toe of a slope or at the project's downgradient perimeter. Linear controls can also be used to prevent sheet and rill erosion. In this case, they are typically installed in strategic places to slow the flow, such as along the face of a slope or where sheet flow discharges to areas of soil disturbance. Linear controls are the most prevalent of all BMPs at construction projects, but even with their popularity, they still seem not to be well understood in what they can and cannot do at a project site. The following are common myths about linear controls that we have observed in the storm water industry.

Myth: Fiber rolls filter storm water. No, they do not! And we can prove it. You probably know the story of the Three Little Pigs. What did one of the pigs use to build his house? Straw. Why, because it filters water? No. Why do many residents in developing countries around the world still use straw on their roofs? Because it, more or less, keeps the water out. Compacted straw does not filter, but rather impedes water. The job of fiber rolls is to slow the flow by creating a miniature dam. When water velocity slows, particles settle out. Don't be fooled by the look of fiber rolls—they don't filter.

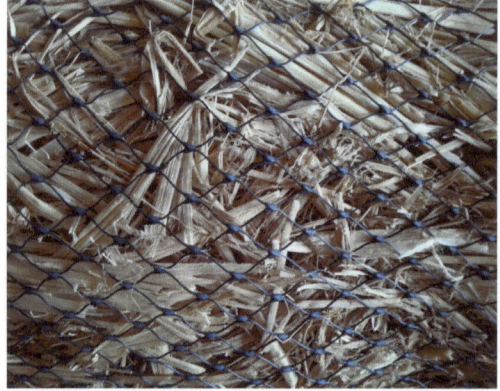

Figure 53 - Does it filter or dam water flow? A familiar bedtime story will help answer the question. (Photo credit: John Teravskis)

Myth: Fiber rolls rolled out on the surface are effective. Unfortunately, this myth is prolific and widely accepted based on the sheer number of construction sites where it occurs. It is very common to find fiber roll surrounding a site that is neither keyed-in (installed in a trench two to three inches deep) nor staked down. We have performed experiments to determine if this typical method of fiber roll installation is effective, and we found the exact opposite to be true. In many cases, instead of allowing particles to settle out, fiber roll that has simply been

Figure 54 - There is no cheaper linear sediment control than this. The problem is that it doesn't work and will probably worsen water quality. (Photo credit: John Teravskis)

laid on the ground worsened turbidity. Remember, these devices do not filter water, they hold water like a dam. If the dam is not firmly secured to the ground, the head pressure of the water behind the fiber roll will cause the water to exploit gaps between the fiber roll and the ground surface. The hydraulic pressure will cause the water to jet from these gaps, eroding the soil. Furthermore, the turbulent water keeps eroded soil particles in suspension. Our experiments show that it is better to not use fiber roll at all than to just lay it on the ground.

Myth: Doubling up fiber roll and silt fence provides better protection. If one is good, two is better. Right? Sorry, not true. Doubling up linear controls mostly just wastes money. And it might indicate that a SWPPP developer lacks confidence in the specified BMPs. Remember, the purpose of these devices is to slow the flow, not filter. When properly installed, fiber roll or silt fence sufficiently slows the flow by itself. No significant additional velocity reduction is gained by doubling up the two devices.

Figure 55 - Show some confidence in your BMPs! Only one linear control is needed to sufficiently slow the flow. (Photo credit: John Teravskis)

Myth: Fiber roll and compost socks do the same thing. Well, this is a half-truth. It is true that they both slow the flow causing sedimentation to occur. However, compost socks do something that fiber rolls cannot do. They filter the water and remove sediment particles and other pollutants by trapping these pollutants in the filter media. Compost socks are much heavier than fiber roll and become even heavier when they are saturated with water and filled up with captured particles. Because of their weight, compost socks are considered "self-anchoring," which helps them conform well to any surface without the need for keying them in and staking them down. In addition, the pass-through rate of water for compost socks helps alleviate the hydraulic pressure. This makes compost socks very effective on paved surfaces.

Figure 56 - One is green and the other is tan. But they appear to do the same thing. Looks can be deceiving. (Photo credit: John Teravskis)

However, when fiber roll is not secured, unlike compost socks, it will become buoyant and float on the water's surface until it acquires a degree of saturation. And because it is lightweight and generally compacted like a tight sausage, it is very difficult for a fiber roll to conform to uneven pavement, which is something the manufacturer doesn't specify anyway. We will revisit compost socks as a treatment option in BMP T-1.

Myth: Curb cutbacks are not BMPs. First let's define a curb cutback. A curb cutback is the transition where water flows from an exposed soil surface to a hardscape surface (e.g., asphalt or concrete). When installed correctly, the soil surface is maintained four to six inches **below** the surface of the hardscape to prevent water from leaving the site *(which happens to be about the same height of a fiber roll)*. In such cases, many people want to install a fiber roll either by properly keying it in and staking it down at the transition or by improperly placing it on top of the hardscape ledge. But what does this accomplish? The curb cutback is already keeping water from flowing off the soil surface and onto the hardscape. Does the runoff know that it has been stopped by concrete instead of straw? No, of course not! It just "knows" that it stopped, and particles need to settle out. The biggest problem with curb cutbacks is that they don't look like BMPs (or at least what we picture as BMPs). This is especially true for untrained crews and an untrained inspector. If your crews don't know what you are trying to accomplish with the curb cutback, they may short circuit it by filling it in as a wheel barrow ramp. Sadly, some inspectors don't know how perimeter controls work and just want to see something that looks like a BMP on their site. So, many projects resort to doing something like what is shown in Figure 57. Other than giving the site a great BMP aesthetic and sifting money out of your pocketbook, this fiber roll isn't accomplishing anything. It is an imposter!

Figure 57 - Where is the BMP in the photo? And which one is the imposter BMP? (Photo credit: John Teravskis)

Myth: Fiber rolls must always be keyed-in. Even though some BMP fact sheets or specifications for fiber rolls seems to indicate that they must be keyed-in (or trenched), the Caltrans BMP fact sheet allows for an alternative method of achieving good surface conformity by using a lashing method. Stakes are driven into the ground on both sides of the fiber roll and a rope or steel cable is used to press the fiber roll down into the surface. This is particularly useful for slopes that are extremely steep or have soils that make trenching impractical. In our Construction Sandbox, we have performed some trials of different

Figure 58 - Evaluation of fiber roll installations on the test slope at our Construction Sandbox. (Photo credit: John Teravskis)

types of fiber roll installations on the test slope. When comparing two side-by-side installations of fiber roll where everything was the same except one was keyed-in but the other was not, we noted similar performances except when it came to the amount of surface runoff between the two studies. The side that had the keyed-in fiber roll had less discharge because it was facilitating the infiltration of runoff into the hillside. The side that was not keyed-in had noticeably more surface flow and, therefore, less infiltration. It should be noted that both sides of the slope had been applied with 3,500 lbs./acre of hydraulic mulch, and erosion was not occurring as evidenced by the very clear runoff. This test taught us a valuable lesson. There are many hillsides which are susceptible to landslides or mass wasting, and when fiber roll, used as a linear-control, is not keyed-in, there will be less infiltration of water into the slope and, therefore, less chance of slope failure. Better yet, a linear control measure that facilitates flow-through, such as compost socks or some proprietary linear control measures, should be specified for these types of conditions.

Myth: Linear controls only need to be installed once and will last the duration of the project. This is the belief held by most project estimators. They typically will only include one initial installation of perimeter controls in their budgets and schedules even for multi-year projects. But it won't take long until your BMP looks like flattened pancakes! All BMPs need maintenance. Fiber roll, compost socks, and silt fence will all take a beating from the sun, wind, and construction activities. They will eventually wear out and need to be replaced. (Refer to BMP

Figure 59 - Pancake wattle is not an effective linear control. BMPs need to be repaired, replenished, and replaced through the life of the project. (Photo credit: Steve Teravskis)

SM-2.) Plus, as site conditions change, the perimeter control strategy will also need to change. Fiber roll might have been a perfectly good sediment control measure during the grading phase, but compost socks or gravel bag berms may be more appropriate during the vertical phase after paving and concrete work has been completed.

Myth: Fiber rolls and silt fence are the only linear control options. Even though you will see fiber rolls or silt fence on the majority of construction projects, they are not the only good options for linear erosion and sediment control. It is also false that they are always the most economical options. True, many SWPPP writers do tend to get in a rut and specify what is customary and familiar. But there are many options available for linear control measures. Sometimes a little creativity can provide an innovative, effective, and cost-efficient alternative to the usual control devices. Table 9 provides a list of linear control measures to consider utilizing at different construction sites.

Figure 60 - Linear sediment controls should be installed so that they are level and secured to the ground. Remember you are building a dam! (Photo credit: John Teravskis)

When specifying or utilizing linear control measures, there are a few important installation considerations:

- The linear control should be kept as level as possible and parallel with the slope contours. It should never be installed to run up or down a slope. Otherwise, runoff will run alongside the linear control, become a path of preferential flow, and form a rill alongside it. If the linear control measure is not level, water will find the low spot and become a point of concentrated flow and a source of erosion. To prevent lateral water migration along linear controls, install cross-barriers periodically along the length of the control measure and "j-hook" the ends of the run upward. This will encourage water to uniformly flow across the control measure or infiltrate into the soil along the length of the control measure.

- When installing a linear control measure, secure it firmly to the soil surface. Try to eliminate gaps or weak points under the control measure that runoff can exploit. Sufficiently overlap joined ends of linear controls so that water does not sneak through the joints. Remember, these tend to act as miniature dams, so make sure your dam will hold water.
- Select a control measure that will have enough capacity to capture and hold the anticipated sediment load. At the toe of a large, unprotected slope, silt fence would be a better choice than fiber roll, because it is taller and has more capacity. The inverse is also true—don't use silt fence for small slopes or in flat areas. The distance from the sediment source should be considered in the BMP design and layout so there is enough room to hold the anticipated storm water and sediment load. In Chapter 5, we will discuss how to quantify soil loss and sediment loads.
- Linear control measures can be used to help prevent sheet erosion from becoming rill erosion. Rills tend to form after ten to fifty feet of sheet flow length. The steeper the slope, the shorter the distance needed to form them. The placement of a linear control will "reset" the travel distance and provide another ten to fifty feet of sheet flow before

Figure 61 - Linear controls walk flow down a slope to prevent the formation of rills. (Photo credit: John Teravskis)

rills form. If this is done along the face of a slope, sheet flow can be effectively managed down the slope. The following spacing for linear controls is recommended:[45]

- ⇒ Ten feet apart for slopes steeper than 2:1 (H:V)
- ⇒ Fifteen feet apart for slopes from 2:1 to 4:1 (H:V)
- ⇒ Twenty feet apart for slopes from 4:1 to 10:1 (H:V)
- ⇒ Fifty feet apart for slopes flatter than 10:1 (H:V)

- Some linear control products can become sources of solid waste or trash or may become an entrapment for wildlife. It is important to understand the life expectancy and durability of the selected control measure and to remove it before it becomes trash or a threat to wildlife.

Myth: Fiber rolls are the most economical option. Well this is half true. Fiber rolls that are not properly installed are considered by many to be the most economical BMP. While it is hard to argue the economics of this practice. It is highly questionable whether a BMP has actually been installed or if a straw-filled adornment had been placed along the perimeter. In Chapter 1, we mentioned the disconnects many people have when it comes to BMPs and effective erosion and sediment control. In particular, we pointed out a BMP we refer to as "miracle roll," which is fiber roll laid on the surface and not keyed in or staked down. As covered in a previous myth, fiber rolls do not filter water but hold water like a miniature dam. When they are not keyed-in or staked-down, they will still operate as a dam but as one that has a design flaw that affects its performance. What would happen if at the base of a dam there was a weak spot where water could escape? It would not be good, right? That is essentially what happens when we have unsecured fiber roll—dam failure! The water being held back by the fiber roll will exploit the weakness at the bottom of the linear control. Head pressure will cause water to jet out from underneath the fiber roll which leads to erosion, turbulence, and increased suspended sediment.

---

45 Caltrans Construction Site BMP Manual May 2017, Fiber Rolls SC-5.

STANDARD FIBER ROLL

When not properly keyed in, the water undermines the fiber roll, causing turbulence and stirring up sediment. Even when keyed in correctly, the water flowing over the device can stir up sediment. Notice that water does not flow through the fiber roll.

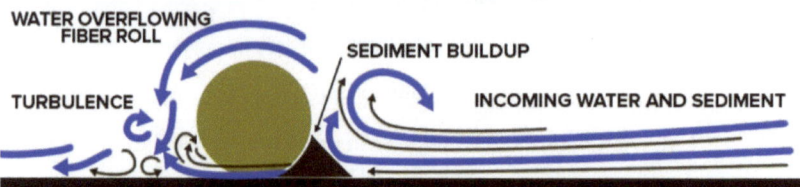

COMPOST FILTER SOCK

Compost socks are heavy enough to block water from passing underneath, even when not keyed in. Most of the water filters through the sock, preventing water turbulence that could stir up sediment.

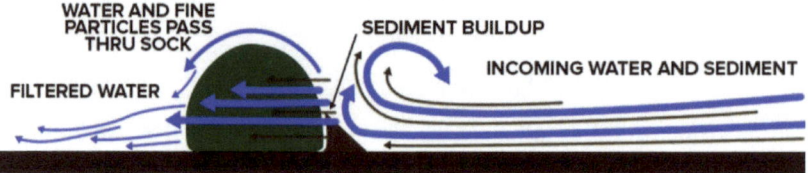

Figure 62 - Improperly installed fiber roll is a liability not an asset!
(Graphic credit: Andrew Teravskis)

Turbidity Test Results

In 2014, the staff at WGR Southwest, Inc. performed an experiment with fiber roll and compost filter socks. Our experiment focused on each sediment control device's ability to reduce water turbidity. We did not perform other tests to measure how each device impacts different aspects of water quality.

During the experiment, we surrounded the test drain in a gravel lot with 8"-diameter fiber roll that we slightly keyed in and staked into the ground. After waiting thirty minutes for any sediment to settle, we carefully collected samples both upstream and downstream of the BMP.

The fiber roll was then replaced with 8"-diameter compost filter socks. After allowing time for sediment from the BMP switch to settle out, we again collected samples both upstream and downstream of the sock.

Here are the results:

Fiber Roll:
- Upstream of BMP: 152 NTU
- Downstream of BMP: 205 NTU

Compost Filter Sock:
- Upstream of BMP: 215 NTU
- Downstream of BMP: 16 NTU

The compost sock obviously outperformed the fiber roll quite a bit, lowering the turbidity results to 16 NTUs—very acceptable numbers. The fiber roll not only didn't lower the numbers, but actually raised them, presumably due to agitation from the turbulence of the water overflowing and undermining the fiber roll.

Watch a video summary of the experiment at:
https://youtu.be/PQ_krMLJ4C4

We have established that laying fiber roll on the ground is not a BMP but only an adornment which could possibly worsen water quality. But is fiber roll really more economical than other linear sediment control measures? Well, you be the judge! The following table provides a cost comparison (based on 2023 dollars) for four common linear control options.

Table 8 – Linear Control Cost Comparisons

Linear Control Device (Assume 1,000 ft.)	Material Purchase Price	Labor and Equipment Cost to Maintain Effective Perimeter for 1 Year[46]	Cost/Linear Foot
Fiber roll *Hand Installed*	$30/25-foot length	90 minutes (installed at 662 ft./hr.) 4 workers @ $35/hr. **2 installations / year**	$2.82
Silt fence *Machine Trenched*	$30/100-foot roll	136 minutes (installed at 440 ft./hr.) Assume $125/hr. equipment charge and $58/hr. for the operator. 2 additional workers @ $35/hr. **1 installation/year**	$0.87
Compost sock *Hand Installed*	$590/200 feet	43 minutes (installed at 1,434 ft./hr.) 2 workers @ $35/hr. **1 installation / year**	$3.00
Curb cutback *Machine Trenched*	$0	Assume $125/hr. equipment charge and $58/hr. for the operator. Assume 4 hours for initial install.	$0.73

---

46 Installation costs for fiber roll, silt fence, and compost socks estimated by MKB Company, LLC / Filtrexx https://www.filtrexx.com/en/resources/bmp-comparison; Equipment costs per Caltrans 2023 rate sheet https://dot.ca.gov/-/media/dot-media/programs/construction/documents/equipment-rental-rates-and-labor-surcharge/book_2023.pdf ; and Equipment Operator rate per 2023 General Prevailing Wage rate sheet https://www.dir.ca.gov/OPRL/2023-2/PWD/Determinations/Southern/SC-023-63-2.pdf.

So you can see that everyone's go-to fiber roll is not the most economical linear sediment control. Silt fence, which many contractors shy away from because of the expense, turns out to be one of the more economical choices. Of course, curb cutback will only work where conditions allow its use, such as a transition from softscape to hardscape. But where it can be used, it is the most cost-effective perimeter control. Other factors that should be considered when deciding upon a linear control and determining its economics include the wear and tear it will receive from construction activities and the elements (sun and wind), the amount of maintenance needed to maintain its effectiveness, the ability to remove and relocate the device, and the amount of storm water treatment needed at that point of discharge (refer to T-1). Fiber roll should always have a place in our BMP toolboxes, but it is important to consider other viable options. Table 9 provides a list of sediment control options.

Table 9 – Linear Control Measures

Type	Description	Variations
Fiber roll	A monofilament polypropylene net or natural-fiber fabric tube sock that is filled with straw. Typically, it is 8" in diameter and comes in 25-foot lengths.	The tube sock can be made of natural fibers or synthetic materials. Fiber rolls can be filled with ordinary straw, certified-weed free straw, coir, flax, rice hulls, or synthetic materials.
Silt fence	An approximate 3-foot high woven or processed mesh fabric that is attached to wooden stakes.	Stakes can be preattached to the fabric or attached upon installation. Fabric comes in different weights and durabilities. For high wind applications, wire backed fabric is available. High visibility orange fabric is available where needed to also provide a visible barrier.

Installation	Advantages	Disadvantages
Typically, fiber roll is installed in a 2-3" deep trench and staked down every 4 feet. Ends should overlap at least 1 foot and be firmly secured. Fiber roll may also be lashed down with a rope or steel cable. In some cases, such as on a slope covered with other erosion controls, trenching in the linear control measure may not be desirable. Because it needs no trench, the tie-down method can be placed on top of a proper blanket installation helping to prevent rill development under the blanket.	✓ Readily available ✓ Comes in biodegradable versions ✓ Light weight makes slope installations easier than other linear control options.	✗ Other than the fully synthetic varieties, they tend to have a maximum life expectancy of one storm season. ✗ Need to be trenched in or otherwise firmly secured to the underlying surface. ✗ Not suitable for use on hardened or paved surfaces or in soils that are not able to be trenched down 2-3 inches. ✗ Cannot be ran over by vehicles. ✗ Monofilament encased fiber roll must be removed at the completion of construction (prior to terminating permit coverage).
Silt fence must be trenched in a minimum of 6" deep and held up by supporting stakes. Stakes should be spaced 5 to 6 feet apart and placed on the downgradient side of the fence so that they support the fabric holding the anticipated storm water/sediment load. The fabric is typically secured to the stakes with staples, zip ties, etc.	✓ Will accommodate higher sediment loads. ✓ Can double as a barrier for an environmentally sensitive area or the work zone boundary. ✓ Can double as wildlife exclusion fencing. ✓ Maintaining a perfectly level installation is a little less crucial, especially if cross-barriers are used. ✓ Can be machine installed.	✗ Tend to be more susceptible to wind damage. ✗ Life expectancy is typically less than one year. ✗ Is not biodegradable and needs to be removed.

Type	Description	Variations
Compost socks	A woven sock that contains "2-inch minus" composted wood mulch.	Compost socks come in a variety of sock materials (synthetic and naturally biodegradable), diameters, and lengths.
Curb cutbacks	When there is a hardscape/soil interface and water is flowing from the area of soil disturbance to the hardscape, the soil can be graded down 4-6 inches at the edge of the hardscape so that water will stop at the interface.	Different depths, widths, and tapering of the excavation.

Connecting the Dots of Best Management Practices

Installation	Advantages	Disadvantages
In places where there is not any concentrated flow, compost socks may be placed directly on the pervious or impervious surface. They are self-weighting and do not need to be trenched in. Where runoff may be more concentrated, compost socks should be secured with staking per the manufacturer's recommendations.	✓ They filter water, and sediment is captured within the sock. ✓ They remove, to varying degrees, other pollutants, such as oils, metals, nutrients, and organic compounds. ✓ They do not always need to be trenched in and staked down, which allows them to be placed on impervious surfaces and easily moved out of and back into position. ✓ They tend to be more durable than fiber roll, often lasting up to two storm seasons. ✓ They can tolerate—to a certain degree—being run over by vehicles. ✓ When done, the fabric can be sliced open and discarded and the compost can usually be utilized on-site.	✗ They are heavy and more difficult to handle than fiber roll. ✗ Even when within USEPA and state limits, detritus such as plastic or metal, etc. may be present and unacceptable near waterbodies unless, after the intended use of the sock when the fabric covering is removed and discarded, the detritus is picked from the spread-out compost being left on-site.
Using a piece of equipment, grade 4-6 inches down a 3-5 foot wide area immediately adjacent to the hardscape. The graded strip can be tapered so that it slopes downward toward the hardscape border.	✓ No materials need to be purchased. ✓ Relatively easy to install and maintain in most instances. ✓ Can be run over by vehicles and equipment. ✓ No undercutting of the control measure by the runoff.	✗ Does not appear to be a BMP; therefore, construction crews and inspectors must be trained to recognize and maintain it. ✗ Not recommended for places where hardscape could be compromised by the runoff. ✗ Not recommended for concentrated flow.

Type	Description	Variations
Gravel bags / sandbags	A row of gravel or sand-filled bags that cause water flow to slow before proceeding beyond it.	Different bag materials, some water can pass through and others are impenetrable to water. Different bag sizes ranging in capacity from 30-40 lb. typical sacks to 1-ton supersacks. Different bag filling materials. Gravel tends to allow water to pass through while sand tends to not allow it to penetrate.
Water bars	A 4 to 6 inch high "speed bump" made of soil, aggregate, or asphalt, placed across an erodible sloped road/path. The water bar, while not a true linear sediment control measure but more of a concentrated flow BMP, redirects sheet flow on the roadway to one or both of the sides of the road, which is stabilized with vegetation or has a stabilized swale equipped with check dams and velocity dissipation.	The water bar can be constructed of a variety of materials. A rolling swale, which is a depression that extends across the roadway/path, can also be used to intercept and redirect sheet flow.
Terracing and grade breaks	Engineered ridges and channels constructed across the slope (parallel with the slope contours) to intercept downslope sheet flow and to redirect the runoff to a place where it can be discharged off the slope in a controlled manner (e.g., stabilized swale or downslope pipe).	The terrace benches can be of varying widths and the channels or swales can be earthen or stabilized with aggregate, geotextiles, or concrete.

Connecting the Dots of Best Management Practices

Installation	Advantages	Disadvantages
Place a row of gravel or sand filled bags to act as a "speed bump" for the water flow. The row can be built up with multiple layers of filled bags.	✓ Can be placed on impervious surfaces. ✓ Can be used in locations with concentrated or channelized flow. ✓ Readily available.	✗ Bags are heavy and hard to handle and place. ✗ Bags can be torn by equipment and vehicles or degraded by sunlight and can become themselves a source of sediment. ✗ Sandbags should not be used by discharge points, especially where subject to being damaged. ✗ Bags must be removed at the completion of construction (prior to filing for permit termination.)
Water bars or rolling swales are typically installed with a piece of grading equipment or by hand. As with other linear control measures, they should be spaced 10 to 50 feet apart depending upon the slope ratio of the roadway/path. Make sure to provide a stabilized path for the redirected flow to travel after the water bar and provide velocity dissipation at the end of the conveyance.	✓ Native materials are typically used to construct them. ✓ Can be easily removed when not needed. ✓ Can be run over by vehicles and equipment.	✗ Earthen water bars or swales are also susceptible to erosion. ✗ Can result in concentrated flow (i.e., directing water to a roadside swale) and must be accompanied with channel stabilization and velocity dissipation control measures.
Must be engineered and part of the approved grading plans. Terrace benches should typically slope back into the hill and they should be spaced 10 to 50 feet apart depending upon the slope ratio. A mechanism for controlled downslope drainage with velocity dissipation at the outlet should be included in the design.	✓ Native materials are typically used to construct them. ✓ They are usually a permanent control measure.	✗ Linear control measures may still be needed until terraces and slopes have been completed and stabilized. ✗ Terraces will typically result in concentrated flow (i.e., directing water into a pipe or swale) that will need energy and velocity dissipation.

Type	Description	Variations
Log erosion barriers[47]	In a natural setting, utilizing downed or intentionally felled trees to intercept and slow downslope runoff.	Burnt or other dead timber from wildfires can be utilized. Felled trees from fire prevention / forest management practices can be used.

---

47 U.S. Department of Agriculture Natural Resources Conservation Service, After the Fire – Log Erosion Barriers, https://www.nrcs.usda.gov/resources/guides-and-instructions/after-the-fire-log-erosion-barriers.

Connecting the Dots of Best Management Practices

Installation	Advantages	Disadvantages
A contour line is marked on the slope to identify the approximate cross slope alignment. Trees along this line are felled on the upstream side of the contour line as much as possible. Stumps are left about 12" high to brace the tree. The logs are cut to a length that permits safe handling and placement for the crew, generally 10 to 30 feet, but longer logs can be difficult to manage and therefore can be broken up into 4-foot segments. Tree limbs are removed to the extent necessary for the log to lie flat on the ground. A shallow trench (about 2 to 6 inches deep) is dug along the contour. The log is placed in the trench and seated with tamped backfill such that water flowing down the slope will not run under it. For this practice to be effective, the gaps between the logs must be blocked by a "joining" log above or below the gap to impede passage of water.	✓ Ideal for erosion control after wildfires, for forest thinning / management activities, and for restoration projects. ✓ Utilizes native materials that do not need to be later removed and can remain in place permanently. ✓ Minimizes concerns regarding solid waste of used BMPs and potential for wildlife entrapment.	✗ Need to have a good supply of logs. Hot burn areas may not have enough remaining logs. ✗ Water can flow under logs that do not have good conformance to the ground. ✗ Labor intensive work.

Type	Description	Variations
Boulders, riprap, and earthen berms.	Often with some creativity, natural materials or features already present at the site can be used effectively as linear sediment control measures.	Natural materials can include boulders or broken-up rock (riprap), logs (as described above), and berms that are either existing or have been created with rock or salvaged organic material.
Vegetative buffers and hedgerows.	A linear stretch of vegetation between the construction area and the project boundary or receiving water.	This can take many different forms, such as preserving 50 feet or more of existing vegetation; planting or preserving a hedgerow of trees, bushes, or vines; or engineering and designing a landscaped area that storm water runoff must pass through.

Connecting the Dots of Best Management Practices

Installation	Advantages	Disadvantages
Use what you have on hand, making sure the material will 1) adequately impede storm water surface flow, and 2) not itself be a source of sediment or pollutants.	✓ Lessens the need for purchased BMPs. ✓ Utilizes (and recycles) materials already present. ✓ May reduce the need for off-hauling of materials from the site. ✓ May be able to become a permanent sediment control feature.	✗ Sometimes it is hard to achieve good conformance to the ground so that flows don't undercut the BMP. ✗ May not have enough supply of natural materials to provide linear control for the entire project. ✗ Earthen berms need to be stabilized or vegetated.
Installation may be as simple as installing ESA fencing to protect an existing area of vegetation. Or it may involve landscape design and engineering and installation to create a vegetative buffer.	✓ Lessens the need for purchased BMPs. ✓ Vegetative buffers are very effective in improving water quality. ✓ Certain species of plants can uptake pollutants and provide phytoremediation. ✓ Vegetative buffers reduce runoff by facilitating infiltration and transpiration. ✓ They can also provide some wind protection to help control wind soil loss. ✓ It provides habitat for birds and other animals.	✗ Can already have paths of preferential flow, channeling, and erosion issues. ✗ Need maintenance to manage vegetative growth and disease. ✗ Can restrict flows too much.

SF-1 Linear Controls:

Linear controls are used to slow the flow along a perimeter or a place within the project to promote sedimentation to occur and to prevent or minimize sheet and rill erosion from occurring. When utilizing linear control measures, the following design and installation criteria is important to consider:

- Determine where linear controls should be placed. Sometimes they are called perimeter controls, but not every project needs or should have them installed around the perimeter. They should never run up or down a hill but should be placed horizontally along the toe of the slope and along the face of the slope. They should also be placed where water runs onto and off the project.
- The linear control device should be installed so that it is as level as possible. You want to have level water backing up behind the length of the control measure. Otherwise water will flow to the low spot and will form a rill or gully at that location. Cross-barriers along the linear control measure will help prevent the lateral movement of water. J-hooking the ends of the control measure upward will also help prevent accumulated water from spilling off the ends of the installed device.
- Linear controls should have good conformance to the underlying soil so that runoff will not exploit weak points or gaps under the device. These devices tend to act as miniature dams, which risk hydraulic pressure from water held behind the device to cause erosion to occur at weak points or gaps.
- Be creative! Utilize resources already on hand like vegetation, logs, rocks, berms, etc. Remember, you don't have to circle the project site with fiber roll or silt fence.
- Plan for the future. Consider the life span of the selected linear control device. Is it biodegradable and can be left in place, or will it need to be removed after its intended purpose has been completed? Can a long term permanent linear control be used instead of a temporary one?

Speed Bumps (SF-2)

When driving in an alley or residential neighborhood, speed bumps are hard to ignore. Even if you were not paying attention, the first bump you "hit" will definitely get your attention and cause you to slow down. In a neighborhood, these bumps are beneficial for the safety of the kids playing in the street. On a construction site, storm water speed bumps also cause a reduction in velocity but, in this case, not for safety reasons but for sedimentation. Remember, when we slow the flow, sedimentation occurs and we get less erosion. In a neighborhood, speed bumps are placed in strategic locations because of a particular safety concern, such as a school or playground. On a construction site, we also place storm water "speed bumps" at places of vulnerability, which include:

- ⇒ Drain inlets
- ⇒ Curb and gutters
- ⇒ Drainage swales
- ⇒ Slopes

Notice that each of these locations have something in common. They all involve the conveyance of storm water. Because the purpose of a storm water conveyance is to move runoff from one point to another efficiently and effectively, these are going to be places where the water velocity is going to be higher. Like a police officer parked on the side of the road with a radar gun, we want to slow things down. However, the police officer cannot always be parked on the side of the road, so a speed bump will also retard traffic, or in our case, reduce the velocity of

Figure 63 - Speed bump BMPs slow the flow at strategic points on the project. These locations tend to be where storm water is "speeding." (Photo credit: John Teravskis)

the runoff, creating another chance to reduce the sediment load in the runoff before it is discharged off-site.

Speed bumps are effective at causing sediment to drop out. But their effectiveness can lead to their ineffectiveness. As more and more sediment is deposited, the bump becomes a ramp and no longer slows the flow or captures sediment. Therefore, it is very important to remove buildup of sediment to maintain the water "bump" so there is room to capture more sediment. A good rule of thumb is to maintain the sediment below one third of the height of the device.

Drain Inlet Protection: I personally think that too much emphasis is placed on drain inlet (DI) protection. For me, it is too little, too late. What I mean is that much of the heavy lifting regarding erosion and sediment control needs to be done elsewhere on the project site. By the time the surface runoff reaches a DI, the water quality should be pretty good. Now, I am not against the use of DI protection as long as it is understood that it is just a safety net or a final chance to do some "polishing" of the discharge. However, at many projects, DI protection is the principal—or only—BMP in place. This is just putting too much confidence in them, and chances are they are not going to be able to handle the sediment load that they will receive. There are also common misconceptions about how DI protection works. Under normal conditions, drain inlets need to be open and in service. They need to remove water efficiently and effectively from the project site, otherwise there will be flooding. This means that the flow rate by design will be relatively fast. The DI protection speed bump needs to be just a "bump," a slight slowing of the water to allow larger particles to settle out. A common mistake we have observed on construction sites is the placement of a filter fabric on or around the drain grate. This will typically plug up with sediment and prevent water from efficiently discharging, which results in flooding. In these cases, usually a frustrated construction operator or maintenance personnel will end up puncturing or ripping off the filter fabric to get the water to drain. However, there are different situations where DI protection is needed, and the approach to each situation needs to be customized for each case. Table 10 provides an overview of the different situations and types of DI protection used to slow the flow and capture sediment.

Table 10 - DI Protection Scenarios

Scenario	Recommended DI Protection	Installation Considerations
DI is located in a soil disturbed area with a significant amount of loose, uncompacted soil where localized ponding is not a concern.	Place silt fence around the drain inlet with at least 12 inches of distance between the edge of the DI opening and the silt fence. The area within the silt fence should be stabilized with geotextile and crushed rock.	If flooding is a concern, this may not be the best type of BMP to use. DO NOT puncture the silt fence. Silt fence will allow some water to weep through it, but typically it is less than 0.5 gallons/minute/square foot of fence material. By making a larger circumference around the DI, more water will discharge to the DI and the design considerations here can be significant. The silt fence's height demands it be around a substantial sump condition such that a diversion away from the DI doesn't occur.
DI is located in a soil disturbed area with a significant amount of loose, uncompacted soil where ponding is not desirable.	Stack either compost socks or gravel bags around the drain inlet with at least 12 inches of distance between the edge of the DI opening and the compost socks or gravel bags and secure them with staking. Stack the socks or bags to an elevation of at least 12 inches above grade (or higher if there are piles of loose soil or sloughing possible near the DI). The area between the DI and your chosen device should be stabilized with geotextile and crushed rock.	A longer circumference around the DI will allow more flow to pass to the DI and help to prevent localized ponding.

Connecting the Dots of Best Management Practices

Scenario	Recommended DI Protection	Installation Considerations
DI is located in a soil disturbed area with minimal amount of loose soil.	Surround the DI with compost socks, gravel bags, or properly installed fiber roll or proprietary fiber roll replacement products (keyed in and staked down).	Vehicle and equipment traffic needs to be considered. Fiber rolls cannot tolerate being run over. Although gravel bags and compost socks can withstand a certain amount of impact from vehicles and equipment, they should be protected from traffic and site personnel should be taught to recognize and respect them as important BMPs.
DI is located on an impervious or highly compacted surface but not in a curb and gutter.	Surround the DI with compost socks or gravel bags.	The socks, the bags, and their respective media must have significant ability to allow flow-through. Traffic of vehicles and equipment needs to be considered. Although gravel bags and compost socks can withstand a certain amount of impact from vehicles and equipment, they should be protected from traffic, and site personnel should be taught to recognize and respect them as important BMPs.

Scenario	Recommended DI Protection	Installation Considerations
DI is located within the curb and gutter of a paved public roadway where the municipality allows sediment control devices to be placed in the curb and gutter.	The constructed configuration should create a venturi of the storm water flow which will allow particles to settle out before water flows over, around, or through the configured device and into the drain inlet (refer to Figure 62). Ideally the gravel bags / compost socks should be 6 inches high (stacked if necessary) and 3-4 feet long. The placement should create a venturi of the storm water flow which will allow particles to settle out before water flows around the berm and into the drain inlet.	Always check to see if the local municipality allows these types of devices to be placed in the curb and gutter. If flow enters from both sides of the DI, a gravel bag / compost sock chevron berm should be placed on both sides.
DI is located within the curb and gutter of a paved public roadway where the municipality does not allow sediment control devices to be placed in the curb and gutter.	Use a flush-mounted DI protection device. These are typically proprietary manufactured devices that range from bags placed in the DI to screens (with high flow bypass holes) installed on the grate or DI opening.	Confirm what the local municipality will allow or not allow. Confirm that the dimensions of the DI grate and subgrade box/chamber will accommodate the selected device. In higher traffic situations, the device may need to be epoxied onto the surface.
Where there is a concern about capturing large particles, leaves, debris, or trash.	Install a proprietary filter bag or drain inlet filter device/cartridge in the DI.	This can be used in conjunction with most of the types of DI scenarios described above. Confirm the dimensions of the DI grate and subgrade box/chamber will accommodate the selected device. Some devices are also equipped with oil absorbent materials.

Curb and Gutter Speed Bumps:
The chevron berms described in Table 10 are not only appropriate for immediately upgradient of a drain inlet but may also be used effectively in the curb and gutter even where there is no nearby drain inlet. This is a very typical situation for roadway and subdivision construction projects. Track-out onto the paved surfaces or wind-blown sediment can make its way to the curb and gutter. Placing the chevron berms every fifty to one hundred feet (or more often where there are steeper grades or more sediment sources) can significantly reduce the amount of sediment in the runoff and take some of the pressure off of the drain inlet protection devices.

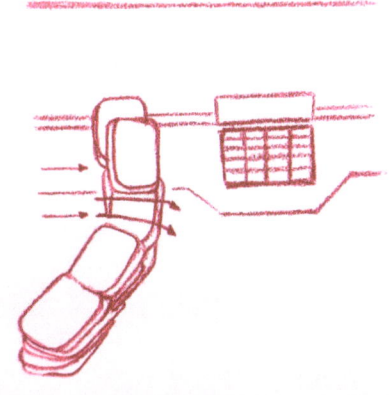

Figure 64 - Curb and gutter placement for gravel bags or compost socks to facilitate sedimentation without impeding flow. (Sketch by Abigail Teravskis)

Drainage Swales and Check Dams: Drainage swales also convey water from one point to another and need to have their speed regulated. In a swale, typically we would utilize check dams to slow the flow and provide opportunities for sediment to fall out. On a relatively flat grade (< 2% slope), the check dams can be spaced every fifty to one hundred feet. However, for swales that have a slope percentage ≥ 2%, the spacing should be as shown in Figure 65. Check dams should only be placed in locations of storm water runoff and not within streams or other natural water bodies. Since check dams are utilized where concentrated flow is expected, they should be secured with staking or weighting. Where high velocity flow is anticipated, weightier check dams can be created from rock-filled gabions, riprap, or larger diameter compost socks that are stacked and secured with staking. All too often, check dams are used as a primary sediment control in a conveyance. They should be viewed as a support practice in a conveyance that has been well constructed and/or stabilized to minimize erosive conditions.

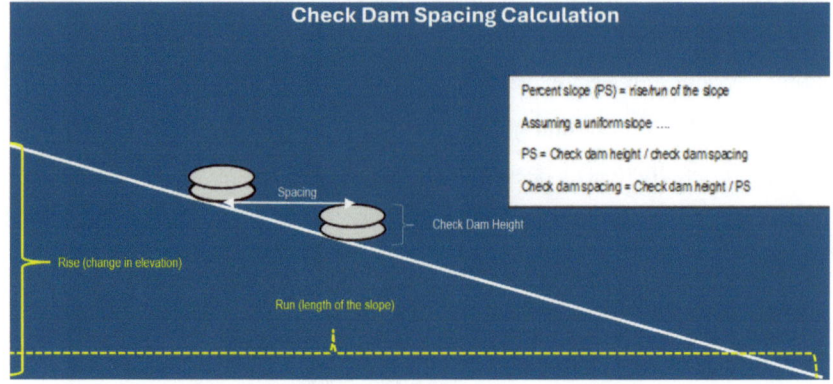

Figure 65 - Calculation for determining the spacing of check dams. For 18-inch-high check dams on a 2% slope, they should be placed 75 feet apart. The same check dams on a 10% slope should be spaced 15 feet apart.

Track Walking: Speed bumps can come in all different sizes. Sometimes one of the best ways to slow flow is with miniature speed bumps on a steep slope, which are created by running a tracked piece of equipment up and down the slope. We call this track walking. But it is very important that the equipment only move up and down the slopes. Otherwise the speed bumps will be turned 90 degrees and will no longer be bumps but raceways for water runoff.

Figure 67 shows a situation where track walking was not performed correctly. The raceways sped up the runoff which then formed rills in each one. If left unchecked,

Figure 66 - Track walk a slope by moving up and down the slope. (Photo credit: John Teravskis)

this could lead to devastating results, including the formation of gullies, slope failure, or mass wasting.

Figure 67 - The effects of track walking in the wrong direction. (Photo credit: John Teravskis)

However, when track walking is performed in the right direction, it not only functions as a sediment control measure but also as a method of erosion control. Note in Figure 68 where the young vegetation is primarily becoming established. It is happening in the depressions. This is where the moisture tends to reside, therefore the depressions are optimal places for germination and will also facilitate a more secure root establishment. As we previously covered, vegetation is a [Raindrop BMP](). As the vegetation grows, it continues to slow the flow and eliminate water borne sediment. But even before the vegetation grows, the track walking speed bumps act as an erosion control measure. Slowing the flow means a reduction of velocity which means less erosion. Track walking alone will not prevent raindrop or sheet erosion, but it can help prevent the formation of rills. Although an

Figure 68 - Track walking is a hybrid control measure acting both as a sediment control and an erosion control. (Photo credit: John Teravskis)

effective soil cover should be applied to exposed slopes as soon as possible, track walking is a BMP that can be in place before other erosion control measures can be installed. Track walking in combination with other Raindrop BMPs provides an effective combination for soil stabilization.

> **SF-2 Speed Bump BMPs:**
> The key to causing sedimentation to occur is to slow the flow of water. We want sedimentation to happen but not off-site. It should occur behind obstacles that we have intentionally placed that have enough capacity to capture and hold sediment until it can be cleaned out. These devices are referred to as speed bump BMPs. We can place them at drain inlets, within curb and gutters or storm water conveyance swales, and on hillsides. When utilizing speed bump measures, the following design and installation criteria is important to consider:
> - Determine the direction of water flow, and place the device in the path upstream of the discharge point.
> - Since these devices are often utilized where there is concentrated flow, make sure they have been sufficiently secured.
> - Spacing between speed bump devices will depend upon the slope. Generally, the bottom elevation of the upgradient device should be the same elevation of the top of the next downgradient device.
> - The speed bumps should be sized for the anticipated sediment load. Regular inspections and maintenance should be performed to ensure that there is adequate sediment storage capacity available. Typically, do not let the sediment build up exceed one third of the height of the device.
> - Track walking should be performed on finished slopes with the tracked equipment moving up and down the slope. Linear sediment controls (SF-1) and an effective soil cover (RD-3) should be installed on the track walked slope to achieve soil stabilization.

Fat Spots (SF-3)

We have already seen that slowing the flow is the key to preventing erosion and encouraging sedimentation to occur. The previous two slow-the-flow control measures accomplished velocity reduction by placing an obstacle in the flow path. Another effective way to slow the flow is to cause a delay for the discharge. You know, like in high school when you were in a hurry to get off campus but needed to go to "detention"—a holding area for kids who need to be slowed down a bit. It results in them being on campus a bit longer than other students, and hopefully some of their less than desirable behaviors will settle out in the detention classroom. That is quite similar to what we do with sediment-containing raindrop delinquents. We put them into detention! These are big spaces from which they cannot quickly race out. I like to call this subcategory of BMPs "Fat Spots."

So let's say Junior and his gang of hoodlum raindrops are moving 1,000 feet across a construction site at 1 ft³/second (cfs) in a shallow trapezoidal-shaped earthen swale. Using Manning's Formula[48], they would cover the unimpeded distance in about seven minutes. That is not much time to settle out solids!

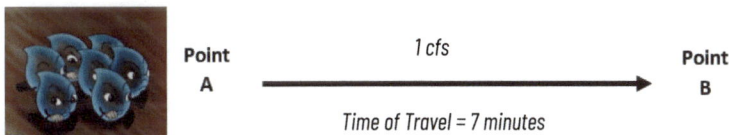

Now, let's introduce these hoodlum raindrops to some detention by making them pass through a pond before leaving the site. Watch what happens when we size the pond to be 10,000 ft³.

---

48   $Q=(1.49/n)(A)(R)^{2/3}(S)^{1/2}$ where n is the Manning coefficient = 0.03, A=flow area, R=hydraulic radius, S=channel slope.

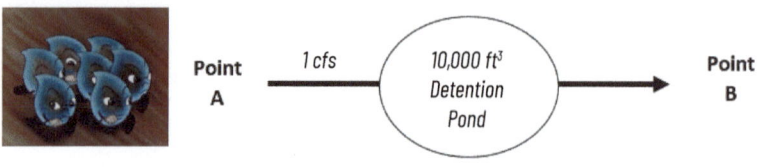

Time of Travel = 2.8 hrs.

The 1 cfs flow into the pond will "hang out" or have a detention time of 2.8 hours, which will allow these hoodlums enough time to let go of some over their dirty baggage (sediment). If we make the pond 1,000,000 ft³, now they will have 11.6 days to think about their behavior.

Fat spot BMPs can be a very effective way to promote sedimentation on projects that have sufficient room for a pond or other detention area. These fat spots can be relatively small or large and can be placed at strategic locations throughout the project site. It is also beneficial to consider the final construction condition and utilize built features to provide the detention. For example, many rural projects are required to have an on-site storm water basin for flood control purposes. These basins are ideal for providing sediment control,

Figure 69 - Stubbed up drain inlets can be used to provide temporary detention during early phases of the project. (Photo credit: John Teravskis)

especially if they are graded and connected to the site's drainage system early during the project. Areas excavated for bioretention cells or swales can also provide detention of storm water runoff during construction. However, you will want to make sure that the sediment load has been significantly decreased before the bioretention cells are completed with the rock and growing media layers and landscaping. Another potential sediment trap can be a drain inlet where the surrounding graded surface is lower than the stubbed-up storm water pipe and a drain frame and grate have not yet been installed. At this point of the project, each of the drain inlets will form a mini-detention pond.

Figure 70 - Bioretention cells can be utilized during construction for storm water detention. However, make sure that sediment loads are minimized before installing the subterranean rock and growing media layers. (Photo credit: John Teravskis)

SF-3 Fat Spot BMPs:

An effective way to slow the flow and encourage sedimentation is to create locations on the project site to detain runoff. This is beneficial for a variety of reasons. First, it slows the flow and provides a period of detention which allows sedimentation to occur. Second, it provides a place where settled soil particles can be collected and managed. Third, if the detention area is on permeable soils, it allows infiltration to occur, which, depending on the soil type, may be significant and may significantly reduce the volume of storm water discharged from the project. When using and selecting "fat spots," it is important to consider the following:

- Large detention areas may need to be designed by an engineer and approved by the local municipality. They may need to be designed and sized in accordance with local, state, and other regulatory standards.
- Make sure that detention areas are adequately stabilized and do not become a source of erosion.
- Velocity and energy dissipation devices may be necessary on both the inlet and outlet of the detention pond.
- When using a future bioretention cell or drainage system feature, make

sure that it is protected from heavy sediment loads or can be cleaned out of accumulated sediment.
- Discharging water from the top of the ponded water using a skimming device can help with improving the water quality of the discharge.
- All methods of detention will require maintenance to remove accumulated sediment.
- Detention is not usually an adequate sediment control for clayey soils or colloidal clay suspensions.

Flow Spreaders and Energy Dissipators (SF-4)

When we are managing storm water, many times the runoff will be concentrated into a single discharge stream. So what does this do to our goal of reducing erosion and soil loss? To find out, let's review the formula for fluid flow rate:

$$\text{Equation 2 - Fluid Flow Rate} \quad Q = v * A$$

Where:

Q is the flow rate at the point of interest measured in cubic feet per second (ft^3/second or cfs),

v is the velocity of the discharge (remember, velocity is directly proportional to soil loss and expressed in feet/second), and

A is the cross-sectional area at the point of interest (i.e., the discharge location) in ft^2.

For our demonstration of this hydraulic calculation, let's assume that the flow rate cannot be altered. As previously stated, the goal of Slow-the-Flow BMPs is to reduce the velocity of the discharge and, thereby, reduce the amount of soil loss due to erosion. Therefore, if we rearrange the above hydraulic equation, we can show that the following is true:

Connecting the Dots of Best Management Practices

$$v = Q / A$$

This rearranged equation reveals that when the cross-sectional area (A) of the discharge point is smaller, the discharge velocity will be faster. But when there is more cross-sectional area (a larger A), the discharge velocity will slow down. Slow flow means less erosion!

So let's consider an 8-inch diameter pipe that discharges water at 3.0 cfs.

If we create a header pipe and attach six 4-inch diameter pipes and we maintain the discharge flow rate the same, we will have an overall flow velocity reduction of 2.8 ft/sec, which is about one third slower than the single pipe configuration.

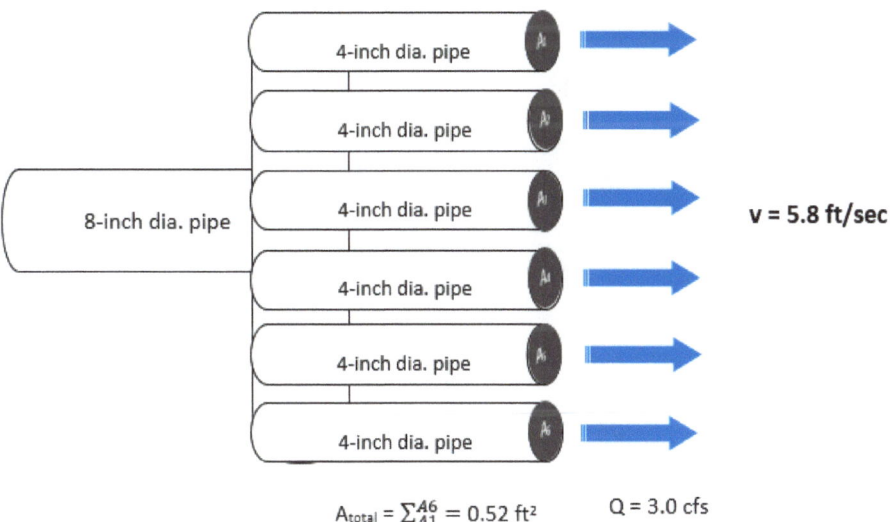

This is the basic concept behind flow spreaders: to create a larger area for the discharge point. Techniques for spreading flow involve creating as many openings as possible from which water can seep or discharge. Perforated pipe is often used for this purpose. An 8-inch diameter perforated pipe can have up to 1.90 square inches of openings per linear foot. That means, if in the above example, we used a 100-foot-long header of 8-inch diameter perforated pipe instead of the six open-ended 4-inch pipe sections, the total cross sectional discharge area (A) would be 1.32 ft^2 and the velocity would now be 2.3 ft/sec for a 74% reduction in the discharge velocity.

Along the same lines of logic is to dissipate energy at the discharge point. Where we have concentrated flow, it is often necessary to install a device that can absorb the energy of the discharge and allow the spreading out of the flow, which will further reduce the velocity. This is typically accomplished through the use of riprap rock placed on a durable geotextile fabric. This allows the concentrated flow to enter the downstream waterbody or watershed at a greatly reduced velocity and will help to prevent channel scour or downgradient erosion.

Figure 71 - Riprap energy dissipation downstream of storm water culvert openings. (Photo credit: John Teravskis)

SF-4 Flow Spreaders and Energy Dissipators:

For a given flow rate, the smaller the cross-section area of the place where water is released, the faster the velocity. Therefore, in order to slow the flow, the discharge openings need to be as big and spacious as possible. Concentrated flow will typically not only have high velocity but will also have high energy. Where concentrated flow exits onto erodible surfaces, it is best to provide a less erodible mechanism to receive the flow, dissipate its energy, and allow it to spread out and exit the area at a slower velocity. When specifying flow spreaders and energy dissipators, it is important to consider the following:

- Many of these devices need to be designed by a professional engineer and approved by the local municipality. They also may need to be designed and sized in accordance with local, state, and other regulatory standards.
- Without other required environmental permits and permissions, these types of devices should never be used in a river, stream, creek, or other natural waterbody.
- Flow spreaders should be installed as level as possible.
- Mechanisms to clear and clean clogged pipes and openings should be provided.
- Usually energy dissipation devices should be placed at the outlets of flow spreaders.
- In temporary settings, it is best to place riprap rock on top of a durable geotextile fabric.
- Rock size should be specified by an engineer to assure it will not wash away during anticipated flow events.

TREATMENT BMPS

So far we have looked at Raindrop BMPs which keep particles from becoming detached by erosion processes and Slow-the-Flow BMPs which settle out particles that have become detached. However, sometimes more aggressive measures are needed to remove soil particles from storm water runoff. These measures are called Treatment BMPs. By "treatment," we mean the removal of soil particles or other pollutants by the means of filtration or other mechanical or chemical processes.

Compost Socks and Berms (T-1)

We have already discussed the use of compost socks as a linear sediment control (Table 9) and for drain inlet protection (Table 10). But compost socks do more than slow the flow, they also grab (physically filter out) soil particles and other pollutants. Pollutants that have been trapped in the compost filter media can then be further treated by microorganisms that reside in the composted materials. These organisms will bioremediate some of the trapped pollutants. The USDA reported, "Compost filter socks have been extensively researched and evaluated at the USDA Agricultural Research Service (ARS) and universities. Research literature has shown that this management practice can physically filter fine and coarse sediment and chemically filter soluble pollutants from stormwater. A USDA ARS study showed that compost filter socks can remove 65 percent of clay and 66 percent of silt particulates; 74 percent of total coliform bacteria and 75 percent of E. coli; 37 percent to 72 percent

Figure 72 - Compost socks provide physical filtering of sediment and other pollutants in storm water runoff. Pollutants trapped within the filter device may be further treated by microorganisms residing within the compost. (Photo credit: John Teravskis)

of Cd, Cr, Cu, Ni, Pb, and Zn; 99 percent of diesel fuel; 84 percent of motor oil; 43 percent of gasoline; 17 percent of ammonium-N; and 11 percent of nitrate-N from stormwater runoff."[49] When slowing the flow is not providing enough removal of pollutants, compost socks can be placed in strategic locations to allow runoff to pass through them. This is particularly important where water is leaving a project and at potential sampling locations. Compost does not have to reside within a sock to provide effective treatment; a compost berm can also provide the same type of treatment and can remain as a permanent storm water control measure.

Compost socks are available in a variety of diameters, lengths, and types of netting. Typical netting is comprised of a fairly durable multifilament polypropylene. The compost fill should be composted organic material (typically wood chips) with 100% passing a 2-inch sieve and only 10–30% passing a 0.375-inch sieve[50].

It is important to procure compost socks from a reputable supplier that has received the U.S. Composting Council Seal of Testing Assurance.[51]

Figure 73 - Stacking compost socks will accommodate a high treatment rate per linear foot and the added weight provides better conformance to the underlying surface and improves treatment effectiveness. (Photo credit: John Teravskis)

When determining the placement and use of compost socks, the anticipated flow should be evaluated and considered. This will determine the type, number, and length of sock needed. According to one compost sock manufacturer, an 8-inch diameter compost sock (the most typical size sold) has a hydraulic flow

---

49   United States Department of Agriculture, Agronomy Technical Note No. 4, Utilization of Compost Filter Socks, February 2014, p. 3.
50   Ibid.
51   https://www.compostingcouncil.org/page/CertifiedCompostSTA .

through rate of 7.5 gallons per minute per linear foot of sock (gpm/ft) and 12-inch diameter sock has a flow through rate of 11.3 gpm/ft[52]. If a higher flow rate is needed, a larger diameter compost sock can be utilized. However, these are less commonly available and have logistical issues (such as weight) associated with them. As an alternative, socks can be stacked. The extra weight actually allows the compost socks to operate more effectively. The added weight causes better conformance to the ground surface and will allow less flow to slip underneath or around the sock. So, if an 8-inch diameter compost sock is stacked three high, it will accommodate a discharge up to 22.5 gpm/ft. When using socks at an outlet or around a drain inlet, a common complaint is that they back up water and cause some localized flooding. A simple solution to prevent such flooding is to create a longer perimeter around the discharge point. This will provide more linear feet of sock and allow a higher pass-through rate.

Compost socks can be effectively used as linear sediment control devices (SF-1), drain inlet protection and check dams (SF-2), and in treatment trains and devices (T-4). Compost berms (compost that has been manually placed in a 6-inch to 24-inch-high windrow) can be used effectively as a long-term perimeter control.

Generally, compost socks will have an effective lifespan of one to two years, but environmental and site conditions can significantly shorten or lengthen the actual effectual duration. Typically solar degradation of the sock material will occur before the compost filter media fills with sediment. When the life expectancy of the compost sock is reached, it can be slit open with a razor blade, the fabric pulled away and discarded or recycled, and many times the spent compost material can be left in place or scattered elsewhere on the project (i.e., in the landscaped areas).

---

52 Filtrexx Design Manual, Section 1.9, Table 9.2 https://www.filtrexx.com/application/files/2616/2022/0572/1.9_Filtrexx_Sediment_Trap.pdf .

T-1 Compost Socks and Berms:

Compost socks and berms not only slow the flow, as do other linear sediment control measures, but they allow water to pass through them, which treats water by physically filtering out pollutants. Once caught in the filter media, many pollutants will undergo further treatment by the means of microorganisms that live in the composted material. The compost materials in the socks should be large enough to allow sufficient pass through but small enough to provide filtering capabilities. Ideally, compost should be what is referred to as "2-inch minus," meaning that 100% passes a 2-inch sieve and only 10-30% of the material passes through a 0.375-inch sieve. When specifying compost use and placement, the following are important considerations:

- Determine the needed flow-through capacity in order to not cause upstream flooding. When using 8-inch diameter sock, use a 7.5 gpm/linear foot figure and, with a 12-inch diameter sock, use a 11.3 gpm/lin. ft. value.
- Although compost socks do not need to be keyed in, make sure that there is good conformance to the ground surface. Uneven surfaces can allow voids under the sock through which untreated water may flow.
- Generally compost socks perform better after an initial wetting. New compost may have a considerable amount of dust. Prewetting socks can help to avoid initial higher turbidity values.
- In places where flow rates may be concentrated, anchor the socks at least every 10 feet.
- Stacking socks often provides better conformance to the underlying surface and will increase the per linear foot flow through flow capacity.
- Use socks and compost sources only from a reputable composter that has the U.S. Composting Council Seal of Testing Assurance.
- Select the sock material type based on the needs of the project such as a high visibility or neutral color and a durable or a biodegradable fabric.
- In many cases, after the project is complete, socks can be ripped open with a razor blade, the fabric gathered up and disposed of or recycled, and the compost spread out on the ground.

Treatment of Tires (T-2)

Water is not the only thing leaving the site that needs to be treated. Equipment and vehicle tires exiting a construction site, especially during wet conditions, need to be cleaned. Otherwise the results will become fairly obvious and will most certainly draw the attention of the public, municipal staff, and storm water inspectors! Tracked-out sediment is problematic for several reasons:

1. During rain events it will cause turbid runoff to enter storm drains and receiving waters.
2. With each passing car or vehicle, it will become more and more spread out.
3. It will cause sediment to be deposited in the roadway gutters and storm water collection system, increasing maintenance needed by the municipality.
4. When it dries, it becomes a source of fugitive dust that is spread beyond the roadway and picked up and mobilized by the next rain event.

Therefore, it is important to keep sediment on the construction site by removing it from the tires of vehicles before they exit. This can be accomplished in several ways.

Figure 74 - Track-out is a red flag shouting at the inspector, "Come inspect me!" (Photo credit: Matt Lewis)

Connecting the Dots of Best Management Practices

Mechanical Removal: This is the most common form of track-out control. It involves driving a vehicle with muddy tires over an uneven surface which will cause the tires to be compressed and flexed to allow sediment and mud clinging to the tire to fall off or be scraped off by the uneven surface. There are a variety of methods used to create an uneven surface including installing a bed of 3-inch to 5-inch jagged rock, structures made of angular steel, and other proprietary manufactured devices. A key design consideration is to have a device large enough to get several rotations of the tire so that contact with the device is maximized. Another design feature is to provide an area for the removed sediment to deposit. An equally important consideration is to have a way to remove accumulated sediment. There has been more than one jobsite I have visited where I commented on the lack of the presence of a track-out control device, to which the site superintendent replied "Oh, it's there, it's buried under the dirt." Without maintenance, your asset can quickly become a liability.

Figure 75 - A construction exit utilizing Fods mats. The mats come in 7' x 12' lengths. They can be secured in place with stakes and picked up and "shaken off" to remove accumulated sediment. (Photo credit: John Teravskis)

Preventative: Another common way to control track-out of sediment is to reduce the likelihood of vehicle tires coming into contact with mud. OK, I know, this isn't exactly treatment of tires, but rather we are "treating" the road surface by providing a stabilized construction pathway for the vehicles to traverse. There are various ways that this can be achieved. When possible, utilizing existing roadways and paved surfaces is a great solution. These may be roadways that are not being demolished or they might be newly established roadways. Most residential subdivision projects will install roadways shortly after grading and before beginning vertical construction of the homes. In recent years, many commercial projects have been learning the value of installing a first lift of asphalt early during the project. This will not only stabilize the surface and prevent muddy tires but will also help avoid the need for purchasing and installing other temporary erosion control measures. Even if some tires get muddy, having extensive stabilized construction roadways will often allow the tire-deposited sediment to remain and be managed on-site rather than on public roadways.

Figure 76 - Stabilized roadways can help keep construction vehicle tires from getting muddy and tracking out sediment. (Photo credit: John Teravskis)

Washing: A less common practice of preventing the track-out of mud onto roadways is to wash the tires of exiting vehicles. This is a particularly useful control measure for sites having sticky, clayey soils not easily removed from tires and underbodies of vehicles. Mechanical removal of such soils is typically not very effective and will quickly become a source of sediment themselves. However, washing tires has its own drawbacks. There is the issue of dealing with the now very turbid wash water. Where tire washing occurs, it is necessary to make sure there is enough storage for the wash water. For sites with clayey soils, the wash water will likely be a colloidal clay suspension and may require treatment using an active treatment system (T-5). Wet tires also present a problem in that, while they have been stripped of mud and clays, they still will cause staining of roadway surfaces. It is best that a tire wash be located quite a distance within the project and have stabilized construction roadways leading from the washing facility to the public roadway.

With all tire treatment methods, maintenance is key. Anything designed to remove sediment will accumulate sediment, therefore, it is necessary to remove the accumulated sediment from time to time. One valuable lesson we learned a few years ago is that there is no such thing as a completely effective track-out control measure. In our Construction Sandbox, we built and installed what we considered to be a better-than-average track-out control measure. It was made fairly consistent to the Caltrans TC-1 specification in that it utilized a bed of 3" x 5" jagged rock placed on a geotextile fabric. It was also equipped with a steel structure to compress and flex tires. The device was long enough to allow four full rotations of a pickup truck tire. We were so proud of our new addition to the Construction Sandbox and we were ready to tell the world about how effective a properly installed track-out control measure is. So, to test it out, we muddied up an 8-foot by 8-foot area behind the track-out control measure and backed up a pick-up into the mud. We gave the tires a good spin (actually only the back tires were in the mud) and then we drove the pickup across the device. What did we see? Clean streets? No! How disappointed we were! There was track-out (deposited sediment, not just staining) extending at least 40 feet from the device. That was from one pickup truck with only the back tires dirtied across a brand new, better-than-average, track-out control measure! So, what did we learn from this unexpected turn of events? We learned that street sweeping (T-3) will always be a necessary function at construction sites having wet, exposed soils.

Figure 77- Construction Sandbox track-out control demonstration. We learned that no matter how well you build it, street sweeping will always be needed. (Photo credit: John Teravskis)

T-2 Treatment of Tires:

To minimize the track-out of sediment off of a construction site and onto public roadways, it is necessary to "treat" the tires of exiting vehicles. Treatment is generally accomplished by one or a combination of the following methods: mechanical removal of mud from tires, prevention by keeping construction vehicles on stabilized roadways, or washing tires. When specifying the use and placement of tire or roadway treating devices, the following are important considerations:

- Consider the largest tire that will be exiting the site and adjust the size of the track-out device to maximize the contact with the tire. A good general rule-of-thumb is to have a length that allows four rotations of the tire.
- To the extent possible, situate the track-out device so that it is sloped to drain back onto the site. Otherwise, storm water runoff will flow across the track-out device and discharge off-site, taking with it the removed sediment. If it is not possible to have the track-out control device slope toward the project site, place sediment control BMPs (i.e., compost socks) downgradient of the device, and avoid use of the exit during rain events.
- Provide a way to easily remove trapped sediment, and clean the device regularly.
- If possible, have vehicles drive on private paved surfaces after exiting the track-out control device and before entering public roadways. This will allow any residual sediment to be deposited and swept up while still on the construction site.
- To the extent possible, locate track-out control devices as far away as practicable from drain inlets.
- Include a way to capture and, if necessary, treat wash water and runoff from the track-out control device. Do not let this water discharge from the site; instead, infiltrate it or capture, treat, and discharge of it in accordance with local, state, and federal regulations.
- Keep in mind that sweeping (T-3) will always be needed.

Treatment of Streets (T-3)

Not only is street sweeping one of the most cost effective and efficient BMPs, but it is probably one of the oldest! Street sweeping was first invented by English engineer, inventor, and philanthropist Joseph Whitworth who created the first model of a mechanical street sweeper in 1843. His street sweeper was horse drawn and made up of a large drum covered in stiff wire bristles that would brush debris (horse poop) onto an elevator system and into a storage area. In 1849, C. S. Bishop brought a similar invention to the United States. Today, mechanical sweepers and vacuum/air sweepers are common sights at construction sites in an effort to control track-out and erosion issues. Aside from aesthetic purposes, street sweeping matters for a variety of reasons. When a lot of earthwork is occurring at a site with vehicles and equipment entering and exiting the site all day, track-out of sediment is a concern—especially during the wet season when it can get liquified in a storm event and wash down the drain. But it's not just dirt that will get washed or blown away from track-out, things like organic debris, metals, trash, microplastics, toxics, bacteria, and more will also be in the mix, causing pollutant concerns. Of course at most construction sites, the main culprit is sediment. Sediment could be coming from track-out, run-on water, wind erosion, or other construction activities generating particulate matter. Fortunately, sediment is almost always visible and can be cleaned up fairly easily. Interestingly, many times we have noticed a direct link between total suspended solids (TSS) and other pollutants—high TSS tends to correlate with high concentrations of metals, nutrients, and toxic substances. So, staying on top of any loose sediment, dust, or dirt on your site can have the added advantage of keeping other pollutants under control. Microplastics are becoming a big water quality concern, and even though it is not currently a regulated monitoring parameter in many states, street sweeping will serve a dual purpose of removing these small particles while cleaning up tracked out sediment. Microplastics at a construction site can come from tire wear, construction activities that include grinding or cutting of plastics, insulation shedding fiberglass filaments, fibers from reinforced concrete, paint, and many times, even from the BMPs themselves. This up-and-coming pollutant has vast detrimental effects on wildlife and human health. Because of plastic's slow degradation, once it is in the environment, it is only accumulating into a bigger problem as time progresses. Studies have been conducted[53] to show that sweeping vastly reduces pollutant concentrations. The more particulate matter collected, the better pollutant removal you achieve. But, because heavy equipment and traffic can often cause dirt to be compacted onto the paved surfaces near the entrances/exits of a site, selecting the right type of street sweeper combination is crucial to getting the most effective BMP. Some sweepers will greatly assist with pollutant removal, while other sweepers tend to just move a problem to another location or make a bigger problem. Equipment choices include the following:[54]

Mechanical broom sweepers: Two varieties of mechanical broom sweepers include the **kick broom sweeper,** which utilizes a spinning brush that sweeps solids off to the side of the unit. This type of sweeper can be used to quickly remove material off of a paved surface, but it has certain disadvantages too. This type of sweeper has no dust collection system and can cause fugitive dust problems. Also the mechanical action of the broom can break down soil particles into smaller and more easily mobilized particles. Some agencies (such as Caltrans) prohibit the use of this type of sweeper.

Figure 78 - While kick broom sweepers can effectively get sediment off of the pavement, the down side is that they can cause fugitive dust and break particles down in size, making them more mobile. (Photo credit: John Teravskis)

---

53   Street and Municipal Sweeping Studies, WorldSweeper.com, https://www.worldsweeper.com/Street/Studies/index.html.
54   Adapted from https://www.worldsweeper.com/Environmental/SutherlandSweepBeforeTreat10.07.html.

Another variation of this type of sweeper is the horizontal rotary broom sweeper, which throws the accumulated material onto a conveyer belt that, in turn, transports it to a self-contained hopper. While this broom is an improvement over the kick broom variety, it still shares many of the same drawbacks.

Regenerative air sweepers: This type of sweeper has a "sweeping hood" spanning the width of the sweeper and is equipped with rubber flaps that maintain an air seal with the pavement. A powerful fan directs an air blast onto the pavement underneath one side of the hood in order to entrain debris, and a corresponding suction system transfers the material to an onboard collection and storage compartment. This is a preferred tool for sweeping up tracked out sediment from construction sites.

Figure 79 - Regenerative sweepers, such as this Schwarze A7 Tornado, use a blast of air to dislodge debris from the roadway and vacuum to capture the loose debris and particles. (Photo credit: Danny Aspiras)

Vacuum sweepers: This type of sweeper only utilizes suction to pick up loose material and deposit it into the onboard storage compartment. Because the suction is usually strong and generally can maintain a consistent seal with the pavement, it is effective in removing loose material and particles from the roadway. It is also the preferred choice for the cleaning of pervious pavement.[55]

---

55   An Overview of Power Sweeping Equipment Technology; Ranger Kidwell-Ross, editor, World Sweeper. com; https://www.worldsweeper.com/ChooseEquipment/overviewofsweepers.html.

T-3 Treatment of Streets:

As demonstrated in section T-2 "Treatment of Tires," no matter how good the track-out control device is, street sweeping is always going to be needed to some extent when construction vehicles are exiting from a site where they came into contact with areas of soil disturbance. When determining the frequency and method of street sweeping, consider the following:

- How big of an area needs to be swept? Can it be done effectively, efficiently, and safely with labor and push brooms, or will a piece of equipment be necessary?
- Is the sediment mostly coarse and can it be deposited onto a shoulder or other adjacent unpaved surface? If so, a kick broom may serve the purpose as long as it does not cause excessive fugitive dust and is not prohibited by the project owner or overseeing agency.
- Is the sediment adhering to the pavement? If so, a regenerative air sweeper may be the best equipment selection.
- Is the sediment mostly loose material, or is the paved surface porous? If so, a vacuum sweeper may be the best choice of equipment.
- Sweeping should be performed as needed with the need determined by site inspections.
- Sweeping should not be performed when it is raining or the pavement is wet. Wet pavement will tend to smear the solids and cause more pollutants to be exposed to storm water. The ideal time to sweep is before anticipated rain events.
- Designate a contained and covered location to dump sweeper waste. If hazardous waste is suspected, characterize and profile the waste stream. Otherwise, dispose of it with other solid waste.
- It is best to have a contract established with a sweeper service before the project starts and to schedule proactive sweeping rather than taking a reactive approach.

Treatment Trains (T-4)

In 2017, we were performing storm water inspections on a project located in San Jose, California, for the construction of a subterranean parking garage. Soon after a recent concrete pour, the project received over three inches of rain, which resulted in the parking garage filling with water. Because of the recent concrete work, the pH of the impounded storm water was in the upper 10s, well above the Construction General Permit's numeric action level (NAL) of 8.5. The contractor needed to get rid of the water but did not know what to do. Our company had been experimenting with something we called a treatment train. We knew it would work, but we were not sure for how long or how much water could be effectively treated. But since the contractor had

Figure 80 - WGR's original treatment train in action at a project in San Jose, California. (Photo credit: Mike Lewis)

no other viable options to quickly resolve the situation, when he heard about our trial system, he asked if we would try it out at his site. So we installed it in a matter of a few hours and soon had water passing through it. This early prototype of a treatment train consisted of a water chute constructed on plastic sheeting with fiber rolls rolled up in the plastic, forming the chute's walls. We constructed three 4-foot by 6-foot cells separated with compost socks. The cells were filled with clean, undyed redwood mulch. There was a final sand filter bay placed at the discharge end of the treatment train. It worked! Well, actually it worked too well. The pH was not only lowered below the upper NAL but also descended below the lower NAL of 6.5. So, we backed off on the use of the redwood mulch and found a sweet spot. The turbidity was also very acceptable—the water being fairly clear except for some coloration from the natural tannins of the mulch. We ended up treating 60,000 gallons of water with the original media. That's not bad for a few hours of labor and under $500 of material costs!

Unless the turbidity that your project is experiencing is caused by a colloidal suspension (e.g., colloidal clay), the sediment particles that cause the water to be turbid will eventually settle out if the water is not disturbed. So, as we observed with the Slow-the-Flow BMPs, a good way to treat high turbidity is to create an area where storm water runoff can slow down and sediment can settle out. The treatment train accomplishes this by using compost socks to create multiple "pools," and by using layers of sand, mulch, and river rock within the pools to disperse and slow down the water flow and encourage sediment to settle out. To prevent additional turbidity problems from arising within the treatment train, the ground beneath the treatment train is lined with a durable black plastic sheeting to create a temporary swale.

As demonstrated with the San Jose project, treatment trains can also be used to bring rogue pH numbers back under control. Wood mulch—especially redwood or cedar mulch—is very effective at lowering pH numbers. Wood mulch not only helps lower pH but can also physically trap sediment particles and help with turbidity issues. However, wood mulch has a limited lifespan for reducing pH, and will need to be occasionally replaced, usually when you start noticing that your pH results are starting to climb back up.

Last but not least, the compost sock check dams in between the "pools" play an important role in treating storm water runoff. As we saw in T-1, compost is a very versatile and effective filtration media and is capable of reducing or removing a large number of pollutants—including nutrients, metals, hydrocarbons, and even bacteria. The heavy socks also help slow the water down in between the pools. In later versions of the treatment train, we have found that we get better performance when we stack an additional layer of compost socks over each check dam. The extra weight helps ensure that water is flowing through the socks instead of undermining them. We also started using passive treatment chemicals (T-6) in the forebay where we get mixing of the influent water. The secured polyacrylamide (PAM) blocks dissolve in this bay and coat the suspended particles. The PAM then makes the particles more likely to be trapped by the downstream media. It also helps to clog any small gaps in the media or along the walls that might let a slipstream of untreated water through.

Treatment trains can be customized and built to accommodate the anticipated flow rate from a particular project and the anticipated sediment load. The general idea is to isolate a storm water outfall so that all of the storm water has to pass through the treatment train before discharging. Using fiber rolls, sand bags, or hay bales, create a "chute" to direct water into the treatment train. The chute should be fairly level with a very slight downward slope toward its exit. Line the chute with durable black plastic sheeting, making sure to wrap it over the sides of the chute. Section off a number of pools within the chute using compost sock check dams that are two socks wide and two socks high, installed in a backward U configuration. Finally, add a layer of treatment media to each pool. Our typical treatment media sequence is to start with wood mulch in the first pool, then sand,

Figure 81 - A later version of WGR's treatment train at a training held at WGR's Construction Sandbox, which uses hay bales instead of fiber rolls for the walls, a double layer of compost socks, a forebay with polyacrylamide (PAM) blocks, a cedar mulch bay, a sand bay, and a final river rock velocity dissipator. (Photo credit: John Teravskis)

and end with river rock right before the outfall. Always install sand downstream of the wood mulch to prevent the mulch from causing any sediment problems of its own.

Again, keep in mind that a treatment train will need to be maintained from time to time. After a while, the wood mulch will no longer effectively treat pH, and the compost socks may become clogged with sediment. For the best results, keep an eye on how the treatment train is doing, and replace media as soon as it begins to look worn out or when your pH levels and turbidity start rising. As mentioned, the San Jose model treated more than 60,000 gallons before needing to be replaced. The later models we developed contain much more media and allow more flow through. We have built and rebuilt several versions in our Construction Sandbox training center and have left them in place for more than two years. Although we have not seen a reduction in their treatment performance, after two years the black plastic and the compost sock fabric starts to degrade.

T-4 Treatment Trains:

A treatment train is not a magic bullet. It is just a consolidation of many of the previously covered BMPs into a small footprint. Depending on your project site, sediment particle size, and sediment loads, it might work great—or it might not work at all. Treatment trains are not active treatment systems, and there will be situations where an active treatment system (T-5) is the only treatment solution that will work. But before you spend the money to acquire the services of an active treatment system contractor, it is worth checking out the performance of a treatment train. For under $1,000 in materials and just a few hours of labor for the installation, you could bring your discharge numbers back under control. When sizing and designing a treatment train, consider the following:

- How much space do you have available for installing a treatment train? A minimum area of 30 feet long by 8 feet wide is typically needed.
- What is the anticipated flow rate that you are needing to treat? The limiting factor of the flow through (treatment) rate are the compost socks. In T-1, we learned that an 8-inch diameter compost sock has a flow through rate of 7.5 gpm/linear foot, and a 12-inch diameter sock has a pass through rate of 11.3 gpm/linear foot. If you stack the socks two-high, you have doubled the flow-through capacity.
- Always use plastic sheeting to eliminate outside influences on the treatment processes, and always include a flow spreader or energy dissipation device (SF-4) at the end of the treatment chute.
- Select redwood or cedar mulch that is fresh, clean, and undyed. We have tried other mulches, such as pine duff, chipped wood, and chipped green waste, but with less than desirable results.
- Select a clean, coarse sand. We prefer buying bagged sandbox or playground sand from a home improvements or hardware store.
- Design the inlet bay for the water flow logistics of the site. Sheet flow can be directed into the forebay by placing the treatment train downgradient of the runoff source and using sand bags to direct the flow into the forebay. If water is pumped, build a containment wall with sandbags at the chute opening. Secure the pipe and install a shutoff valve so that the inflow can be regulated with the valve. As an option, secure blocks of PAM (T-6) in the forebay where there is the most amount of water movement.
- Test the treatment performance at the discharge point from each cell and at the discharge end of the treatment train. Compare these numbers to those of the influent and to any applicable numeric action levels or permit limits. Adjust the treatment system design and flow rate accordingly. We have noticed we typically get better performance after the system has operated for a while.

Active Treatment Systems (T-5)

In Chapter 3, we discussed that the settling time for colloidal clay suspensions can exceed 200 years, and we just don't have that much time to wait for things to settle out. Therefore, in cases like this, it is necessary to remove the particles from the water. However, filtration will not work, because these clay particles are so small, they will pass right through compost socks or sand filters. But remember, the reason these particles stay in suspension is because they are negatively charged. Like charges repel, so a pond of water with a colloidal clay suspension is essentially self-agitating and keeps the trillions of small particles in suspension because they are constantly trying to get away from each other. You can think of it as a microscopic magnetic stirrer.

Figure 82 - An active treatment system deployed on a Northern California site. (Photo courtesy of Active Treatment Systems, Inc.)

If the problem is electrochemical, the solution must also be electrochemical. Active treatment works by introducing positively charged chemicals that attract and bind up the small negatively charged clay particles. The chemical used to accomplish this is a cationic polymer and is often referred to as a flocculant. The newly formed larger particles that have coagulated together (and are called floc) can now settle out by gravity or be caught in filters.

Sounds wonderful, right? Better living by chemistry! Well, there is a downside to this marvel of technology. Not only do clay particles have a negative charge but so do fish gills. If there is an excess of cationic (positively charged) polymer in a waterbody, it will cling to gills of fish, suffocate them, and can result in significant fish kills. Therefore, when using this treatment technology, it is vital to have sufficient controls in place to assure that water is not overdosed with the polymer. This is accomplished through the selection criteria of the polymer, the dosing method, and the monitoring for residual polymer. The California

Connecting the Dots of Best Management Practices

Construction General Permit and other construction storm water permits contain provisions for the use of active treatment systems to make sure they are operated in a way that does not harm the environment. The technology really does work. It can reduce turbidity from 10,000 NTU to less than 1 NTU. But it must have some controls in place to assure that the receiving water and the organisms living it are protected. Typically an Active Treatment System Plan is required to be prepared and submitted to the oversight agency (in California, the Water Board) prior to operating a system. Individuals who design and operate the systems must have received adequate training.

T-5 Active Treatment Systems:
When nothing else is working to remove suspended sediment, it may be necessary to utilize an active treatment system. Specialty contractors design, provide, and operate these systems. Active treatment systems (ATS) are typically not utilized at smaller projects (except in cases of de-watering discharges) primarily because of economics. At smaller sites, it is usually much less expensive to spray a robust hydraulic mulch on the disturbed soils (even several times a year) rather than pay for the deployment and use of an ATS. Sites that need to utilize an ATS are typically larger, have extensive areas of exposed clayey or silty soils, and have the ability to impound water. When sizing and designing an active treatment system, the following items need to be considered:
- There tends to be extensive regulatory requirements for the utilization of active treatment systems; therefore, carefully review and become knowledgeable about the NPDES and other potential local requirements concerning the use of these systems.
- Designate adequate space for the impoundment of water (ponds or portable tanks) and the location of the ATS control center (trailer), sand filters, pumps, generators, piping, and control valves.

- Have an engineer design the ATS discharge point with level spreaders and velocity/energy dissipation devices (SF-4).
- The ATS contractor will need to perform some bench tests on the effectiveness of the various types of available polymers for treating the site's suspended soil particles. Select a polymer that will not only be effective but will also comply with the requirements of the Construction General Permit.
- Make sure to utilize an effective combination of site management, raindrop, slow-the-flow, and treatment BMPs to minimize the sediment load as much as possible. Although these systems will do wonders for removing suspended solids, they can get into impossible situations. Also, keep in mind that the more suspended sediment present, the more polymer is needed to remove it, which means more dollars! Traditional BMPs will always be more cost effective than active treatment.
- Using the rational equation (Equation 6), size the treatment system to capture and treat, within a 72-hour period, a minimum volume equivalent of storm water runoff generated from a 10-year, 24-hour storm event assuming a runoff coefficient of 1 (100% runoff).
- Submit an Active Treatment System Plan to the NPDES oversight agency for review and approval.
- Provide spill prevention and secondary containment for the storage and use of the treatment chemicals.
- Utilize an experienced and knowledgeable ATS contractor and, if using your own personnel to perform some of the ATS monitoring, ask the ATS contractor to provide on-the-job training.

Passive Treatment Measures (T-6)

When it comes to implementing passive treatment, the key is to get sufficient contact of the polymer-containing products with the turbid water, which means movement and mixing. But, equally important is to provide a place for "floc" particles to settle out before discharging off-site.

Products like Floc Logs[56] or Floc Roll / Floc Tabs[57] are blocks of semi-hydrated anionic (negatively charged polymers), usually containing polyacrylamide (PAM). These are large linear-chain polymer chemicals that are highly water-absorbent and form a soft gel when hydrated. The linear polymers are water soluble and dissolve in water, and the cross-linked polymers are what form hydrogels and absorb a significant amount of water. Similar gels are used in potting soil, baby diapers, and sweat bands; however, these linear water-soluble polymers do not form gels and are used in water treatment and passive treatment. Being an anionic chemical, they carry a negative charge. Cationic, or positively charged, polymers are prohibited from passive treatment and may only be used in the more controlled active treatment applications. This is because these positively charged molecules are attracted to the negatively charged gills of fish (opposites attract) and cause the fish to suffocate. Which is also why cationic chemicals are so effective at removing suspended sediment from turbid water. The small, suspended clay or silt particles generally have a negative electric charge. The positive cationic chemicals attract the negatively charged particles, form larger and heavier particles (called floc), and settle out in sediment basins or tanks. So if suspended soil particles have negative charges, how does introducing a negatively charged anionic polymer help? Wouldn't it make matters worse? Well, you would

Figure 83 - Blocks of polymer "Floc Logs" utilized in a swale for passive treatment of turbid water. (Photo used courtesy of Applied Polymer Systems, Inc.)

---

56   Floc Logs is a registered trademark of Applied Polymer Systems, Inc.
57   Floc Roll and Floc Tabs are registered trademarks of LSC Environmental Products

think so; but it works because of a process often referred to as "bridging," which involves ion exchange. Anionic PAM can work with anionic charged particles in soils, in that small amounts of positive calcium ions (Ca^{+2}) attach to the anionic polymer creating a bridging and binding of the soil particles and enabling flocculation.[58]

The blocks of PAM are typically installed in storm water conveyance swales or ditches. Turbid water flowing past them cause the blocks to slowly dissolve and release the anionic polymer. The ideal placement for them is within ditches averaging three feet wide by two feet deep. Block spacing and quantity is based on the anticipated flow rate of the swale. Typically they have built-in ropes with attachment loops that can be looped over stakes to ensure they remain in place. However, as previously stated, mixing is the key! If the flow rate is too slow, adding sand bags, cinder blocks, etc., can create the turbulence required for proper mixing. A settling basin or other sediment collection system should be located downgradient of the placement of the floc blocks.

In lieu of blocks, granular or powder PAM can be applied to the surface of drainage swales that have been stabilized with jute mesh or another type of erosion control mat. The PAM is then hydrated either by humidity, wet soil conditions, or by manually wetting the material with a water hose. Once wetted, the material becomes a sticky, gel-like substance that clings to the jute mesh and will gradually dissolve with the storm water flow in the swale. The swale should then be directed to a sediment basin, trap, or other sediment control structure that adequately captures and removes the floc.

Anionic polymers can also be applied to a sediment basin to treat turbid water, but in this case it will be necessary to use a pump to recirculate the pond water

---

58 Wallace, A., and Wallace, G. A. (1996). Need for solution or exchangeable calcium and/or critical EC level for flocculation of clay by polyacrylamides. In "Proceedings of the Managing Irrigation-Induced Erosion and Infiltration with Polyacrylamide" (R. E. Sojka and R. D. Lentz, Eds.), May 6–8, 1996, College of Southern Idaho, Twin Falls, ID. University of Idaho Misc. Pub. 101-96, pp. 59–63.

so that it comes in contact with the product. This can be accomplished by pumping the water into a swale equipped with blocks of polymer that leads back into the pond or by inserting and securing blocks of polymer into an oversized pipe and allowing the pumped water to flow across it. It is less effective, and likely ineffective, to just place the product in the pond.

PAM can also be land applied (with or without a hydraulic mulch) as an erosion control or soil binder. The same bridging and binding that forms floc and causes sedimentation to occur will also keep particles from breaking loose in the first place.

> **T-6 Passive Treatment:**
> Passive treatment techniques are particularly useful for turbid water caused by the suspension of silt and clay particles. Passive treatment chemicals consist of anionic (negatively charged) polymers that attract negatively charged soil particles through a process called ion exchange or bridging, which involves a positively charged intermediate constituent (such as calcium). Passive treatment consists of introducing the anionic polymer, dissolving and thoroughly mixing it in the water, and providing a place or method for sedimentation to occur. When implementing passive treatment, the following should be considered:
> - Choose a passive treatment chemical and delivery system that will work for your site's logistics. There are a variety of anionic polymers available, and some may be a better fit for the soil conditions and chemistry at a particular site. Possible delivery systems include blocks, tablets, granules, powder, or liquid versions of the polymer. Federal and California CGPs both require that performance (jar) testing is completed to ensure that the polymers used will react and work on each site's unique soil and water.
> - Maximize the flow and mixing of water in the presence of the polymer. Consult with the product manufacturer on the appropriate dose rate for your particular site and conditions.

- Provide a method and location for post-treatment sedimentation to occur. It may be a retention basin or other fat spot BMP (SF-3), a treatment train (T-4), sand filters, or portable tanks.
- A professional engineer should perform calculations and design work to properly size sediment basins and design discharge locations for dissipation of the discharge energy.
- Prepare a written passive treatment plan that documents the above considerations and provides health and safety information and spill prevention and response measures for the treatment chemicals.
- Always use passive treatment techniques in conjunction with other traditional erosion and sediment control BMPs.
- Monitor the consumption of the applied polymers and replace as needed.

De-watering (T-7)

Kind of like treatment trains, de-watering involves a combination of many of the BMPs we have covered thus far. It often includes sedimentation, filtration, treatment, velocity dissipation, and other slow-the-flow measures. However, de-watering deserves its own category because it can occur at any time during the year and involves non-storm water discharges (primarily, groundwater). De-watering can be categorized into two different types of discharges—reactive and proactive. Reactive de-watering is quite common and is usually the result of shallow groundwater seeping into a deep excavation (such as a utility trench or basement excavation). Reactive de-watering occurs when the contractor empties the excavation of accumulated water by pumping it

Figure 84 - De-watering is not always a "knee-jerk" reaction. It is often a premeditated, proactive measure to depress groundwater in order to facilitate construction. However, discharges from de-watering activities not only need their own suite of BMPs but may very likely require their own NPDES permit. (Photo used with permission from Malcolm Drilling.)

out and discharging it off-site. Proactive de-watering is a result of the depression of groundwater levels by pumping water from temporary on-site wells in order to facilitate construction in areas of shallow groundwater. Water pumped from the wells usually needs to be discharged off-site (sometimes at considerable volumes). Although there can be other concerning pollutants in discharges from de-watering activities (such as toxics, metals, nutrients, and pH-altering substances), the main constituent of concern with construction site de-watering is usually suspended solids. Therefore, the removal of solids is where most of the effort will be made. The options for sediment removal will be largely dependent upon the type of suspended particles. Basins, tanks, sediment traps, and filter bags will work well with larger particles that settle out fairly easily. To remove suspended silts and clays, other treatment measures, including a treatment train (T-4), an active treatment system (T-5), or passive treatment techniques (T-6), will most likely be necessary. When water is being impounded or controlled, a concentrated discharge flow will typically occur. This concentrated discharge will need to be managed with flow spreaders and/or velocity dissipators (SF-4) to prevent downstream erosion.

Another important consideration when it comes to de-watering is to make sure that the appropriate permits are in place to cover the discharge. If the de-watering is going to be directed to a municipal sanitary or industrial wastewater connection, a publicly owned treatment works (POTW) permit will most likely be required by the municipality. If the water will be discharged to a MS4 or a receiving water, then a NPDES permit will be required by the state water quality agency or the USEPA. In some instances, the NPDES permit will be the same permit covering discharges of storm water from the construction project, but in other cases, coverage by another NPDES permit may be required for the de-watering discharges. It is always best to check with your local NPDES oversight agency (in California, the Regional Water Quality Control Board) to determine if another NPDES permit will be applicable. Whether the de-watering discharge is covered by a POTW permit or by another NPDES permit, the governing permit will usually contain its own requirements for managing discharges and implementing control measures.

T-7 De-watering:

If there is a possibility of groundwater from excavations or wells to be discharged from the project, some preplanning is in order. It should be determined where will the water be discharged and whether another permit (POTW or NPDES) will be required by the local oversight agency. The main concern for construction site de-watering is typically suspended sediment. Control measures needed will largely depend upon the site's soil texture. Sands and other easily settable soils can be adequately addressed with basins, tanks, or filters. Removing suspended silts and clays will typically require more advanced treatment. When planning for de-watering, the following should be considered:

- How much water is anticipated to be generated (volume and flow rate).
- The location and capacity of the water storage mechanism (ponds or tanks).
- The soil texture at the source of the groundwater. (Keep in mind that the soil texture of deeper soils may be quite different from that of surface soils.)
- The type of sediment control or treatment control measures needed to reduce suspended solids.
- The potential for other pollutants of concern to be present. If so, then additional filtering and treatment may be needed to remove or neutralize the pollutants (i.e., pH buffering or utilizing a metals absorbing media).
- The location and method where water will be discharged. If the location or downstream conditions are erodible, an energy and velocity dissipation technique (SF-4) will need to be implemented.

CORRECTIVE ACTION AND MAINTENANCE

A common misconception about BMPs is that once you have implemented them you can forget about them. Nothing could be farther from the truth! BMPs, from fiber roll at a project's perimeter to an educational sign at the project's entrance, all need a certain amount of maintenance. The same elements that erode soil (wind and rain) as well as the sun on bright sunny days will cause BMPs to fall apart. BMPs are also a victim of their success. Sediment-capturing devices tend to fill up with sediment and need to be cleaned out in order to maintain their effectiveness. Under the Site Management BMP, Budgeting and Procurement (SM-2), we discussed the need to adequately budget for the procurement of BMPs, which includes taking into consideration the life-expectancy of the control measure. For a multiyear project, one installation of fiber roll is not going to be sufficient to adequately control sedimentation for the project duration. But sometimes, we also fail to plan for the success of the control measure. These devices work! Therefore, they are going to collect sediment. The sediment needs to be removed from them so that they will continue to be an asset and not turn into a sediment liability themselves. We need to connect the dots of our BMP program by providing sufficient labor and materials to perform routine maintenance and repairs. In Chapter 6, we will talk about the purposes of a monitoring program. A primary reason for monitoring is to see how the BMPs are holding up. An effective monitoring program will identify corrective actions needed to either reestablish the sediment capturing capacity of an installed device, or to refresh or replace worn out or damaged

Figure 85 - All BMPs require maintenance. Wind, rain, and the sun will all take their toll on them, not to mention human activities. (Photo credit: John Teravskis)

sections of the BMP. But it goes beyond just documentation. Inspection reports are full of items needing attention, but this is where another dot often does not get connected—and that is to actually do something about it. The dots become connected when there is an expectation and a process in place to assure that items needing attention (as identified in the inspection reports) are recognized by site managers and addressed in a timely manner. You know there is a disconnect when the same deficiency shows up on multiple sequential inspection reports. Site management BMP, Expectations and Enforcement (SM-6), will go a long way in keeping these dots connected. In addition, tracking tools (typically software or spreadsheets) can help to manage identified deficiencies and document the resolution of each concern. When documenting corrective actions, it is important to photograph the corrected issue. It is common to have photos of the problems on a project, but we often forget or fail to take photos of the resolution, which helps to document that the item of concern is once again in compliance and has been successfully resolved. These photos of the resolution can help to limit the potential for regulatory enforcement or litigation by nongovernmental organizations.

CHAPTER 5
Connecting the Dots of SWPPP Development

Now that we have connected the dots of erosion theory, identifying pollutants and their sources, and the types of BMPs necessary to have an effective program, it is time to put those ideas to paper (literally or electronically) in a way that will help the construction personnel understand the logic of the program and, hopefully, help them perceive why the specified BMPs are needed. The document through which this is accomplished is referred to as the Storm Water Pollution Prevention Plan (SWPPP). Although in our storm water industry we may all agree on the purpose and intent of this document, there is little consensus on how we pronounce the SWPPP acronym. I have heard *swĭppee*, *swămp*, S-W-P-P-P (spelled out), and a host of other pronunciations. But my personal preference is to simply say *swĭp* (not swipe!). Regardless of what you call it, it remains the core guidance document on how to control erosion and sedimentation and how to prevent pollutants from discharging with storm water runoff.

Unfortunately, over the years SWPPPs have been victimized by standardization, templates, and large committees. Now I get it—we all want to have a document that is fully compliant, standardized, easy to use, and readily accepted. But over the last two decades, this has led us to a place where I now hand an LRP or contractor a 350 to 400-page document which, of course, I expect them to read and understand before next Monday when the project starts. True, the SWPPP template used to create this treatise has been evaluated by a committee and includes almost everything that possibly might need to be present, including a few things that probably will never apply to the project. But I can't help thinking that this three-inch thick SWPPP binder is self-defeating—after all, who wants to read it? I don't, and I wrote it!

Figure 86 - Is this document self-defeating? Does the mere size intimidate people from reading it? Would on-site personnel be more apt to read a streamlined version? You decide! (Photo credit: John Teravskis)

Part of connecting the dots of erosion, sediment, and pollutant control at construction sites involves telling the erosion and sediment control story in a way that will not alienate, confuse, or discourage the intended audience. This is accomplished through clear, concise, and consistent language used in the SWPPP and on the supporting maps and attachments. I am sure everything that committees decide to put into SWPPP templates are important pieces of information to a regulator, consultant, or someone in the storm water industry. But when I prepare SWPPPs, I try to streamline them to include information that is important to the intended audience: the contractors and other personnel in the field who are relying on the document for guidance. Information (albeit important) that they don't need just clutters the story we are trying to tell.

Connecting the Dots of SWPPP Development 211

You can think of the SWPPP as the paper on which the dot-to-dot drawing comes together. Up until now, in this book we have identified a collection of dots and have made some mental connections with them. But to get those connections out of our minds and into the minds of the individuals working on the project, we will need to put them down on paper. The dots needing to be connected for developing an effective SWPPP document include:

- Determining who requires the SWPPP, what information that entity requires to be included in the document, and what, if any, template needs to be used to create the document;
- Making sure that the document preparer meets the state and local SWPPP developer requirements;
- Preparing to write the plan by doing your homework first and learning all you can about the jobsite;
- Crunching the numbers to get the "big picture" when it comes to hydrology, topography, soil type, anticipated soil loss, and the sequencing of the project and how those features interact with each other;
- Identifying all of the players who will be involved in the SWPPP implementation; and
- Incorporating the pollutant source assessment discussed in [Chapter 3](#) with a selection of appropriate BMPs from [Chapter 4](#) to address the identified potential pollutants.

CHOOSE THE RIGHT SWPPP DOCUMENT FORMAT

Of course, compliance is of utmost importance when it comes to developing a SWPPP. If the NPDES permit requires certain information to be included in the SWPPP, it needs to be there. So before choosing a template or SWPPP resource, or before preparing one from scratch, it is important to know what the applicable

NPDES permit requires. Table 11 contains a list of the CGP requirements for each of the fifty states of the Union and, where applicable, provides a link to that state's SWPPP template. In California, the 2022 CGP[59] requires the following to be included in construction SWPPPs:

IV.O.2. The SWPPP shall include:
  a. Identification of all pollutants, their sources, and control mechanisms, including sources of sediment associated with all construction activities (e.g., sediment, paint, cement, stucco, cleaners, site erosion);
  b. Pollutant source assessments, including a list of potential pollutant sources and identification of site areas where additional BMPs are necessary to reduce or prevent pollutants in stormwater and authorized non-stormwater discharges, per the following minimum requirements when developing the pollutant source assessment:
     i. Consider all potential sources of pollutants, including non-visible pollutants which are known, or should be known to occur on-site including those that:
        1. Are used in construction activities;
        2. Are stored on-site;
        3. Were spilled or released during construction activities or past land use activities and not cleaned up; and
        4. Were applied to land as part of past land use activities.
     ii. Consider all potential sources of pollutants associated with applicable TMDLs listed in Attachment H, and state whether or not sources of those pollutants are present on-site;
     iii. Consider the quantity, physical characteristics (e.g., liquid, powder, solid), and locations of each potential pollutant exposed, source handled, produced, stored, recycled, or disposed of on-site;
     iv. Consider the degree to which pollutants associated with those materials may be exposed to and mobilized by contact with stormwater; and
     v. Consider the direct and indirect pathways that pollutants may be exposed to stormwater or authorized non-stormwater discharges. This shall include an assessment of past spills or leaks, non-stormwater discharges, and discharges from adjoining areas.

---

59 Order 2022-0057-DWQ, pages 31–35.

Connecting the Dots of SWPPP Development

c. Description of site-specific BMPs implemented to reduce or eliminate stormwater pollution, including the following, if applicable:
   i. Minimum sediment and erosion control BMPs as outlined in Attachments D and E of this General Permit;
   ii. Active treatment systems as included in an Active Treatment System Plan (as required in Section E.1 of Attachment F);
   iii. Passive treatment technologies as included in a Passive Treatment Plan (as required in Section D.2 of Attachment G);
   iv. BMPs implemented to address applicable TMDL implementation requirements (as required by Attachment H); and
   v. Dewatering systems (as required by Attachment J).
d. Site-specific BMPs initialized immediately to temporarily stabilize an area disturbed by construction where construction activities will not be resumed within 14 days;
e. Identification, elimination, control, or treatment information for all non-stormwater discharges from the site not regulated by this or another NPDES permit;
f. Description of efforts and BMPs used to minimize and control pollutants discharged from equipment and vehicle washing, wheel wash water, and other wash waters. Wash waters must be captured and properly disposed of and/or treated to mitigate impacts to water quality;
g. Description of efforts and BMPs used to minimize exposure of building materials, building products, construction wastes, trash, landscape materials, fertilizers, pesticides, herbicides, detergents, sanitary waste, and other materials present on the site to precipitation and to stormwater;
h. Description of spill and leak prevention and response plan including:
   i. Procedures that effectively address hazardous and non-hazardous spills in accordance with law;
   ii. Spill and leak response equipment and materials to be available on-site, cleaned up immediately, and disposed of properly; and
   iii. Personnel are assigned and trained for spill and leak prevention and response.

i. Construction Site Monitoring Program that describes methods and procedures for monitoring discharges in accordance with the applicable Attachment D or E that includes the following:
   i. Visual inspection locations, inspection procedures, and follow-up tracking procedures.
   ii. Applicable sampling locations, collection, and handling procedures shall include detailed procedures for field analysis, sample collection, storage, preservation, and shipping to the laboratory to ensure consistent quality assurance and control is maintained.
   iii. A copy of the Chain of Custody form used when handling and shipping samples.
   iv. Identification of the analytical methods and related method detection limits (if applicable) for each parameter.
   v. Watershed Monitoring Option:
      1. If the discharger is part of a qualified regional watershed-based monitoring program approved by the Regional Water Board Executive Officer or their delegate, the discharger may be eligible for relief from the monitoring requirements in the applicable Attachment D or E. The Regional Water Board may approve proposals to substitute a qualified watershed-based monitoring program if it determines the program will provide information to determine each discharger's compliance with the requirements of this General Permit.

In addition, the 2022 CGP requires a title sheet (more likely to be multiple cover sheets) for the SWPPP to include the following information:

j. Title Sheet(s) with:
   i. Project name;
   ii. Project location (vicinity map);
   iii. Preliminary schedule of activities;
   iv. Site operating hours (hours when construction activities are occurring);
   v. Index of attachments;
   vi. Contact information for QSD(s), QSP(s), and trained delegates (name, phone numbers, license or certification number); and
   vii. Signature of the QSD(s) who prepared the SWPPP.

Connecting the Dots of SWPPP Development

The 2022 CGP also has specific requirements regarding SWPPP maps. It requires a minimum of two maps that contain the following information:

k. Pre-Earthwork Drawing with:
  i. Site and project boundaries;
  ii. Areas disturbed during geotechnical or other preconstruction investigation work;
  iii. Existing roads and trails;
  iv. Drainage areas;
  v. Discharge locations;
  vi. Existing storm drain system if applicable; and
  vii. Proposed locations of storage areas for waste, construction materials, project staging areas, stockpiles, vehicles, equipment and vehicle maintenance, loading/unloading of materials, site access (entrance/exits), fueling, water storage, water transfer for dust control, demolition, and areas of other construction support activities.

and:

l. Construction and Earthwork Drawing(s) with:
  i. Site layout (grading plans) including roads;
  ii. Site and project boundaries;
  iii. Drainage areas;
  iv. Discharge locations;
  v. Sampling locations;
  vi. Areas of soil disturbance (temporary or permanent);
  vii. Proposed active areas of soil disturbance (cut or fill);
  viii. Proposed locations of erosion control BMPs;
  ix. Proposed locations of sediment control BMPs;
  x. Proposed locations of run-off BMPs;
  xi. Temporary and/or permanent run-on conveyance (if applicable);
  xii. Proposed locations of active treatment systems(s) (if applicable);
  xiii. Locations of storage areas for waste, construction materials, project staging areas, stockpiles, vehicles, equipment and vehicle maintenance, loading/unloading of materials, site access (entrance/exits), fueling, water storage, water transfer for dust control, demolition, and areas of other construction support activities; and
  xiv. Site-specific procedures to implement final stabilization BMPs as soon as reasonably practicable.

It is good to utilize the NPDES requirements as a minimum checklist for the contents of the SWPPP and to develop a template SWPPP based on the specific requirements of the applicable permit (as you will see later, I developed a SWPPP template based on the 2022 California CGP).

Certain project owners (especially large agencies like Caltrans or the San Francisco Public Utilities Commission) will have their own SWPPP requirements and SWPPP templates. Contractual obligations necessitate the use of these owner-specific templates for those working under their auspices. Otherwise, SWPPP preparers should be cognizant of the state NPDES requirements or, where applicable, the USEPA CGP requirements for SWPPPs. Some states utilize and/or require the use of a standardized SWPPP template or fillable form. Other states, to a lesser or greater degree, specify what the SWPPP should address or contain.

In California, the choices for a construction SWPPP template are generally from:

- California Stormwater Quality Association (CASQA);
- Caltrans; or
- Your own creation or a hybrid of the above templates.

The CASQA Template: In California, this is the most widely used and recognized of the SWPPP source documents. The California Stormwater Quality Association (CASQA)[60] has released several versions of this template over the years (with the most recent in 2023). Anyone who has been extensively writing and reviewing SWPPPs since approximately 2010 will probably recognize the different versions of the CASQA templates in SWPPPs still being produced to date.

During the last couple of decades, I have utilized the CASQA template for the creation of project-specific SWPPPs. There are very good reasons to do so. First,

---

60 California Stormwater Quality Association - https://www.casqa.org/

the SWPPP writer can have confidence that the original template takes California's CGP requirements well into account. CASQA has utilized a team of collaborators who have created a well thought out and reliable document. This document has also undergone the test of time and has been reviewed by countless consultants, engineers, agencies, and storm water professionals. With each revision of the template, the document becomes that much more robust and refined. Another motivating reason to utilize the CASQA template is that it is widely used and recognized. Reviewing agencies and contractors will be familiar with the layout and will know exactly where to look for information. The CASQA template also utilizes a treasure-trove of BMP fact sheets that enable the SWPPP writer to provide detailed instructions on BMP installation, inspections, and maintenance. All in all, the CASQA SWPPP template is a very good choice for SWPPP writers, especially those who may be relatively new to the industry. To obtain permission to utilize the CASQA template, a subscription is required. But it will be dollars well spent, because the subscription and a CASQA membership will also provide access to many other invaluable resources for storm water professionals.

However, I have found the CASQA template to also have some drawbacks. The first is the size. As previously mentioned, these documents along with their attachments can easily be over 350 pages long. We mentioned that the size of the document may defeat the purpose of the document—which is to be read! I believe there is another negative aspect that also arises from the document size. SWPPPs generated from CASQA templates tend to remain too much of a template (or what many refer to as "boilerplate") and not site specific enough. Of course that is not CASQA's fault, but the fault of the SWPPP developer. Certainly, the CASQA template can be customized with a good amount of site specifics. But, again, I believe the size and amount of verbiage in the SWPPP tends to discourage a SWPPP writer, who is often under a budget and time constraint, to get overly creative on making the document customized to the project site.

The CASQA fact sheets have been a huge asset to the storm water community. Maybe because I started my career in California and have become somewhat California-centric, but it has always been my impression that CASQA pioneered these fact sheets that are now seen in many other states' storm water programs. The storm water industry owes much of its understanding of BMPs to this wonderful resource. But like anything, given enough time and familiarity, we can take them for granted and utilize them in a way that perhaps was not originally intended. This brings me to another drawback of the CASQA template. For many, it has become a little too formulaic. Rather than really thinking through the concepts we discussed in Chapters 2 and 3, with the CASQA template, we can fall into a trap or bad habit of, what I refer to as "window shopping" BMPs. With the tables in Section 3 of the CASQA template and the inclusion of BMP fact sheets, we can be tempted to shortcut the process by using a formula for SWPPP writing rather than a well thought out plan. For example, I will take one of these (sediment control), and two of these (materials management), and another of these (an erosion control measure) for my SWPPP. Now, don't get me wrong—taking that approach is not always a problem nor will it result in an unprotected site. But it allows the SWPPP writer to somewhat check out mentally from the process of determining an effective erosion and sediment control strategy for the project. For the majority of the sites, it might not even matter especially if the SWPPP developer has some good experience.

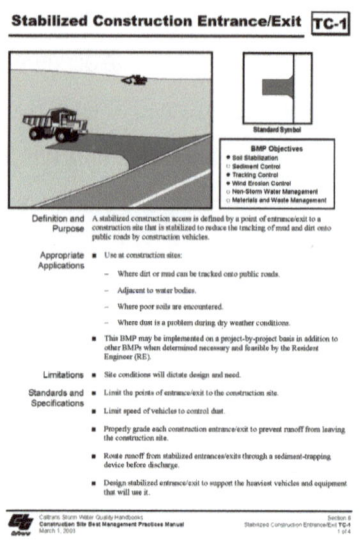

Figure 87 - BMP factsheets such as this one for stabilized construction entrances and exits have been a huge asset to the storm water industry. The one shown here was issued by Caltrans which is very similar to the CASQA version. (Taken from the Caltrans 2003 Construction Site Best Management Practices Manual (TC-1)). http://website.dot.ca.gov/hq/construc/stormwater/TC-1.pdf

But there will be a handful of projects, where subtle clues and details about the site really do need to be considered and "window shopping" BMPs may lead the SWPPP writer to prepare a plan that is not sufficient for a particular situation. This is a big reason why I recategorized BMPs in Chapter 4. It was my hope that by changing the names and categories of the BMPs, it might allow even experienced SWPPP writers to see them in a new light and to encourage the development of SWPPPs based on sound erosion and sedimentation control principles.

The Caltrans Template: You have to give them credit for having the most creative approach for SWPPP templates. No Microsoft Word document is used in preparing Caltrans SWPPPs! The concept is rather novel. Caltrans utilizes a database software, Microsoft Access (2007 or later version), to receive inputs from the SWPPP developer which is then used to populate a PDF document. It is kind of a fill-in-the-blank SWPPP, supposedly to make the SWPPP writing process easier. But I am probably not the only SWPPP writer who longs to return to the Microsoft Word world after a few frustrating sessions

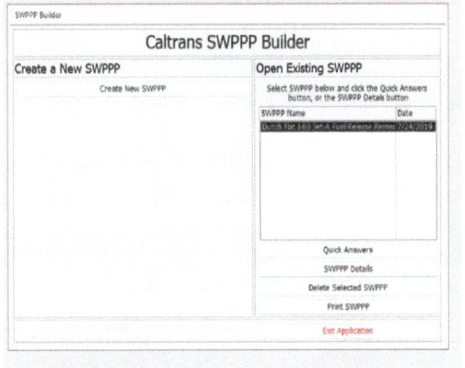

Figure 88 - The Caltrans SWPPP template ... love it or hate it, you have no choice but to use it if you are doing a Caltrans project. (Image from the Microsoft Access Caltrans SWPPP Builder.)

with the database Q&A. And as they say about databases, "garbage in, garbage out." I am not saying that the makers of the Caltrans SWPPP template did not do a good job. I am sure the problem is entirely with me. But I find that some of the questions asked by the database are not intuitive to me or I had understood them to be asking something a bit different. Therefore, when I read a draft of the compiled information in the PDF that was produced, I found that the answer I supplied for the associated question is not at all what this particular section of the SWPPP is addressing. OK, so back to the database! If you are a neat freak like me, formatting also tends to be an issue with these automated compilations. I have seen the cover page cut into two halves. Although Adobe Acrobat has recently developed some convenient editing tools, only so much editing can be done post-production with these SWPPP PDFs without making a mess of things or needing to just go back to the drawing board. Of course the more you use this tool, the more familiar you will become with it, and it should go much smoother with each successive SWPPP preparation. So, have some patience please!

Another huge consideration about the Caltrans SWPPPs is that they really only apply to roadway projects. It would be like trying to put a square peg into a round hole to use the Caltrans template for a home subdivision. It just won't work. Over the past years, we have had nontraditional (i.e., non-roadway) Caltrans projects that were also extremely difficult to address with this fairly inflexible template. Also, the SWPPP template has been developed for the Caltrans specifications and culture. The database will be asking questions that only pertain to Caltrans projects, such as providing information about the Resident Engineer, Water Pollution Control Manager, and contract numbers. It utilizes Caltrans specific inspection reports (like the CEM-2030) that are so completely oriented to Caltrans projects, it would be difficult to utilize them anywhere else. With that said, there is a segment of non-Caltrans projects that do commonly require the use of the Caltrans SWPPP

Figure 89 - Although they are subject to the California CGP, Caltrans projects have their own culture and way of doing things and, therefore, require a specific SWPPP template to be used. (Photo credit: John Teravskis)

Connecting the Dots of SWPPP Development 221

and forms. It includes roadway projects involving Caltrans rights-of-way that are overseen by a different local agency (typically a city or county). In addition, some municipalities have adopted the Caltrans standards and specifications for their roadway projects and require (or allow) the use of the Caltrans templates and forms. But, if you are doing a Caltrans construction project, you don't have a choice; for projects with one acre or more of soil disturbance, you will need to utilize the most recent version of the Caltrans SWPPP, and for projects with less than one acre of soil disturbance, you will need still need to prepare a SWPPP-like document: the Water Pollution Control Plan (WPCP).[61]

Create Your Own Templates: It is important to remember that, in California, the CGP does not require the use of a template in developing a SWPPP. At the beginning of this chapter, we provided excerpts from the California 2022 CGP regarding the permit-required information to be included in the SWPPP. As long as those mandatory items are contained in the site-specific plan, you have met the permit requirements. You are free to develop your own version of a SWPPP. Over the years, many SWPPP writers have done this to a certain extent by modifying one of the templates already discussed. Our company, probably like many other consultants, developed an array of SWPPP templates for different risk levels, types of projects (such as residential, commercial, roadway, traditional, or LUP), and

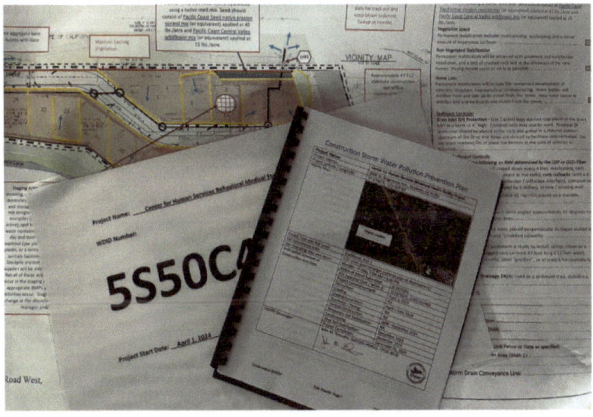

Figure 90 - Download this free SWPPP template. (Photo credit: John Teravskis)

---

61   Also see: https://dot.ca.gov/programs/construction/storm-water-and-water-pollution-control.

locations and watersheds. For example, we utilize previously prepared SWPPPs as templates. In my template library, I might have a Risk Level 1 residential SWPPP for the Bay Area, a Risk Level 2 commercial SWPPP for a project in the Central Valley, a Risk Level 3 ecological restoration SWPPP for the coastal range, and a Type 1 LUP SWPPP for in-road pipeline installations, etc.

With the issuance of the California 2022 CGP, to address some of the drawbacks previously mentioned regarding other SWPPP templates, and as a part of the creation of this textbook, we have prepared a SWPPP template that our readers can download and use for their projects. You can access it for free with the following link:

https://wgr-sw.com/TheRaindropConnection/

We had several objectives in mind when we were creating our new SWPPP template:

1. It had to be fully compliant with the California 2022 CGP. We made sure that every item required to be included or addressed in the SWPPP by the CGP was present.
2. It had to be streamlined. We wanted a document that was not intimidating to the intended audience. We did not want them to look at the size and think *"there's no way I am going to read that!"* Although it is not as concise as we were hoping to achieve, it is less than a third of the size of other templates with all of their attachments. We tried to not include too much beyond what the CGP was requiring; however, we did identify a few nonrequired but very useful pieces of information to include, like the permit (WDID) number and risk level.
3. We wanted a document that was relevant to the intended audience (the project owner and contractors) and was mostly

specific to that particular project. As important as it might be to someone in the storm water community, we really tried to cut out the fluff and boilerplate material. If it wasn't specifically required by the CGP or relevant to the intended audience, it was cut from the template.

As previously mentioned in regard to Caltrans projects, the type of project needs to be considered when selecting the template you will use as the foundation of your SWPPP. Prior to selecting the starting document, take time to consider the following:

- ☑ Review the SWPPP requirements in the project bid specifications. Sometimes there are none or the requirements are quite ambiguous. But other times, there are very specific SWPPP requirements that should influence your template selection. Recently, I was reviewing the bid specification for a landfill excavation and liner installation project, and it stated that the *"SWPPP must comply with the Caltrans Stormwater Pollution Prevention Plan (SWPPP) and Water Pollution Control Program (WPCP) Preparation Manual and must be prepared using the latest template posted on the Construction stormwater website."* Most likely, this is just some boilerplate that got past the reviewer and was not replaced for this bid specification, but before writing a SWPPP, it certainly merits submitting a request for information (RFI) to the project owner to see if this is truly required and if they would accept a non-Caltrans SWPPP. I have also observed bid specifications by municipalities and other agencies requiring the inclusion of CASQA BMP standards within the SWPPP.
- ☑ Review the local municipal code for where the project is located for specific SWPPP requirements. One Northern California municipality has a municipal code stating, *"The applicant…must comply with the terms, conditions, and requirements imposed by the City to ensure compliance*

with this chapter and any applicable permit. Such terms, conditions, and requirements may include, but are not limited to, **requirements consistent with CASQA's Construction Best Management Practice Manual**, in the version adopted by resolution of the City Council, and requirements for erosion and sediment controls, soil stabilization, de-watering, source controls, pollution prevention measures and illicit discharges." In this case, after consulting with the municipality, we were able to utilize a non-CASQA SWPPP template because we could show that the BMPs were "consistent" with the CASQA BMPs. Had they not agreed that the proposed BMPs were consistent with CASQA BMPs, we would have needed to utilize the CASQA template.

☑ If your project is in another state, outside of California, check to see if that state utilizes or provides a SWPPP template. Table 11 provides a listing of state SWPPP preparation requirements and a link to permits and templates.

☑ Regardless of the origin of the template, experienced SWPPP writers will most likely develop their own library of SWPPP templates, allowing them to select a template that is as closely relevant as possible to the new project. You may have a library of templates for LUP and traditional projects, for different types of development (commercial, residential, industrial, landfills, roadways, and restoration projects), for different risk levels (1, 2, or 3), and for different watersheds (that include watershed-specific information such as name, HUC-12 number, impairments and TMDLs). Such a selection of templates can really help facilitate the SWPPP preparation process.

Connecting the Dots of SWPPP Development

Figure 91 - Make the template you are using feel like there was no template. Use photos, maps, and narrative to make it specific to the project and location. (Image from WGR's SWPPP template.)

The number one rule when using a template is to make it customized for your project and project's location. As a SWPPP writer, my goal is to make people think that I didn't even use a template because the document has so much project-specific information in it.

This can be accomplished by:

- Including aerial imagery, topographic maps, and soil maps.
- Including photos of the pre-construction conditions (from Google Earth ™ or your own reconnaissance).
- For each selected BMP, including a brief narrative description in the SWPPP and on the SWPPP map of how it will be implemented at this particular project. Two sentences with site-specific content is better than two paragraphs of generic fluff.

- Including owner requirements and specifications that were identified in the bid specification documents such as restrictions regarding the type of sediment or erosion controls that may be used on the project (i.e., prohibition of plastic or monofilament containing BMPs) and specifications for erosion control products (e.g., hydraulic mulch manufacturer and application rate information, and seed type and application rates for seeding).
- Including municipal information such as the contact information for the municipal storm water compliance officer or program manager and any applicable requirements or prohibitions that the municipality may have relevant to the project's storm water management program.
- Provide a good amount of detail about site-specific drainage management areas (DMAs) including how they may change throughout the project, and provide details about the discharge locations, which usually will be the inspection and monitoring points. Discuss how water flows onto, across, and off of the project site.
- Identify the watershed in which the project is located and any applicable TMDLs or water quality impairments.
- Call out specific resources for the project (e.g., spill response contractors, BMP providers/installers, hydraulic mulch / hydroseed specifications, treatment contractors, laboratories, etc.) including contact information.
- Include contact information for the project owner, project developer, general contractor, subcontractors (at least the ones who will have a significant role on site, such as the grading contractor), storm water inspectors, and SWPPP developer.
- Provide customized forms (or links to electronic online forms/apps).
- Identify the overseeing storm water regulatory agency and provide contact information. In California, identify the Regional Water Quality Control Board and provide contact information for the staff person who oversees compliance with the CGP.

- Identify other environmental permits that have been or will be obtained for the project and are relevant to SWPPP implementation and BMP selection, such as the 401 Water Quality Certification, the 404 U.S. Army Corps dredge/fill permit, Department of Fish and Wildlife lake and streambed alteration agreements, and other NPDES permits required for de-watering or for other non-storm water discharges.
- Provide a project schedule that contains the anticipated starting and ending dates for the project as well as dates when various phases of the project will occur. The schedule should also include information about when BMPs will be installed or removed and anticipated weather patterns (such as months when rain is expected and seasons of the year when windy conditions normally prevail.)
- Identify the post-construction development features utilized at the project to meet the low impact development and storm water treatment goals of local or state agencies.
- Discuss how the project will achieve final stabilization and meet the qualifications for CGP termination.

In Chapter 2, we discussed the various forms of erosion we need to address in SWPPPs. But there is one more type of erosion SWPPP writers especially need to beware of: **template erosion**.

Erosion tends to occur in SWPPPs when we utilize a template of a template of a template. As discussed above, we want to create SWPPPs as site specific as possible. Therefore, we tend to remove items in the SWPPP template we are using that are not applicable to a particular project. This sets up the ideal conditions for template erosion to occur. It is not a problem for that particular SWPPP because what was removed is not applicable to it. But, as we often do, we grab that SWPPP to use as a template for a future project. In doing so, we frequently forget that we had removed one or more sections or phrases for the previous project—this is where erosion occurs! With each generation of SWPPPs, the erosion can become more and more pronounced as additional items or wording is removed or replaced. It can lead to producing a SWPPP that is not fully compliant with the CGP requirements or is deficient in one or more aspects. To prevent template erosion, it is best to frequently return to a master template that contains all of the required information or at least use it for a comparison to a late generation template that you chose to use because of convenience.

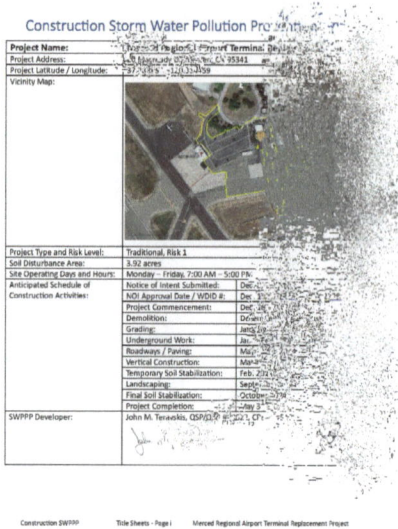

Figure 92 - Beware of SWPPP template erosion!

MAKE SURE THE SWPPP DEVELOPER MEETS THE REQUIREMENTS OF THE REGULATORY AGENCY THAT HAS JURISDICTION OVER THE PROJECT

When connecting the dots for developing a compliant SWPPP, one dot that needs to be identified early on in the process is *"Who is authorized to prepare the SWPPP?"* There are still some places in the United States where there is no particular SWPPP developer credential required by the overseeing NPDES permit agency for SWPPP developers. For example, as of February 2024, the state of Nevada does not require a particular credential or level of expertise for the person who is completing the state's construction SWPPP template.[62] The Nevada Construction General Permit only specifies that the SWPPP should be prepared and implemented

---

[62] State of Nevada NPDES General Permit NVR100000, https://ndep.nv.gov/water/water-pollution-control/permitting/stormwater-discharge]-permits/construction-sites-greater-than-1-acre.

Connecting the Dots of SWPPP Development

"in accordance with good engineering practices." Table 11 provides an overview of what the various states require for SWPPPs and of the SWPPP developers. Since NPDES permits are normally issued for a period of five years, it is important to check with the local NPDES permitting authority to see if the construction SWPPP requirements have changed.

Table 11 – Construction SWPPP Development Requirements by State[63]

State	Regulating Agency	Permit	
Alabama	Alabama Department of Environmental Management	Alabama Construction General Permit ALR100000 https://adem.alabama.gov/programs/water/permits/ALR10ConGen.pdf	
Alaska	Alaska Department of Environmental Conservation	Alaska Construction General Permit No. AKR100000 https://dec.alaska.gov/media/22136/2021-cgp-pmt-akr10-fnl-20201217.pdf	

---

63   Table compiled in February 2025 and adapted partially from The Stormwater Practitioners Guide, U.S. Department of Transportation, Federal Highway Administration, December 2018, Version 1, https://highways.dot.gov/sites/fhwa.dot.gov/files/docs/federal-lands/construction/27396/cfl-stormwater-guide.pdf, Appendix A current as of March 7, 2022, https://highways.dot.gov/sites/fhwa.dot.gov/files/docs/subdoc/2116/cfl-appendix-state-requirements-april-2021.pdf ; for an up-to-date version of Table 11, go to https://wgr-sw.com/TheRaindropConnection/

64   Some States refer to SWPPP by another name. For example, in Colorado it is called a Stormwater Management Plan (SWMP).

SWPPP[64] Template Available	Who Can Prepare a SWPPP
Yes, https://adem.alabama.gov/programs/water/waterforms/CSW-CBMPPTemplate.pdf	Qualified Credentialed Professional (QCP) who is *"a licensed (in the State of Alabama) professional engineer (PE) or a Certified Professional in Erosion and Sediment Control (CPESC) as determined by EnviroCert International. Other registered or certified professionals eligible to be classified as a QCP include registered landscape architect, licensed land surveyor, registered geologist, registered forester, Registered Environmental Manager as determined by the National Registry of Environmental Professionals (NREP), or Certified Professional and Soil Scientist (CPSS) as determined by the Soil Science Society of America."*
Yes, https://dec.alaska.gov/media/22241/2021-cgp-swppp-template.docx	Qualified Person *"A person knowledgeable in the principles and practice of erosion and sediment controls who possesses the skills to assess conditions at the construction site that could impact storm water quality, the effectiveness of any erosion and sediment control measures selected to control the quality of storm water discharges from the construction activity and is familiar with the State's SWPPP requirements as a means to implement this permit."*

State	Regulating Agency	Permit
Arizona	Arizona Department of Environmental Quality	General Permit for Stormwater Discharges Associated with Construction Activity to Waters of the United States (AZG2020-001) https://azdeq.gov/node/524
Arkansas	Arkansas Department of Energy & Environment	Construction Stormwater Permit: ARR150000 Large Site (5 Acres or More) https://www.adeq.state.ar.us/water/permits/npdes/stormwater/pdfs/construction/arr150000_final_permit_signed_ajy.pdf Construction Stormwater Permit: ARR150000 Small Site (AUTOMATIC COVERAGE for 1 Acre or More but Less than 5 Acres) https://www.adeq.state.ar.us/water/permits/npdes/stormwater/pdfs/construction/arr150000_final_permit_signed_ajy.pdf
California	California State Water Resources Control Board	Construction Stormwater General Permit Order 2022-0057-DWQ https://www.waterboards.ca.gov/water_issues/programs/stormwater/construction/general_permit_reissuance.html
Colorado	Colorado Department of Public Health & Environment	Construction Stormwater Discharge Permits COR400000 https://cdphe.colorado.gov/cor400000-stormwater-discharge

SWPPP[64] Template Available	Who Can Prepare a SWPPP
Yes https://www.azdeq.gov/what-swppp	Anyone
Yes Large Site: https://www.adeq.state.ar.us/water/permits/npdes/stormwater/pdfs/construction/arr150000_swppp_template_large_site.pdf Small Site: https://www.adeq.state.ar.uwater/permits/npdes/stormwater/pdfs/construction/arr150000_swppp_template_small_site.pdf	Qualified Personnel "A person knowledgeable in the principles and practice of erosion and sediment controls who possesses the skills to assess conditions at the construction site that could impact stormwater quality and to assess the effectiveness of any sediment and erosion control measures selected to control the quality of stormwater discharges from the construction activity."
No	Qualified SWPPP Developer (QSD) as defined in the permit.
Guidance is provided, but not a template. https://oitco.hylandcloud.com/pop/docpop/docpop.aspx and https://oitco.hylandcloud.com/pop/docpop/docpop.aspx	Anyone

State	Regulating Agency	Permit
Connecticut	Connecticut Department of Energy & Environmental Protection	The General Permit for the Discharge of Stormwater and De-watering Wastewaters from Construction Activities https://portal.ct.gov/-/media/DEEP/Permits_and_Licenses/Water_Discharge_General_Permits/stormconstgppdf.pdf
Delaware	Delaware Department of Natural Resources and Environmental Control	Delaware Construction General Permit State Permit Number WPCC 3082/20 and NPDES Permit Number DE 0051268 https://documents.dnrec.delaware.gov/Watershed/Sediment-Stormwater/Permits/Construction-General-Permit.pdf
Florida	Florida Department of Environmental Protection	Construction Generic Permit https://floridadep.gov/sites/default/files/Construction_Generic_Permit_0.pdf
Georgia	Georgia Environmental Protection Division	2023 NPDES General Permits Nos. GAR100001 (Stand Alone CGP), GAR100002 (Infrastructure CGP), and GAR100003 (Common Development CGP)

SWPPP[64] Template Available	Who Can Prepare a SWPPP
Guidance is provided in the Permit, but no template is available.	Anyone
Guidance is provided, but not a template. https://documents.dnrec.delaware.gov/Watershed/Sediment-Stormwater/Handbook/Erosion-and-Sediment-Control-Handbook.pdf	Owner
Yes https://floridadep.gov/sites/default/files/ConstructionSWPPP_0.pdf	Anyone
No	Design Professional: "A professional licensed by the State of Georgia in the field of: engineering, architecture, landscape architecture, forestry, geology, or land surveying; or a person that is a Certified Professional in Erosion and Sediment Control (CPESC) with a current certification by EnviroCert International, Inc. and that has completed the appropriate certification course approved by the Georgia Soil and Water Conservation Commission in accordance with O.C.G.A 12-7-9."

State	Regulating Agency	Permit
Hawaii	Hawaii Department of Health, Clean Water Branch	HAR 11-55 Appendix C - NPDES General Permit Authorizing Discharges of Storm Water Associated with Construction Activity https://health.hawaii.gov/cwb/files/2024/01/11-55-Appendix-C-January-29-2024.pdf
Idaho	Idaho Department of Environmental Quality	Construction General Permit IDR100000 https://www2.deq.idaho.gov/admin/LEIA/api/document/download/16509
Illinois	Illinois Environmental Protection Agency	Construction General Permit https://epa.illinois.gov/content/dam/soi/en/web/epa/topics/forms/water-permits/storm-water/documents/General-Npdes-Permit-ilr10-Construction.pdf
Indiana	Indiana Department of Environmental Management	Construction Stormwater General Permit (CSGP) https://www.in.gov/idem/stormwater/files/final_gen_permit_inra00000_construction.pdf

SWPPP[64] Template Available	Who Can Prepare a SWPPP
No	Anyone
Guidance is provided, but not a template. https://www2.deq.idaho.gov/admin/LEIA/api/document/download/14821	Anyone
Guidance is provided, but not a template. https://epa.illinois.gov/topics/forms/water-permits/storm-water/pollution-prevention-plan.html	Anyone
No, but guidance is provided: https://www.in.gov/idem/stormwater/files/csgp_development_guidance.pdf	Anyone, but must be signed by a trained individual. "An individual who is trained and experienced in the principles of stormwater management, including erosion and sediment control as is demonstrated by completion of coursework, State registration, professional certification, or annual training that enable the individual to make judgments regarding stormwater management, treatment, and monitoring."

State	Regulating Agency	Permit
Iowa	Iowa Department of Natural Resources	Iowa Department Of Natural Resources NPDES General Permit No. 2 Storm Water Discharge Associated with Industrial Activity For Construction Activities https://www.iowadnr.gov/media/7475/download?inline
Kansas	Kansas Department of Health & Environment, Division of Environment	Construction Stormwater General Permit S-MCST-1703-1 https://www.kdhe.ks.gov/DocumentCenter/View/6315/Stormwater-Runoff-from-Construction-Activities-General-NPDES-Permit---Effective-08-01-2017-PDF
Kentucky	Kentucky Energy & Environment Cabinet	Kentucky Pollutant Discharge Elimination System Permit NO.: KYR100000 https://eec.ky.gov/Environmental-Protection/Water/PermitCert/KPDES/Documents/KYR10Permit.pdf
Louisiana	Louisiana Department of Environmental Quality	Storm Water General Permit For Large Construction Activities https://deq.louisiana.gov/assets/docs/Permits/LAR100000.pdf
Maine	State of Maine Department of Environmental Protection	Maine Construction General Permit https://www.maine.gov/dep/land/stormwater/2025-01-13_Final-MCGP.pdf
Maryland	Maryland Department of the Environment	Maryland General Permit No. 20-CP https://mde.maryland.gov/programs/water/wwp/Documents/20CP-Final/20CP-Permit-ModA-Final.pdf

SWPPP[64] Template Available	Who Can Prepare a SWPPP
No, but guidance is provided. https://www.iowadnr.gov/media/5843/download?inline	Anyone
No	"Stormwater Pollution Prevention (SWP2) Plans shall be developed and prepared under the supervision of a licensed Kansas professional engineer, geologist, architect, or landscape architect or a Certified Professional in Erosion and Sediment Control."
Yes, guidance is also provided. https://eec.ky.gov/Environmental-Protection/Water/PermitCert/KPDES/Documents/SWPPPPermitPage.pdf	Anyone
Yes, https://deq.louisiana.gov/assets/docs/Water/Stormwater/BlankLargeConstructionSWPP.doc	Anyone
No	Anyone
Yes, guidance documents also available. https://mde.maryland.gov/programs/water/wwp/Documents/20CP-TD/20CP-SWPPPTemplate.docx https://mde.maryland.gov/programs/water/wwp/Documents/20CP-Final/CP-SWPPP-Guidance.pdf	Anyone

State	Regulating Agency	Permit
Massachusetts	U.S. EPA	National Pollutant Discharge Elimination System (NPDES) Construction General Permit (CGP) for Stormwater Discharges from Construction Activities https://www.epa.gov/npdes/2022-construction-general-permit-cgp
Michigan	Department of Environment, Great Lakes, & Energy (EGLE)	EGLE's Water Resources Division (WRD) has adopted a process called "Permit-by Rule" (Rule 2190, promulgated under Part 31, NREPA) for issuing the necessary storm water coverage. https://www.michigan.gov/egle/-/media/Project/Websites/egle/Documents/Programs/WRD/Storm-Water-SESC/Construction-Storm-Water-Permit-by-Rule-Rule2190.pdf?rev=30dcd41e8a964eb-7861de1841c87c811&hash=911DFAEA0B-963D2732E8F47041FD016F
Minnesota	Minnesota Pollution Control Agency	2023 NPDES/SDS Permit number MNR100001 https://www.pca.state.mn.us/sites/default/files/wq-strm2-81a.pdf
Mississippi	Mississippi Department of Environmental Quality	Large Construction General Permit https://www.mdeq.ms.gov/wp-content/uploads/2017/06/Large-Construction-General-Permit-final.pdf
Missouri	Missouri Department of Natural Resources	Area-Wide Land Disturbance Permit MO-R100000 https://dnr.mo.gov/water/business-industry-other-entities/permits-certification-engineering-fees/stormwater/area-wide-land-disturbance-mo-r100000

SWPPP[64] Template Available	Who Can Prepare a SWPPP
Yes https://www.epa.gov/npdes/construction-general-permit-resources-tools-and-templates#swppp	Anyone
No, but guidance available. https://www.michigan.gov/egle/about/organization/water-resources/soil-erosion/plan-development-review-resources	Anyone
Yes https://www.pca.state.mn.us/sites/default/files/wq-strm2-12.docx Guidance: https://www.pca.state.mn.us/sites/default/files/wq-strm2-29.pdf	Anyone
No, but guidance is available. https://www.mdeq.ms.gov/wp-content/uploads/2017/06/ConstructionGM.pdf	Anyone
No	Anyone

State	Regulating Agency	Permit
Montana	Montana Department of Environmental Quality	Storm Water Construction (SWC) - MTR100000 https://deq.mt.gov/files/Water/WQInfo/Documents/2021%20Public%20Notices/PN-MT_21-31/FINAL/2023-FPER-MTR100000-S%20Sign.pdf
Nebraska	Nebraska Department of Environment & Energy	NER210000 Construction Stormwater General Permit https://dee.nebraska.gov/sites/default/files/publications/NER210000%20CSW%20General%20Permit%20-%20Revised.pdf
Nevada	Division of Environmental Protection	Construction Stormwater General Permit NVR100000 https://ndep.nv.gov/uploads/documents/Construction_SW_GPermit_2015_.pdf
New Hampshire	U.S. EPA	National Pollutant Discharge Elimination System (NPDES) Construction General Permit (CGP) for Stormwater Discharges from Construction Activities https://www.epa.gov/npdes/2022-construction-general-permit-cgp

SWPPP[64] Template Available	Who Can Prepare a SWPPP
No	SWPPP Administrator or Preparer "All SWPPP Administrators and Preparers must be certified by a DEQ-approved training provider (no reciprocity with certification from other States). All approved providers meet the minimum training requirements for SWPPP Administrators and Preparers set forth by DEQ." "A SWPPP Administrator is a designated individual who is responsible for developing, implementing, maintaining, revising, and updating the SWPPP."
No	Qualified Personnel "A person knowledgeable in the principles and practice of erosion and sediment controls that possesses the skills to implement and assess the effectiveness of any erosion and sediment control measures. The qualified personnel must possess the skills to assess conditions at the construction site that could impact storm water quality and possess the skills to assess the effectiveness of any storm water controls selected and installed to meet the requirements of this permit."
Yes https://ndep.nv.gov/uploads/water-wpc-permitting-stormwater-construction-docs/nvr100000-const-swppp-template-2017.pdf	Anyone
Yes https://www.epa.gov/npdes/construction-general-permit-resources-tools-and-templates#swppp	Anyone

State	Regulating Agency	Permit
New Jersey	New Jersey Department of Environmental Protection	DST210001 Stormwater Discharge Master General Permit No. NJ0088323 https://dep.nj.gov/wp-content/uploads/njpdes-stormwater/5g3_final_permit.pdf
New Mexico	U.S. EPA	National Pollutant Discharge Elimination System (NPDES) Construction General Permit (CGP) for Stormwater Discharges from Construction Activities https://www.epa.gov/npdes/2022-construction-general-permit-cgp
New York	New York Department of Environmental Conservation	SPDES General Permit for Stormwater Discharges from Construction Activity - GP-0-20-001 https://extapps.dec.ny.gov/docs/water_pdf/constgp020001.pdf
North Carolina	North Carolina Environmental Quality	The NCG01 Permit https://www.deq.nc.gov/energy-mineral-and-land-resources/stormwater/npdes-general-permits/ncg010000-general-permit-april-2019/download The NCG25 Permit https://www.deq.nc.gov/energy-mineral-and-land-resources/stormwater/npdes-general-permits/ncg250000-permit-final-20200925/download

SWPPP[64] Template Available	Who Can Prepare a SWPPP
No	Anyone
Yes https://www.epa.gov/npdes/construction-general-permit-resources-tools-and-templates#swppp	Anyone
No	Anyone
No	Anyone

State	Regulating Agency	Permit
North Dakota	North Dakota Environmental Quality	Construction Permit https://deq.nd.gov/publications/wq/2_NDPDES/Stormwater/Construction/NDR11per20200401F.pdf
Ohio	Ohio Environmental Protection Agency	General Permit OHC000006 https://epa.ohio.gov/static/Portals/35/permits/OHC000006.pdf
Oklahoma	Oklahoma Environmental Quality	General Permit OKR10 https://www.deq.ok.gov/wp-content/uploads/water-division/OKR10-permit-mod2-final-1.pdf
Oregon	Oregon Department of Environmental Quality	Construction Stormwater Discharge Permit 1200-C https://www.oregon.gov/deq/FilterPermitsDocs/1200Cpermit.pdf
Pennsylvania	Pennsylvania Department of Environmental Protection	PAG-02 General Permit https://greenport.pa.gov/elibrary//GetFolder?FolderID=90982

SWPPP[64] Template Available	Who Can Prepare a SWPPP
Yes https://deq.nd.gov/publications/wq/2_NDPDES/Stormwater/Construction/SWPPP2_012016.docm?v=2	Anyone
No	Anyone
Yes https://www.deq.ok.gov/wp-content/uploads/water-division/OKR10-SWP3-Template-112822.pdf	Qualified Person "Those persons (either the operator's employees or outside personnel) who are knowledgeable in the principles and practice of erosion and sediment controls and pollution prevention, who possess the skills and training to assess conditions at the construction site that could impact stormwater quality, and who possess the skills and training to assess the effectiveness of any control measures selected to control the quality of stormwater discharges from the construction activity."
No	Anyone
No	Anyone

State	Regulating Agency	Permit
Rhode Island	Rhode Island Department of Environmental Management	2020 RIPDES Construction General Permit https://dem.ri.gov/media/30076/download
South Carolina	South Carolina Department of Health & Environmental Control	NPDES General Permit SCR100000 https://des.sc.gov/sites/des/files/media/document/BOW_NPDESStormwaterDischargesGP_01292021_0.pdf
South Dakota	South Dakota Department of Agriculture & Natural Resources	South Dakota General Permit Number: SDR100000 https://danr.sd.gov/OfficeOfWater/SurfaceWaterQuality/docs/DANR_ConstructionGeneralPermit2023.pdf
Tennessee	Tennessee Department of Environment & Conservation	General NPDES Permit for Storm Water Discharges Associated with Construction Activity Permit Number TNR100000 https://dataviewers.tdec.tn.gov/data-viewers/apex_util.count_click?p_url=B-GWPC.GET_WPC_DOCUMENTS?p_file=540656813282722325&p_cat=DOCS&p_id=540656813282722325&p_user=GUEST&p_workspace=19833722515258996

Connecting the Dots of SWPPP Development

SWPPP[64] Template Available	Who Can Prepare a SWPPP
No	Anyone
Yes https://des.sc.gov/sites/des/files/docs/Environment/docs/SWPPP-CGP-template.doc	For projects that disturb more than 2 acres, the C-SWPPP must be prepared and certified by one of the following licensed individuals: • Registered professional engineers as described in Title 40, Chapter 22; • Registered landscape architects as described in Title 40, Chapter 28, Section 10, item (b); • Tier B land surveyors as described in Title 40, Chapter 22; or • Federal government employees as described by Title 40, Chapter 22, Section 280(A)(3).
No	Anyone
Yes https://www.tn.gov/content/dam/tn/environment/water/policy-and-guidance/dwr-nr-g-02-cgp-non-engineering-swppp-final-051719-template.docx	Anyone

State	Regulating Agency	Permit
Texas	Texas Commission On Environmental Quality	TPDES Construction General Permit TXR150000 https://www.tceq.texas.gov/downloads/permitting/stormwater/general/construction/2023-cgp-txr150000.pdf
Utah	Utah Department of Environmental Quality	Construction General UPDES Permit No. UTRC00000 https://lf-public.deq.utah.gov/WebLink/DocView.aspx?id=424911&eqdocs=DWQ-2024-004974&cr=1
Vermont	Agency of Natural Resources; Department of Environmental Conservation	General Permit 3-9020 For Stormwater Runoff From Construction Sites https://dec.vermont.gov/sites/dec/files/wsm/stormwater/docs/StormwaterConstructionDischargePermits/3-9020_Stormwater_ConstructionGeneralPermit_2020-02-19.pdf
Virginia	Commonwealth of Virginia Department of Environmental Quality	General Permit No.: VAR10 https://www.deq.virginia.gov/home/showpublisheddocument/8525/637547667064630000
Washington	State of Washington Department of Ecology	Construction General Stormwater Permit https://apps.ecology.wa.gov/paris/DownloadDocument.aspx?Id=348923

Connecting the Dots of SWPPP Development

SWPPP[64] Template Available	Who Can Prepare a SWPPP
Yes https://www.tceq.texas.gov/downloads/assistance/publications/rg-639.docx	Anyone
Yes https://lf-public.deq.utah.gov/WebLink/DocView.aspx?id=424549&eqdocs=DWQ-2024-004705	Anyone
No, but guidance is provided. https://dec.vermont.gov/sites/dec/files/wsm/stormwater/docs/StormwaterConstructionDischargePermits/VermontStandardsAndSpecificationsForErosionPreventionAndSedimentControl_2020-02-19.pdf	Anyone
Only for single family home SWPPPs. https://www.deq.virginia.gov/home/showpublisheddocument/8504/637546761330070000	Anyone
No	Anyone

State	Regulating Agency	Permit
West Virginia	West Virginia Department of Environmental Protection	Draft General Permit for Reissuance https://dep.wv.gov/WWE/Programs/stormwater/csw/Documents/2024%20CGP/Reissued%20permit%20WV0115924%20-12-13-23-CLEAN.pdf
Wisconsin	State of Wisconsin Department of Natural Resources	General Permit To Discharge Under The Wisconsin Pollutant Discharge Elimination System WPDES Permit No. WI-S067831-6 https://dnr.wisconsin.gov/sites/default/files/topic/Stormwater/FINAL_CSGP_WI-S067831-6_for_reissuance_September_2021_signed.pdf
Wyoming	Wyoming Department of Environmental Quality	State of Wyoming Large Construction General Permit No. WYR100000 https://deq.wyoming.gov/water-quality/wypdes/discharge-permitting/storm-water-permitting/large-and-small-construction-general-permit/

SWPPP[64] Template Available	Who Can Prepare a SWPPP
Yes https://dep.wv.gov/WWE/Programs/stormwater/csw/Documents/Blank%20Construction%20SWPPP.doc	Qualified Person "A person who is knowledgeable in the principles and practices of sediment and erosion controls, pollution prevention, and possesses the education and abilities to assess conditions at the proposed site that could impact stormwater quality and to assess the effectiveness of proposed stormwater controls to meet the requirements of this permit."
No, but guidance is provided. https://dnr.wisconsin.gov/topic/Stormwater/construction/erosion_control.html	Anyone
Yes https://deq.wyoming.gov/water-quality/wypdes/discharge-permitting/storm-water-permitting/large-and-small-construction-general-permit/	Anyone

Perhaps because I live and work in California and am a bit California-centric, it seems to me that our Golden State tends to be on the forefront of environmental regulatory requirements. This is certainly true when it comes to qualifications for SWPPP developers. In the 2009 Construction General Permit, the state introduced the concept of requiring credentialed individuals to prepare SWPPPs and inspect construction sites. But as evidenced on Table 11, many other states have also implemented SWPPP writer requirements.

Figure 93 - California QSPs and QSDs are professionals who have fundamental knowledge of erosion and sedimentation processes. (Photo credit: John Teravskis)

In California, Qualified SWPPP Developers (QSDs) are the professionals required to prepare or amend the written plans, and Qualified SWPPP Practitioners (QSPs) are those required to perform or oversee inspections. (Because the QSD is considered to be a higher credential, the state considers QSDs to also be QSPs.) The state expects QSDs and QSPs to have fundamental knowledge of erosion and sedimentation processes, best management practices, and their implementation to control pollutants in storm water discharges. Therefore, these individuals are required by the state to demonstrate they have this knowledge by either **1)** being a California licensed Professional Engineer (PE) or Professional Geologist (PG) and self-certifying their eligibility to serve as a QSP/QSD on the State Water Board's website; or **2)** taking a state-approved class (two days for QSPs and three days for QSDs) given by a CASQA-approved Trainer of Record, passing the corresponding exam, and obtaining one of the following state-approved prerequisite underlying credentials:

Connecting the Dots of SWPPP Development

For QSDs:

- A California landscape architect registration;
- A professional hydrologist registration through the American Institute of Hydrology;
- A Certified Professional in Erosion and Sediment Control (CPESC) registration through EnviroCert International, Inc.;
- A Certified Professional in Stormwater Quality (CPSWQ)™ registration through EnviroCert International, Inc.; or
- Any prerequisite course approved by the State Water Board's Division of Water Quality Deputy Director.[65]

For QSPs:

- A Certified Erosion, Sediment, and Stormwater Inspector (CESSWI)™ registered through Enviro Cert International, Inc.;
- A certified inspector of sediment and erosion control (CISEC)™ registered through Certified Inspector of Sediment and Erosion Control Inc. (now under Ecopliant™);
- A construction management degree from an accredited four-year institution that includes coursework that covers the underlying principles of erosion and sediment control and practices of reducing pollution in storm water; or
- Any prerequisite course approved by the State Water Board's Division of Water Quality Deputy Director.[66]

---

[65] The State Water Board will post on their Construction General Permit website other prerequisite courses that they have approved. For more information, refer to the Water Board's guidance on the 2022 CGP Additional QSD & QSP Prerequisite Criteria https://www.waterboards.ca.gov/water_issues/programs/stormwater/construction/docs/2024/2022-cgp-qsdqsp-prereq.pdf.

[66] For more information about the CASQA QSP / QSD certifications and training programs, go to https://www.casqa.org/resources/training/cgp-training-program/qsd-qsp-qualification

In addition, to remain in good standing with their certification, QSDs and QSPs who took a course from a CASQA Trainer of Record need to annually complete six hours of continuing education (or comply with the continuing education requirements of their underlying credential) and complete the online QSP/QSD renewal process every two years. The State Water Board may suspend or rescind the QSP or QSD credential from any individual who, in the course of acting as one, demonstrates a lack of knowledge or training or is willfully or negligently causing a violation of the Construction General Permit.

But these are not the only professional storm water credentials that a Construction SWPPP writer may need in California. QSDs (and QSPs) who implement SWPPPs for Caltrans projects will also need to become a Caltrans Water Pollution Control Manager (WPCM)[67]. This involves taking an eight-hour class by one of the Caltrans-approved instructors[68] and also completing a four-hour online Title 22 Hazardous Waste Generator Training course.

So you think you have all the necessary credentials for writing a SWPPP by being a QSD and a WPCM? Not necessarily! Some large developers (such as Walmart)[69] also have their own in-house mandatory classes/certifications or require SWPPP writers and contractors working on their projects to obtain training from a third-party training organization.

---

67 As defined in Caltrans Standard Specification 13-1.01D(4) https://dot.ca.gov/programs/design/july-2023-ccs-standard-plans-and-standard-specifications

68 A list of approved instructors can be found at https://dot.ca.gov/programs/construction/storm-water-and-water-pollution-control

69 International Erosion Control Association News, Impact of Wal-Mart's Stormwater Compliance Program May Spread Throughout the Industry, July/August 2005, https://cdn.corporate.walmart.com/5d/98/6f-55c9094ac5bea2dcb846714cb8/1285_erosioncontrolmagazineJuly2005_2117323889.pdf

DO YOUR HOMEWORK FIRST BY GETTING TO KNOW THE PROJECT SITE

Don't be in such a hurry to get your SWPPP written that you don't take adequate time to get to know the site and the project about which you will be writing. I have found taking an hour or two (sometimes more) to familiarize myself with the situation will pay off with efficiencies later on in the process. There has been more than one occasion when I rushed into SWPPP writing only later to find that I had to change the discharge monitoring locations or BMP configurations because I failed to adequately comprehend the site dynamics or the project details. Had I slowed down to do my homework first, not only would I have been much further ahead in the process, but also would have saved myself the aggravation of having to redo some work. A homework list for SWPPP writers should include the following:

Studying the site on Google Earth: What did we do before we had Google Earth? What an amazing resource! Taking some time to examine the project site using this powerful tool can greatly enhance a SWPPP writer's knowledge about a location. This tool works quite well for many locations and provides aerial, topographic, and street-view perspectives of the pre-construction conditions of a site. Information that can be gained by viewing a location on Google Earth includes:

- ☑ **General site layout**

  From the above Google Earth imagery, we can see that the 23.7-acre proposed industrial park site is undeveloped, somewhat vegetated, and is elongated. Zooming in, we can observe signs of fairly recent soil disturbance and the stockpiling of soil. We also observe an entrance onto the project site off the cul-de-sac located on the east side.

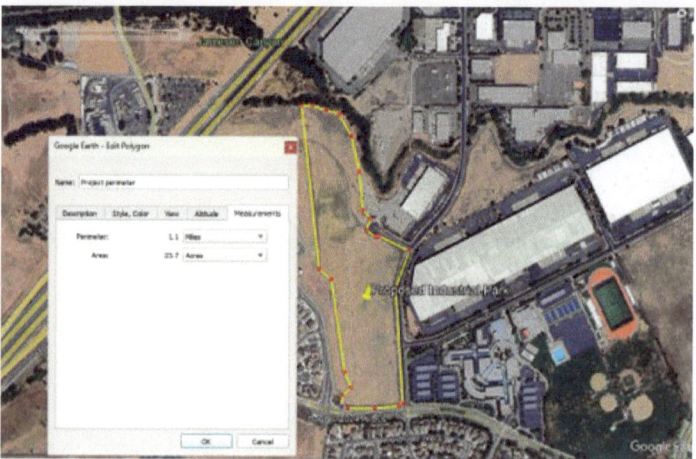

Figure 94 - Google Earth is a powerful tool for the SWPPP writer and provides useful insight into how to manage storm water runoff. (Photo credit: Google Earth™, 2024)

☑ **Adjacent and nearby properties and water bodies**

Based on the aerial imagery, industrial facilities border the site to the northeast and east, a school campus to the southeast, residential neighborhoods to the south and west, a strip of undeveloped land along the west perimeter, and a water course flowing along the north–northeast border.

☑ Changes in topography and elevation

When hovering the mouse over a certain point, the elevation of that point will be displayed in the lower right corner of the screen. Although perhaps not as accurate and detailed as a pre-development contour map from the civil drawings, this will allow us to get a general idea of the changes in topography at the site. Using the measuring tool in Google Earth, we can also measure the distance from point A to point B and find that the sheet flow length between them is approximately 325 feet. By using the formula "rise over run" to determine the slope percentage, we can estimate the average percent slope between those two points to be 26 feet (rise or, in other words, the elevation difference) divided by the run or 325 feet, which equates to an 8% slope (fairly steep!). By the way, this information will be used to calculate soil loss.

Figure 95 - Google Earth can also be used help determine sheet flow directions and slope percentages. Red numbers are elevations in feet above mean sea level, and blue arrows are flow directions. (Photo credit: Google Earth™, 2024)

Figure 96 - Google Earth street views can also be very useful for visualizing the project's topography and for identifying other existing site features such as drain inlets on- and off-site. (Photo credit: Google Earth™, 2024)

Does the street view correspond to this calculation? Yes it does; although it does appear that most of the elevation change occurs on the west side of the property. From these images, we have learned that our perimeter sediment control measures are going to need to be focused on the eastern perimeter.

☑ Drainage patterns and historical ponding

By viewing historical aerial images on Google Earth, we can observe historic areas of ponding and drainage across the property. It is helpful to view photos of the site taken during previous wet months. From Figure 97, an aerial image taken in 2001, we can observe that the site receives significant run-on from the west, which exits from the property in two separate locations.

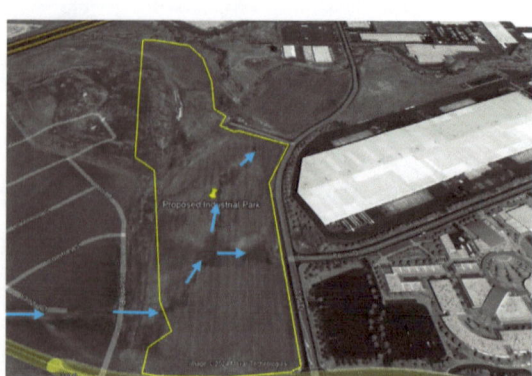

Figure 97 - Historic aerial photos can help identify run-on and run-off locations as well as actual flow patterns across the site. (Photo credit: Google Earth™, 2024)

☑ Drain inlets on and off site

Google Earth has saved me many trips to project locations to identify nearby off-site drain inlets. A field visit may still be needed if there were cars parked along the street on the day the Google camera passed by, but in cases like this, it helps us to positively identify the drain inlet locations and provide some insight into what type of protection should be utilized.

Figure 98 - There's the storm drain! I love it when Google Earth saves me a trip to the site. (Photo credit: Google Earth™, 2024)

☑ Information about project perimeters

Many times, even with a good set of civil drawings, it is difficult to visualize what type of perimeter sediment control measure should be used, especially for the early phases of the project. Should we use fiber roll? Silt fence? Curb cutback? What would be best for this particular location? That is where

Figure 99 - What an ideal spot for fiber roll! (Photo credit: Google Earth™, 2024)

Google Earth street-view images really help. We can see from Figure 99 that on the south side of this project it is fairly flat. As we saw earlier from Google Earth, the flow at this location is generally moving away from the street. We also can observe a fairly ideal location for the proper installation of fiber roll or silt fence. Therefore, since we are not anticipating a heavy sediment load at this location, fiber roll would be our preferred choice for perimeter control.

☑ **Past uses or sources of contamination**

The historic aerial imagery also reveals that this property was not previously developed but had been farmed in the relatively recent past. This is relevant information for the Pollutant Source Assessment that we discussed in [Chapter 3](); particularly for identifying materials that may have been spilled or used on this site. We would not expect to have any historic industrial pollutants at this location. But if the site is located where a TMDL has been established for a pesticide, we may need to include the past farming activities in the pollutant source assessment

Figure 100 - Historic aerial imagery can help us with the Pollutant Source Assessment. If this location is in an area with a TMDL for a pesticide, then we would probably want to do some more research to see if it had been applied in the past. (Photo credit: Google Earth™, 2024)

if we believe that the pesticide of interest might had been previously applied at this location. County Agriculture Commissioner records can help determine if a certain pesticide was applied at the project site.

Studying the civil drawings: Do not shortcut this homework assignment! It is the most important thing to do in preparing for the SWPPP development. Learn to read civil drawings. For some writers, they grew up through the trades and have been reading plans for years. However, other SWPPP writers may come from a science or academic background and have never needed to read plans. For those with limited experience with construction plans, there are some very good books available on how to read and understand blueprints. (A quick search on Amazon will produce several good options.) But regardless of how much or little you know about civil drawings, it is worth spending some time absorbing the information. Quite a bit of what is on the plans is fairly intuitive and will start to make more sense as you spend time absorbing the information.

Here are a few things to which a SWPPP writer should pay particular attention:

☑ **Scale and direction**

To get oriented to the project site, the scale and north arrow on the civil plans will greatly assist you. Although it may seem overly elementary to point this out, checking the north arrow first will help you to correctly visualize the project. There have been several projects on which I had a hard time visualizing it because I had it oriented wrongly in my head. Scale is also something you should take a moment to familiarize yourself with. Because

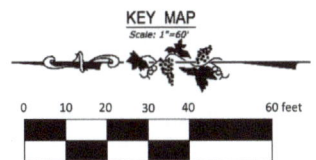

Figure 101 - The north arrow and scale will allow the SWPPP writer to get the correct orientation for the project. But be careful about what scale you use! (Courtesy of Baumbach & Piazza, Inc. Civil Engineers and Land Surveyors)

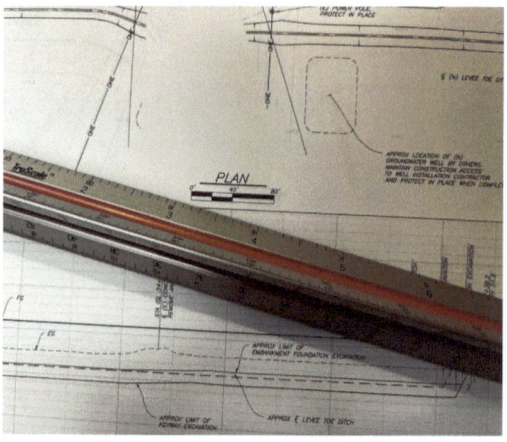

Figure 102 - Using an engineer scale and a printed bar (or graphic) scale, you can determine a project's size and lengths. (Photo credit: John Teravskis)

SWPPP writers often receive PDFs of civil plans that are formatted or printed as an 11" x 17" plan sheet, the best scale to utilize is a bar (or graphic) scale. When a drawing says something like "1 inch = 60 feet," it means when printed at 100% scaling on a certain sized drawing—for civil plans, generally it would be a 24" x 36" (D size) drawing. Therefore, if you use a ruler and are basing measurements taken off of the 11" x 17" plan sheet having a scale of "1 inch = 60 feet," you will have underestimated the project's size and lengths. However, using your ruler or engineer scale with a printed bar scale will produce the correct values. But sometimes drawings only have "1 inch = 60 feet" (or some similar scale) and no graphic scale. If you suspect that the drawing has not been printed to full scale (i.e., on a smaller sheet of paper), using Google Earth, you can produce a close approximation of the scale for the drawing. Do this by first identifying an existing physical feature (like a building or a roadway) that is viewable both on the civil drawing and on Google Earth. Next, use the measuring tool on Google Earth to determine the length or width of the selected physical feature. Using your engineer scale or ruler, now measure the same feature on the civil drawing. If the selected physical feature measured 131 feet on Google

Earth, and it measured 1.6 inches on the civil drawing, then the scale for the printed civil drawing would be determined by dividing 131 feet by 1.6 inches and would result in an approximate scale of 1 inch = 82 feet. Your scale is now calibrated for the printed 11" x 17" drawing. Of course anytime you zoom in or out or rescale the image on your SWPPP map, you will need to recalibrate your scale. (Perhaps this method is not accurate enough for constructing the project, but it is certainly close enough for developing a SWPPP!)

☑ **Legend**

After orienting to the direction and scale, take a look at the legend for the drawing. For a set of civil plans, sometimes you will find the legend included on the drawing you are reviewing, other times it may be found on the first or second page of the civil drawing set, or there may be applicable legends in both locations. Study the legend to help you identify areas of cut and fill, grade breaks (where surface flow will head in a different direction), project or grading boundaries, drainage systems, surface flow direction (denoted with arrows or elevations), and types of surface coverings. As we will discuss later, when preparing a SWPPP map using a civil map as the base map, I will often include the civil map legend and have a separate legend for the SWPPP map that includes information about the BMPs and other site features relevant to the CGP.

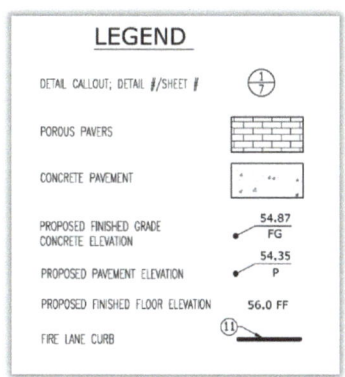

Figure 103 - The legend is the key to unlocking your understanding of the drawings. (Courtesy of Baumbach & Piazza, Inc. Civil Engineers and Land Surveyors)

☑ Notes

Details, details, and more details! Since we are talking about taking time to do your homework, while reviewing civil drawings don't forget to get out your magnifying glass (or zoom in 300% on the PDF) and read the construction notes. As with the legend, these can be located in several locations throughout the civil drawings. Sometimes there are one or two whole pages dedicated to them. By not reviewing them, you can miss some pretty vital information that you will need for preparing the SWPPP. This information may include details about the phasing of the project, what gets demolished or protected in-place, the storm water drainage system, and post-construction storm water measures. For example, note #5 shown in Figure 104 indicates that soil will be hauled off-site, which is an activity we would want to include in the SWPPP. Note #7 suggests that lime treating at this site may occur. We would want to include this in our Pollutant Source Assessment.

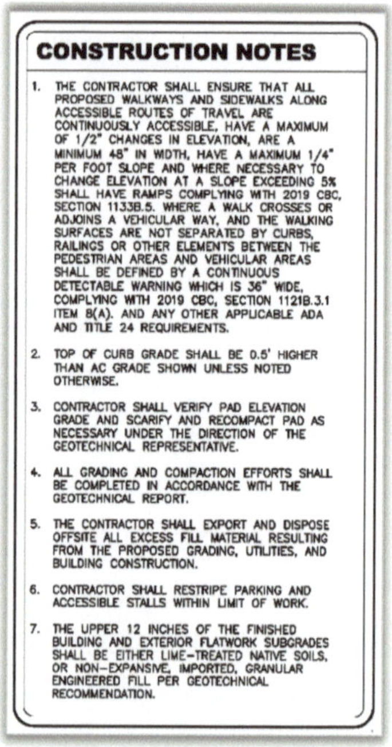

CONSTRUCTION NOTES

1. THE CONTRACTOR SHALL ENSURE THAT ALL PROPOSED WALKWAYS AND SIDEWALKS ALONG ACCESSIBLE ROUTES OF TRAVEL ARE CONTINUOUSLY ACCESSIBLE, HAVE A MAXIMUM OF 1/2" CHANGES IN ELEVATION, ARE A MINIMUM 48" IN WIDTH, HAVE A MAXIMUM 1/4" PER FOOT SLOPE AND WHERE NECESSARY TO CHANGE ELEVATION AT A SLOPE EXCEEDING 5% SHALL HAVE RAMPS COMPLYING WITH 2019 CBC, SECTION 1133B.5. WHERE A WALK CROSSES OR ADJOINS A VEHICULAR WAY, AND THE WALKING SURFACES ARE NOT SEPARATED BY CURBS, RAILINGS OR OTHER ELEMENTS BETWEEN THE PEDESTRIAN AREAS AND VEHICULAR AREAS SHALL BE DEFINED BY A CONTINUOUS DETECTABLE WARNING WHICH IS 36" WIDE, COMPLYING WITH 2019 CBC, SECTION 1121B.3.1 ITEM 8(A). AND ANY OTHER APPLICABLE ADA AND TITLE 24 REQUIREMENTS.
2. TOP OF CURB GRADE SHALL BE 0.5' HIGHER THAN AC GRADE SHOWN UNLESS NOTED OTHERWISE.
3. CONTRACTOR SHALL VERIFY PAD ELEVATION GRADE AND SCARIFY AND RECOMPACT PAD AS NECESSARY UNDER THE DIRECTION OF THE GEOTECHNICAL REPRESENTATIVE.
4. ALL GRADING AND COMPACTION EFFORTS SHALL BE COMPLETED IN ACCORDANCE WITH THE GEOTECHNICAL REPORT.
5. THE CONTRACTOR SHALL EXPORT AND DISPOSE OFFSITE ALL EXCESS FILL MATERIAL RESULTING FROM THE PROPOSED GRADING, UTILITIES, AND BUILDING CONSTRUCTION.
6. CONTRACTOR SHALL RESTRIPE PARKING AND ACCESSIBLE STALLS WITHIN LIMIT OF WORK.
7. THE UPPER 12 INCHES OF THE FINISHED BUILDING AND EXTERIOR FLATWORK SUBGRADES SHALL BE EITHER LIME-TREATED NATIVE SOILS, OR NON-EXPANSIVE, IMPORTED, GRANULAR ENGINEERED FILL PER GEOTECHNICAL RECOMMENDATION.

Figure 104 - Details, details, details...don't forget to read the details! (Photo credit: RSC Engineering, Inc. The notes referenced are provided solely as an example. The author assumes no responsibility for their application or interpretation by the reader.)

☑ Demolition plans / pre-construction drawings

Many times civil drawings will include a sheet that shows the pre-construction elevations or contours and a sheet that contains the demolition plans. (With the advent of the California 2022 CGP, these civil drawings are now going to be utilized more often than in the past because of the State Water Board's requirement to include in the SWPPP a pre-construction drawing.) When orienting myself to a new project, I will study these drawings to determine the project's starting point. Depending the proposed development, the ending condition may not at all resemble the early phases of the project. A SWPPP writer will want to know what the BMP configuration should look like during these early phases. Too often, SWPPP maps only show BMP layouts for the final phases of the project. I remember one time I visited a levee project along the Sacramento River for which I had written a SWPPP and prepared SWPPP maps based on the final construction phase of the project. As I walked the project with SWPPP map in hand, I could not even recognize the project site or get an orientation for the BMPs I had specified. This was because the early phases and features of this project were so dramatically different than the later phases. This project merited multiple SWPPP maps—one for each phase.

☑ **Grading contours**

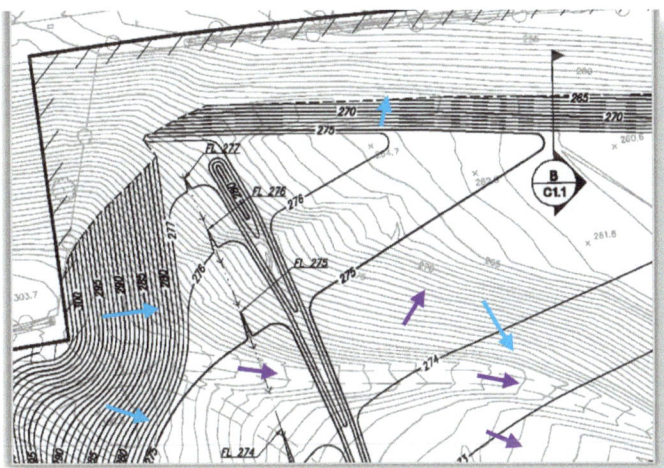

Figure 105 - Going up or going down? SWPPP writers should never have water flowing uphill. The purple arrows show the pre-grading surface flow directions and the blue arrows show the post-grading flow directions. (Photo credit: Ruggeri-Jensen-Azar Engineers, Planners, and Surveyors)

It is vital for a SWPPP writer to know how to read grading contours. Otherwise, you might find yourself in a very embarrassing situation where you show water flowing uphill on your SWPPP map. Most of the time, grading contours will be labeled with an elevation value for every one to ten feet of elevation change. The higher the number, the higher the elevation is. Therefore, water flows from a higher number to a lower number. If we see a series of concentric rings of elevation contours, how do we know whether we are looking at a depression or a mound? If the center rings have a higher value than the outer rings, it is a mound. If the center rings have a lower value, it is a depression. It is common for civil grading plans to show dark contour lines placed on top of lighter contours as shown in Figure 105. The lighter elevation contours are for the existing site conditions. The darker contours show where grading and cut and fill work will be occurring. Often a dashed line around the darker lines will be used to delineate the grading limits. Another common denotation on grading plans are contours that are "V" shaped. These usually indicate a natural or constructed drainage swale. But how do you know which way the water is flowing in the swale? Sometimes it is fairly obvious, but I have seen many cases where a closer look is needed and I learn that water is actually flowing the opposite direction than I first thought. The swale shown in Figure 105 is flowing toward the bottom of the figure.

☑ Cross sections

On Figure 105, there is a circle with a darkened triangle pointing to the right of it that says "B/C1.1". This indicates that the engineer is providing a cross section view of that location. The large, darkened triangle arrow points to the perspective (or view) of the cross section. The line connecting to the smaller darkened triangle shows the extent of the cross section. The nomenclature "B/C1.1" indicates that it is Section B found on the civil drawing page C1.1. Going to that sheet, we find Section B (shown in Figure 106). These cross sections can be very helpful to SWPPP writers in understanding the nuances of certain locations. For example, on Figure 106, we can see that there is an existing concrete ditch at the base of the slope. We also see that the earthwork will most likely be occurring within the upper one third portion of the slope. Based on this cross section, it may be appropriate to install fiber roll or silt fence upgradient of the existing chain-link fence. I will often include cross sections with the SWPPP map and show on them the BMP placements. This will provide the contractor with a better understanding of how the BMPs should be configured than just showing them on a plan view.

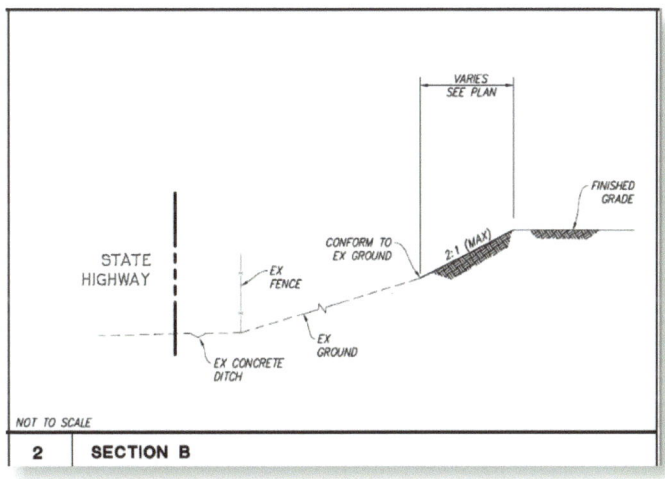

Figure 106 - Cross sections can be very useful for SWPPP writers to understand the nuances of certain project areas. (Photo credit: Ruggeri-Jensen-Azar Engineers, Planners, and Surveyors)

☑ **Surface types**

Civil drawings will usually have both the pre-construction and post-construction surface types called out. As shown in Figure 107, the surface types may have a hatch pattern defined in the legend or will be denoted with text on the drawing. A SWPPP writer will need to determine the percent imperviousness of the pre-construction conditions and compare it to that of the post-construction development. The pre-construction SWPPP map should identify impervious surfaces that will remain in place and those that will be removed. The post-construction SWPPP map should show new impervious surfaces, such as paving and buildings, and permeable surfaces such as landscaping, bioretention cells, permeable pavement, and other low-impact development measures.

Figure 107 - A SWPPP writer needs to identify both the pre-construction and post-construction surface types. Determine what surfaces are impermeable. (Courtesy of Baumbach & Piazza, Inc. Civil Engineers and Land Surveyors)

☑ **Drainage system**

In order to properly manage storm water and control erosion and sedimentation it is necessary to adequately understand the flow of water across the project site throughout the duration of the project. In the previous discussion about elevation contours, we saw how to discern surface flow in a pre-construction and graded condition. But during the vertical phase of the project, storm water does not always strictly follow the surface contours. A drainage system will collect runoff at distinct points and convey it off-site or to a different location on the project site, such as the bioretention facility shown in Figure 108. In addition, as we learned about Slow-the-Flow BMPs in Chapter 4, in particular with Speed

Connecting the Dots of SWPPP Development

Bump BMPs SF-2, drain inlets are crucial locations to provide sediment with an opportunity to drop out before entering the drainage system. We will want to identify all of the existing and new drain inlets on our SWPPP maps. Another storm water drainage system feature that should be shown on the SWPPP maps include the Fat Spot BMPs SF-3, such as retention basins or, as shown in Figure 108, bioretention basins. During grading these features can serve as sediment traps.

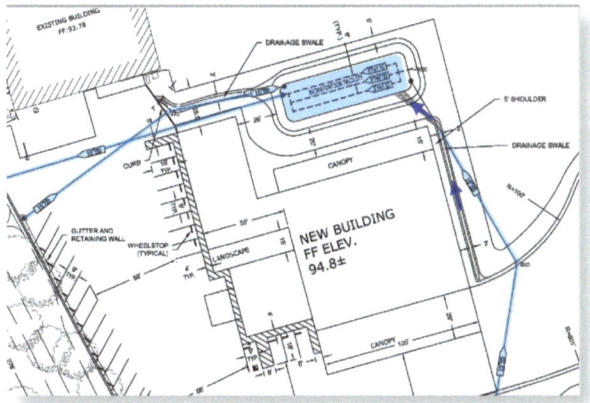

Figure 108 - At some point during the project, storm water runoff will be managed by a storm water drainage system. A SWPPP writer needs to understand when this will occur and to where water will be conveyed. (Courtesy of Baumbach & Piazza, Inc. Civil Engineers and Land Surveyors)

☑ **Drainage Management Areas**

Along the lines of understanding the drainage system, step back and take a more macroscopic approach by evaluating the drainage areas. These are often referred to as Drainage Management Areas (DMAs). In Chapter 7, we will discuss post-construction design standards that are required of most new construction projects. In that context, a DMA is typically defined as an area of the project (and at times, it can be the entire project area) that flows to a unique off-site discharge point and in which storm water is managed (or treated) in a similar manner. DMAs

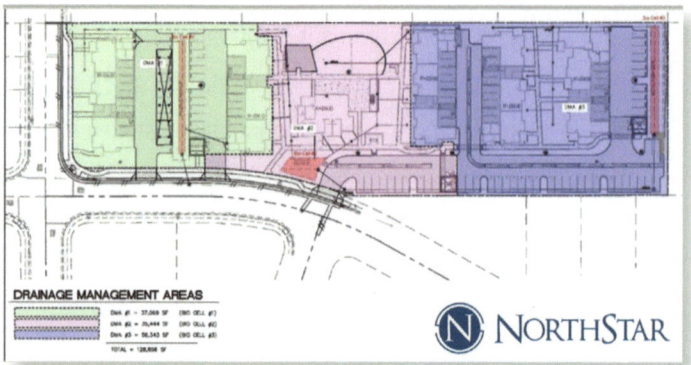

Figure 109 - A project with three DMAs. Each DMA has a unique discharge point and each DMA has its own bioretention facility for treating storm water. (Drawing used with the permission of NorthStar Engineering.)

are utilized to calculate and evaluate the runoff for pre-construction and post-construction conditions. In the case shown in Figure 109, there are three areas of the project that have unique discharge points. All runoff in each of these three DMAs flows into a separate bioretention facility where it is allowed to infiltrate into the soil, and excess water then discharges to the unique discharge location.

☑ **Erosion and Sediment Control Plans**

Most civil plan drawings include an Erosion and Sediment Control Plan (ESCP) sheet. At first glance, a SWPPP writer gets excited thinking that perhaps their job just got a lot easier and they won't have to prepare one or more of the SWPPP maps. Calm down! It's not usually that simple for a variety of reasons. First, although many of the civil engineers with whom I work have a really good understanding of erosion and sediment control and the Construction General Permit requirements, I still find that I will rarely be in 100% agreement with their approach to the plan. For some of the better ESCPs, I may end up using it as my SWPPP base map and just add some additional details to it. But, quite frequently, I find that

Connecting the Dots of SWPPP Development

their approach is wrong or not compliant with the permit requirements, such as having a linear sediment control installation going uphill. In those cases, I find it easier to use the grading, utility, or DMA plan as the basis for my SWPPP map. Another reason for not just inserting the ESCP into the SWPPP as the SWPPP map is because the Construction General Permit requires quite a bit more information on the SWPPP map than what is typically included on the ESCP. As we discussed in Chapter 4 under site management BMPs, pollution prevention measures are not normally included on ESCPs prepared by engineering firms.

Reviewing the soils report and/or the USDA's Web Soil Survey: Understanding the site's soils will allow the SWPPP writer to develop a plan that is appropriate for the location. BMPs that are effective in a sandy loam will not be nearly as effective in silty clay. Before diving into the SWPPP preparation, take some time to study the soil type(s) at the site. Resources that may be available to a SWPPP preparer include a site-specific geotechnical report, the Web Soil Survey, and site reconnaissance. Regardless of the resource utilized, the SWPPP developer should be able to classify the soil conditions by soil texture and hydrologic soil group classification.

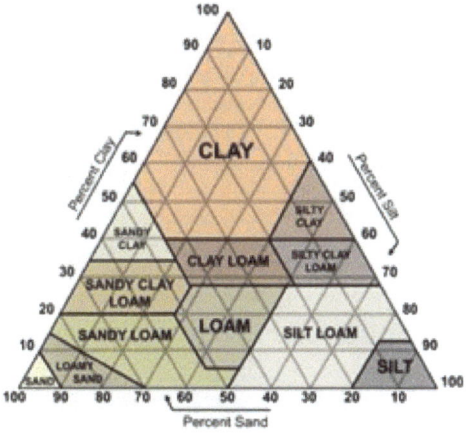

Figure 110 - Soil texture triangle from the United State Department of Agriculture, Natural Resource Conservation Service.

As discussed in Chapter 2, there are three basic soil textures: sand, silt, and clay. Sandy soils generally have larger particle sizes. Clays are made of the smallest soil particles. Most types of soil are a combination of the three textures. The triangle shown in Figure 110 is used to determine the soil type based on the percentage of each texture found to be present in the soil. For example, a soil that has 30% clay, 40% silt, and 30% sand would be known as a clay loam. When the word "loam" is used in the soil type name, it is indicative of a soil type that is well suited for growing crops.

The hydrologic soil group (HSG) of the soil type should also be identified. There are four HSG classifications, designated with letters A, B, C, and D, which indicate the ability of the soil to infiltrate water and, conversely, the potential for runoff. Classification "A" has the highest infiltration rate and lowest runoff rate and "D" has the lowest infiltration rate and highest runoff rate.

According to the United States Department of Agriculture[70], the hydrologic soil groups are defined as the following:

> **Hydrologic Soil Group A:** The soils have a high infiltration rate even when thoroughly wetted. They chiefly consist of deep, well drained to excessively drained sands or gravels. They have a high rate of water transmission. (Low runoff potential). Infiltration rate is typically >0.45 inches/hour.
>
> **Hydrologic Soil Group B:** The soils have a moderate infiltration rate when thoroughly wetted. They chiefly are moderately deep to deep, moderately well drained to well drained soils that have moderately fine to moderately coarse textures. They have a moderate rate of water transmission. Infiltration rate is typically 0.15 to 0.30 inches/hour.

---

70 https://efotg.sc.egov.usda.gov/references/Agency/SD/Archived_hydgrp_100415.pdf and United States Environmental Protection Agency, National Stormwater Calculator User's Guide – Version 2.0.0.1, by Rossman, Lewis A., and Bernagros, Jason T., EPA/600/R-13/085g, Revised July 2019, https://www.epa.gov/sites/default/files/2019-04/documents/swc_users_guide_desktop_v1.2.0.3_april_2019.pdf.

Hydrologic Soil Group C: The soils have a slow infiltration rate when thoroughly wetted. They chiefly have a layer that impedes downward movement of water or have moderately fine to fine texture. They have a slow rate of water transmission. Infiltration rate is typically 0.05 to 0.15 inches/hour.

Hydrologic Soil Group D: The soils have a very slow infiltration rate when thoroughly wetted. They chiefly consist of clay soils that have a high swelling potential, soils that have a permanent high water table, soils that have a claypan or clay layer at or near the surface, and shallow soils over nearly impervious material. They have a very slow rate of water transmission. (High runoff potential). Infiltration rate is typically 0 to 0.05 inches/hour.

Dual Hydrologic Soil Groups: Dual hydrologic soil groups, A/D, B/D, and C/D, are given for certain wet soils that can be adequately drained. The first letter applies to the drained condition, the second to the undrained. Only soils that are rated D in their natural condition are assigned to dual classes. Soils may be assigned to dual groups if drainage is feasible and practical. In the examples listed above, the "D" assignment could be due to a high water table but should the area be drained, the first letter now defines the resulting condition for infiltration.

Based on the definitions of these soil groups and what we know about the soil textures, we would expect the following to generally be true:[71]

⇒ HSG A soils to be comprised of sand, loamy sand, or sandy loam types of soils.
⇒ HSG B soils to be comprised of silt loam or loam.
⇒ HSG C soils to be comprised of sandy clay loam.
⇒ HSG D soils to be comprised of clay loam, silty clay loam, sandy clay, silty clay, or clay.

☑ **Site Specific Geotechnical Report**
For many projects, a geotechnical or soils report will have been prepared and may be available to the SWPPP preparer. The soils report is prepared by a geotechnical engineer or soils engineer and will contain information about the soils and subsurface conditions based on a field investigation, soil borings, and other tests performed at the proposed project site. Soils reports will identify the soil textures and horizons below the surface and tell the builder what they can expect during construction. The soils report will also typically contain information about the depth to groundwater or, at least, whether or not it was encountered in the soil borings. Some soils reports will contain information from a sieve analysis of the collected soil samples that will identify the particle size and distribution of sizes in the soil sample. Percolation testing results may also be included in some soils reports, which will identify the percolation rates of the soil. Usually the municipality issuing the grading permit will require a soils report for projects having significant grading or where a structure will be constructed, but they are not required of all types of projects (e.g., a restoration project). If a soils report has been

---

[71] Minnesota Stormwater Manual – Design Infiltration Rates https://stormwater.pca.state.mn.us/index.php?title=Design_infiltration_rates.

Connecting the Dots of SWPPP Development

prepared for a project, typically, a copy of it may be obtained from the project owner or civil engineer.

☑ **Web Soil Survey**

For projects where no soils report has been prepared or is not readily available, the USDA's Natural Resource Conservation Service (NRCS) Web Soil Survey[72] is an excellent option for obtaining some basic soil information about native soils for a particular location. It is an online tool that allows the user to identify and delineate an area of interest using aerial map imagery. Once the area of interest has been defined, under the "soil map" tab, the soil type or types are identified. Clicking on the supplied hyperlinks will direct the user to where they can identify the Hydrologic Soil Group classification for each soil type and the erodibility constant (K value) for the soil type. However, please note there are limitations to this data, and a site-specific soils report is always preferable. One limitation is that it only provides data for native soils. If a project location has had significant import of soils in the past, the

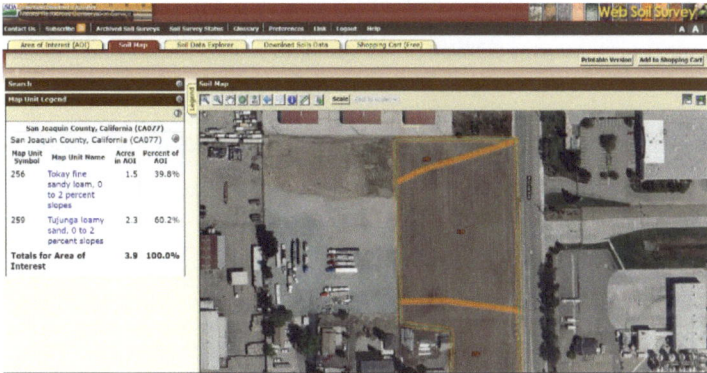

Figure 111 - The USDA Web Soil Survey online tool is a useful tool in helping SWPPP developers to identify the soil type(s) at the project site.

---

72   United States Department of Agriculture Natural Resource Conservation Service Online Web Soil Survey; https://websoilsurvey.nrcs.usda.gov/app/.

data provided by this online tool will not be accurate. I have also found that the Web Soil Survey does not have data for all locations. It is not uncommon to have a soil within an urbanized area to be classified as "Urban Land" with no other soil data available, which is most likely recognizing that this area has had significant disturbance to the native soils and imported nonnative soil types.

☑ **Field Reconnaissance**

Soil type, at least of the near surface soils, can also be determined by a site visit. The USDA has a flow chart [73] that can be used to determine soil textures in the field with some very simple manual exercises—all you need are your hands and a little bit of water.

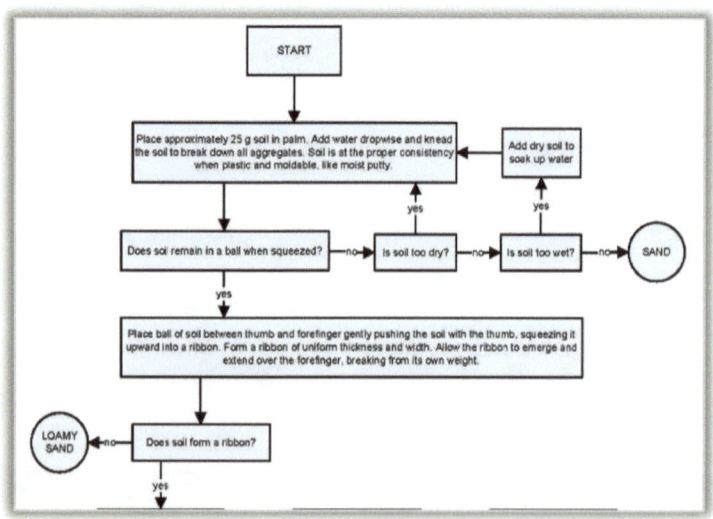

Figure 112 - Download and laminate this field guide to help you identify soil textures at your next site inspection. (USDA, NRCS Guide to Texture by Feel, https://www.nrcs.usda.gov/sites/default/files/2022-11/texture-by-feel.pdf.)

---

73   USDA, NRCS Guide to Texture by Feel, Modified from S.J. Thien. 1979. A flow diagram for teaching texture by feel analysis. Journal of Agronomic Education. 8:54–55, https://www.nrcs.usda.gov/sites/default/files/2022-11/texture-by-feel.pdf.

Connecting the Dots of SWPPP Development

Reading the owner's specifications: As we discussed in Chapter 4 regarding Standards for BMPs, it is absolutely necessary to review the owner's specifications prior to preparing the SWPPP. For some projects, the specifications don't exist or say very little that affects how the SWPPP is prepared and what it includes. But for other projects, the owner's specifications will have much information that will need to be embodied into the SWPPP. This information is not just limited to BMPs. When reviewing the specifications, look to see if any of the following items are addressed:

⇒ **Permit applicability and, for California projects, risk level.** Some specifications will state that the CGP does not apply to this project and it will provide the rationale. It may be that the project qualifies for the Small Construction Site Erosivity Waiver, has less than one acre of soil disturbance, or is occurring within a landfill or wastewater treatment plant. You might not agree with the owner's claim of exemption, but it is good to know their expectation and to start a dialogue with the owner's representative regarding permit applicability before diving into the SWPPP preparation.

⇒ **Project schedule and sequencing of events.** This information will need to be included in the SWPPP and can greatly affect how, when, and where BMPs are implemented.

⇒ **SWPPP status.** Sometimes the owner's specification will state that the construction SWPPP has already been prepared or will be prepared by others. Some specifications will include a prepared SWPPP or a skeleton SWPPP, which is a document that will need to be updated by the contractor's SWPPP preparer. The owner may also specify which SWPPP template needs to be utilized for the project.

⇒ **SWPPP approval process.** Specifications will often identify the submittal and approval process for the prepared SWPPP. It may require submission of the prepared plan a certain number of weeks before construction commencement and a certain quantity of hard copies to be delivered to the owner's reviewer. Some projects will require a pre-SWPPP development meeting and/or site visit.

⇒ **Other environmental permits.** The owner's specifications will usually call out other applicable environmental permits and provide copies of them. These permits should be reviewed for work restrictions, prohibitions, and BMP specifications. The environmental impact report or mitigated negative declaration prepared for the project as required by the California Environmental Quality Act (CEQA) or the National Environmental Policy Act (NEPA) may also be included with the owner's specifications and include prohibitions or mitigation measures relevant to the SWPPP.

⇒ **Site logistics.** Operating days and hours, access gates, haul roads, borrow pits, staging areas, environmentally sensitive areas, and other restricted areas may be identified in the owner's specifications. The SWPPP preparer will want to make sure that the SWPPP map and narrative are in line with these site features and restrictions.

⇒ **BMP requirements and restrictions.** The owner may require or prohibit the use of certain BMPs. More and more organizations are prohibiting the use of plastic or monofilament-containing BMPs. Owner specifications will commonly call out the type of erosion control to be utilized, including the hydraulic mulch brand and application rate; type and rate of seed applied; the inclusion of fertilizers, soil binders, or mycorrhizal fungi; and the use of jute netting or straw mulch as part of a two or three-step process. Some owners will also specify when BMPs should be applied and how often they should be inspected and/or maintained.

Connecting the Dots of SWPPP Development

Going to the site: One of the questions I get asked most often by new SWPPP preparers is *"Do I need to visit the site before writing the SWPPP?"* The answer to that question is: not necessarily. Now please don't misunderstand me. I think pre-SWPPP development site visits can be very useful and sometimes absolutely essential. It is interesting that they are not required by the 2022 California Construction General Permit even though several other field visits are required to be performed by the Qualified SWPPP Developer (QSD) after the project is permitted. So I have developed some rules of thumb for when I personally perform pre-SWPPP development site reconnaissance.

- ☑ **When available online or provided imagery does not allow the project to be clearly viewed from above.** This may be because the site is covered with trees and cannot be viewed because of the tree canopy. It may also be due to poor or missing imagery. The area depicted in Figure 113 is mostly obscured by the tree canopy. However, we can detect that there are one or more water bodies present and some changes in topography. This site would merit a pre-SWPPP development site visit.

Figure 113 - Tree canopy can obscure the view and hide details that a SWPPP developer needs to identify and address. (Photo credit: Google Earth™, 2024)

☑ **When topography is complex.** Even with a good set of civil drawings, at some locations, it may be difficult to perceive the scale of the project or the nuances of the changes in terrain. I have found that a site visit can greatly assist in comprehending the civil plans. This can be a time saver for a SWPPP preparer, especially when the site is not too far away. A quick trip to the site will enable the preparer to understand the location features more easily and will, likely, reduce the overall time needed for the plan preparation.

Figure 114 - Complex topography as shown in this aerial photo can more readily be comprehended when the SWPPP preparer's boots are on the ground. (Photo credit: Google Earth™, 2024)

☑ **When there are significant environmental receptors.** Whenever the stakes are high environmentally, that is when a pre-SWPPP development site visit is crucial. If there are significant environmental receptors on or adjacent to the site, it is worth taking the extra time and energy to make sure that adequate protection measures are included in the SWPPP. Significant environmental receptors would include, but not be limited to, bodies of water, Areas of Special Biological Significance[74], sites with suspected threatened or endangered species, locations with historic or cultural archaeological resources, locations with known environmental contamination (natural or human-caused), and recreational or protected open space areas.

Figure 115 - Some places absolutely require a pre-SWPPP development site visit... especially national parks! (Photo credit: Andrew Teravskis)

---

74   Area of Special Biological Significance (ASBS). In California, these are thirty-four ocean areas monitored and maintained for water quality by the State Water Resources Control Board. ASBS cover much of the length of California's coastal waters. They support an unusual variety of aquatic life and often host unique individual species. ASBS are basic building blocks for a sustainable, resilient coastal environment and economy. For a map of these locations, refer to: https://www.waterboards.ca.gov/water_issues/programs/ocean/asbs_map.shtml.

CRUNCH THE NUMBERS

Just as a dot-to-dot drawing has numbers that need to be connected, so does an effective construction SWPPP. Although you may not need a college degree in mathematics, there is a certain amount of number crunching needed in order to be able to understand the site's dynamics and runoff characteristics. Now, don't worry you may not need to break out your old trigonometry and calculus books. Some of the number crunching will involve a calculator, but much of it is simply knowing where to look to find the answers.

Area: Project area is obviously quite important, especially when we are comparing it to the permit requirements. One acre (43,560 ft^2) or more of soil disturbance will require permit coverage. But this is just for starters when it comes to our analysis of project areas. SWPPP writers will also need to be able to identify drainage management areas (DMAs), impervious and permeable areas, completed or stabilized areas, and calculate the areas where erosion controls will need to be applied. As illustrated in Figure 94, Google Earth is a powerful tool the SWPPP writer can use to calculate the area of the site or existing site features. Civil drawings, post-construction storm water control plans, and DMA maps are also good resources for identifying the areas of the pre-construction and post-construction conditions.

The surface land use type and runoff coefficients: If there are three 1,000 ft^2 plots of land all on a consistent 2% slope and one is covered with asphalt (A), the second is bare dirt (B), and the third is vegetated with native grasses (C), which one would produce the most amount of discharge? Well, intuitively, we would answer the paved plot, right? But why does it have a larger volume of discharge? It is because of the runoff coefficient. Of the other two remaining plots, which one would produce the least amount of discharge? This is where we need to look at a few other factors to help identify the runoff coefficient.

Figure 116 - Which one will produce the most runoff? Which will produce the least amount of runoff?

Surface covering or land use will certainly affect the amount of runoff; but so will the slope and the type of soil. When we were doing our homework to prepare for the SWPPP development, we learned that different soils can be categorized in one of the four Hydrologic Soil Groups: A, B, C, or D. HSG "A" soils have the highest infiltration rates and HSG "D" soils have the lowest infiltration rates. Using Table 12, a more precise runoff coefficient can be determined if we know the soil type and the slope percentage. So, if the plot of bare soil is "rough," meaning not compacted but broken up, the runoff coefficient would range from 0.20 to 0.50. The vegetated plot, if it were planted on a steep slope on "heavy soil" (meaning silty or clayey soil) would have a coefficient range of 0.25 to 0.35 and could produce the same amount of runoff as the unvegetated plot.

Table 12 – Runoff Coefficients for Various Surface and Soil Type[75]

Land Use	Runoff Coefficient (C)
Business:	
Downtown areas	0.70-0.95
Neighborhood areas	0.50-0.70
Residential:	
Single-family areas	0.30-0.50
Multi units, detached	0.40-0.60
Multi units, attached	0.60-0.75
Suburban	0.25-0.40
Lawns:	
Sandy soil, flat, 2%	0.05-0.10
Sandy soil, avg., 2-7%	0.10-0.15
Sandy soil, steep, 7%	0.15-0.20
Heavy soil, flat, 2%	0.13-0.17
Heavy soil, avg., 2-7%	0.18-0.22
Heavy soil, steep, 7%	0.25-0.35
Agricultural land:	
Bare packed soil	
• Smooth	0.30-0.60
• Rough	0.20-0.50
Cultivated rows	
• Heavy soil, no crop	0.30-0.60
• Heavy soil, with crop	0.20-0.50
• Sandy soil, no crop	0.20-0.40
• Sandy soil, with crop	0.10-0.25
Pasture	
• Heavy soil	0.15-0.45
• Sandy soil	0.05-0.25
• Woodlands	0.05-0.25

---

75   California State Water Resources Control Board (Water Board), The Clean Water Team Guidance Compendium for Watershed Monitoring and Assessment State Water Resources Control Board 5.1.3 FS-(RC) 2011; https://www.waterboards.ca.gov/water_issues/programs/swamp/docs/cwt/guidance/513.pdf.

Land Use	Runoff Coefficient (C) [76]
Industrial: Light areas Heavy areas	0.50–0.80 0.60–0.90
Streets: Asphaltic Concrete Brick	0.70–0.95 0.80–0.95 0.70–0.85
Unimproved areas	0.10–0.30
Drives and walks	0.75–0.85
Roofs	0.75–0.95
Parks, cemeteries	0.10–0.25
Playgrounds	0.20–0.35
Railroad yard areas	0.20–0.40

---

76 The Water Board notes, "The designer must use judgment to select the appropriate "C" value within the range. Generally, larger areas with permeable soils, flat slopes and dense vegetation should have the lowest "C" values. Smaller areas with dense soils, moderate to steep slopes, and sparse vegetation should assigned the highest "C" values."

Runoff coefficients are typically provided for an entire property. Therefore, if the developed project site has three different types of land uses or surface coverings, it will be necessary to do some averaging. Let's suppose we have a site with the three surface coverings shown in Figure 116, the site has a consistent 2% slope, and it is situated on sandy soils. What would be the average runoff coefficient (C_{avg}) if there were four acres of "A" asphalt, two acres of "B" bare smooth soil, and four acres of "C" native grass cover? For this exercise, we will use the higher coefficient value provided in the ranges presented in Table 12. We will need to calculate a weighted average by doing the following:

Equation 3 - Weighted Runoff Coefficient

$$C_{avg} = \left(C_A \frac{Acres\ A}{Total\ Acres}\right) + \left(C_B \frac{Acres\ B}{Total\ Acres}\right) + \left(C_C \frac{Acres\ C}{Total\ Acres}\right)$$

$$C_{avg} = \left(0.95 \frac{4\ acres}{10\ acres}\right) + \left(0.60 \frac{2\ acres}{10\ acres}\right) + \left(0.10 \frac{4\ acres}{10\ acres}\right) = 0.54$$

The weighted average runoff coefficient is usually identified for the pre-construction and post-construction conditions.

Storm water runoff volume: Over the years, I have had more than one contractor tell me that their solution to managing the storm water runoff from their completely exposed site was renting a 20,000-gallon mobile temporary tank. I am sure they honestly believed that a single tank would more than accommodate the site's runoff. I would then ask, "How big is the site's drainage area?"

"Five acres," they might respond.

Connecting the Dots of SWPPP Development

While pulling out a calculator and crunching some numbers, I would say "Well, we are expecting an inch of rain in the next forty-eight hours...so, five acres, with a runoff coefficient of 0.54 for roughened soils would mean...you will need about four 20,000-gallon tanks."

Calculating the anticipated runoff volume (V_{runoff}) will help a SWPPP writer be able to understand the magnitude of the discharge and to size storm water control measures. The calculation is as follows:

Equation 4 - Runoff volume

$$V_{\text{runoff in gallons}} = \text{Acres} \times 43{,}560 \text{ ft}^2/\text{acre} \times \left(\frac{\text{inches of rain}}{12 \text{ inches/ft.}}\right) \times 7.48 \text{ gal./ft}^3 \times C_{avg}$$

$$V_{\text{runoff in acre-feet}} = \text{Acres} \times \left(\frac{\text{inches of rain}}{12 \text{ inches/ft.}}\right) \times C_{avg}$$

Where C_{avg} is from Equation 3. The "inches of rain" is dependent on the actual forecast, or it can be set as 1 so as to determine the runoff volume for each inch of rain. Equation 4 provides two different methods so that the units of measurement for V_{runoff} can be calculated either as gallons or acre-feet.[77]

Runoff time of concentration: From the time it starts to rain to the moment discharge begins in earnest, how long will it take? Is it immediate? Or will it take hours to begin? According to the United States Department of Agriculture, "Time of concentration (Tc) is the time required for runoff to travel from the hydraulically most distant point in the watershed to the outlet. The hydraulically most distant point is the point with the longest travel time to the watershed outlet, and not necessarily the point with the longest flow distance to the outlet. Time of

---

77   One acre-foot of water is the equivalent volume as would be one acre (43,560 ft²) covered with exactly 1 foot of water, which equals 43,560 ft³, or approximately 325,829 gallons.

concentration is generally applied only to surface runoff and may be computed using many different methods. Time of concentration will vary depending upon slope and character of the watershed and the flow path."[78] There are several empirical equation options for estimating Time of Concentration (Tc), and calculating the actual pre- and post-project values should be left to a professional engineer. A SWPPP developer would be best served by obtaining this information from the project's civil engineer. However, for a relatively quick and easy estimation of the Time of Concentration (expressed in hours), the Watershed Lag Method[79] may be utilized as shown in Equation 5.

Equation 5 - Time of Concentration

$$Tc = \frac{\ell^{0.8}(S+1)^{0.7}}{1,140 Y^{0.5}}$$

Where:

ℓ = flow length (feet), defined as the longest path along which water flows in the watershed to the outlet (or in context of the project, the length from the farthest point on the project to the discharge point)

Y = the average land slope percentage (feet rise/feet run or %). It can be determined by drawing three or four lines on a topographic map perpendicular to the contour lines and determining the average weighted slope of these lines.

S = the maximum potential retention (inches) = (1,000 / cn') − 10

cn' = the retardance factor, which is a measure of surface conditions relating to the rate of runoff. Low retardance factors are associated

---

[78] United States Department of Agriculture, Natural Resources Conservation Service, Part 630 Hydrology National Engineering Handbook, Chapter 15, Time of Concentration, May 2010, https://irrigationtoolbox.com/NEH/Part630_Hydrology/NEH630-ch15draft.pdf.
[79] Ibid. Section 630.1502 (a), p. 15–5

Connecting the Dots of SWPPP Development

with rough surfaces having high degrees of flow retardance, or surfaces over which flow will be impeded. High retardance factors are associated with smooth surfaces having low degrees of flow retardance, or surfaces over which flow moves rapidly. The USDA states that the retardance factor (cn') is approximately the same as the hydrologic curve number (CN), which can be used as a surrogate value for cn'. Curve numbers[80] are somewhat similar in concept to runoff coefficients in that they indicate the amount of runoff for certain types of surface cover / land usage and hydrologic soil groups. Once a curve number has been established, it is used to translate rainfall amounts into runoff volumes. Table 13 contains some curve numbers for a variety of common soil covers.

Table 13 - Runoff Curve Numbers [81]

Land Use / Soil Cover	CN for Hydrologic Soil Group			
	A	B	C	D
Bare soil	77	86	91	94
Vegetated open space <50% ground cover 50-75% ground cover >75% ground cover	68 49 39	79 69 61	86 79 74	89 84 80
Wooded or orchard	36	60	73	79
Paved	98	98	98	98
Commercial development	89	92	94	95
Residential 1/4-acre lots	61	75	83	87

---

80   For more information on curve numbers, refer to USDA, NRCS, Part 630 Hydrology National Engineering Handbook, Chapter 9, Hydrologic Soil-Cover Complexes, July 2004, https://irrigationtoolbox.com/NEH/Part630_Hydrology/H_210_630_09.pdf
81   Ibid.

So let's determine the Time of Concentration (Tc), expressed in hours, for a typical project site. In this case, we want to calculate the value for the pre-construction condition as shown in Figure 117. The site has a single discharge point on the east end. There is 1 acre of existing paved roadway, 0.5 acres of 1/4-acre residential lots, 3 acres of wooded terrain, and 7 acres of >75% grass-covered open space. Assume the flow length (ℓ) is 1,000 feet, the average slope percentage is 8%, and the soils are HSG "C."

Figure 117 - What is the Time of Concentration for this project watershed?
(Photo credit: Google Earth™, 2024)

Putting it together:

ℓ = 1,000 feet

Y = 8% (or the decimal values of 0.08 used in the equation)

S = (1,000 / CN_{avg}) - 10 = (1,000/76.2) - 10 = 3.12 inches

As we did with the runoff coefficient, we had to calculate the weighted average CN value, which we did using the information on Table 13.

Connecting the Dots of SWPPP Development

$$CN_{avg} = \left(CN_{roadway}\frac{Acres\ Roadway}{Total\ Acres}\right) + \left(CN_{homes}\frac{Acres\ Homes}{Total\ Acres}\right) + \left(CN_{woods}\frac{Acres\ Woods}{Total\ Acres}\right) + \left(CN_{open\ space}\frac{Acres\ open\ space}{Total\ Acres}\right)$$

$$CN_{avg} = \left(98\frac{1\ acre}{11.5\ acres}\right) + \left(83\frac{0.5\ acres}{11.5\ acres}\right) + \left(73\frac{3\ acres}{11.5\ acres}\right) + \left(74\frac{7\ acres}{11.5\ acres}\right) = 76.2$$

Now by inserting the values of these variables into Equation 5, we get:

$$T_c = \frac{\ell^{0.8}(S+1)^{0.7}}{1{,}140 Y^{0.5}} = \frac{(1{,}000\ ft)^{0.8}(3.12\ inches + 1)^{0.7}}{1{,}140(0.08)^{0.5}} = 2.12\ \text{hours}$$

This tells us that it will take a little more than two hours for runoff to travel from the farthest point on the project to the discharge point.

Peak flow rates: Storm events resemble bell curves both when looking at graphs of their forecast and the resulting runoff. Storms typically start slow, build to a crescendo, and then taper off. Discharge follows suit, usually delayed by a lag time and the time of concentration that we evaluated in the previous section. Storm water conveyances and treatment devices, such as low impact development (LID) techniques, are typically sized to accommodate the peak discharge flow rate (Q_p) expressed in ft³/second or cfs. To demonstrate the proper utilization of LID measures, we will often compare the Q_p of the pre-development conditions to that of the post-development conditions. If the post Q_p is equal to or less than the pre Q_p, then we have demonstrated that the LID measures have successfully mitigated the hydrologic impacts of the development. The formula for calculating peak flow is known as the Rational Equation.

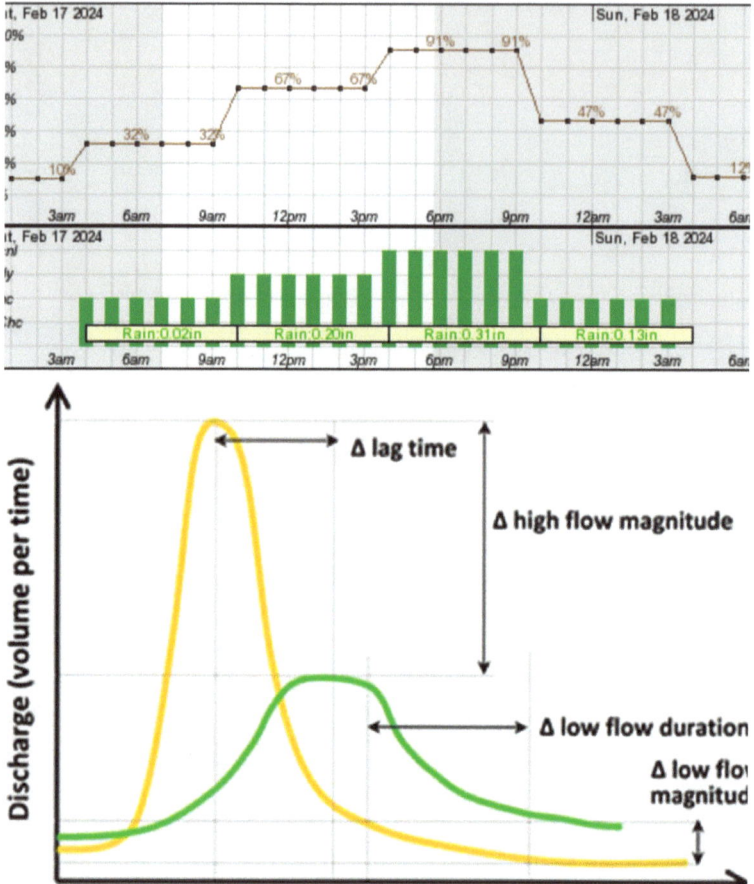

Figure 118 - Storm events look like bell curves both on graphs of their forecast and runoff. The forecast imagery is from the National Weather Service. The hydrograph is from the USEPA. https://www.epa.gov/caddis-vol2/urbanization-hydrology

Equation 6 - Rational Equation $\quad Q_p = CiA$

Where:

Q_p = Peak flow, ft³/sec or cfs

C = Runoff coefficient (dimensionless)

i = Rainfall intensity, in/hr (for a specified storm frequency and duration)

A = Drainage area, acres

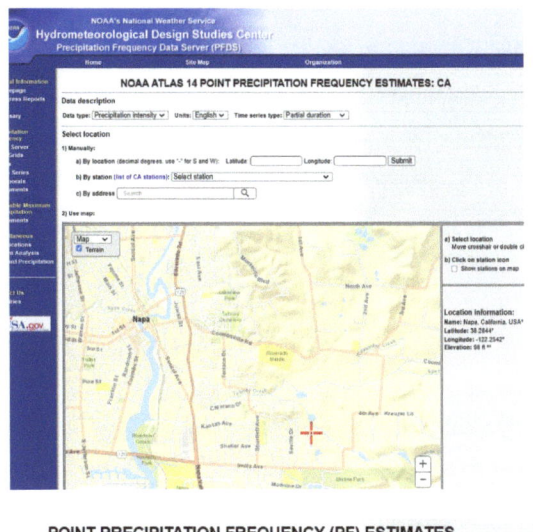

Figure 119 - The National Weather Service look up tool to find rainfall intensities for a variety of recurrence intervals and durations. https://hdsc.nws.noaa.gov/pfds/

The variables "C" and "A" we have already discussed and have seen how to derive them. But let's explore the "i" variable—for rainfall intensity. This variable will need to be defined by the user. It represents the top of the bell curve for whatever size of a storm event we want to specify. It is the point in the storm, when it is really coming down at maximum inches/hour. This value will not only be different for different types of storms based on their recurrence intervals and durations but also for different locations. For example, utilizing the National Weather Service's Hydrometeorological Design Studies Center Precipitation Frequency Data Server[82], we can look up values for a variety of storm sizes for locations all across the United States. For the example project depicted in Figure 117, using Equation 6 let's calculate the peak flow rate (Q_p) for the pre-development conditions.

$$Q_p = CiA$$

The weighted average runoff coefficient (C_{avg}) is calculated as follows:
Area (A) = 11.5 acres

$$C_{avg} = \left(C_{roadway} \frac{Acres\ Roadway}{Total\ Acres}\right) + \left(C_{homes} \frac{Acres\ Homes}{Total\ Acres}\right) + \left(C_{woods} \frac{Acres\ Woods}{Total\ Acres}\right) + \left(C_{open\ space} \frac{Acres\ open\ space}{Total\ Acres}\right)$$

Therefore, using the values from Table 12:

$$C_{avg} = \left(0.95 \frac{1\ acre}{11.5\ acres}\right) + \left(0.40 \frac{0.5\ acres}{11.5\ acres}\right) + \left(0.25 \frac{3\ acres}{11.5\ acres}\right) + \left(0.45 \frac{7\ acres}{11.5\ acres}\right) = 0.44$$

Intensity "i" selected from the National Weather Service for a two-year, twenty-four-hour event for this location is equal to 0.117 inches/hour.

Therefore:

$$Q_P = CiA = 0.44 \times 0.117 \frac{inches}{hr.} \times 11.5\ acres = 0.59\ ft^3/sec$$

---

[82] National Weather Service's Hydrometeorological Design Studies Center Precipitation Frequency Data Server (PFDS) online look up tool https://hdsc.nws.noaa.gov/pfds/.

Connecting the Dots of SWPPP Development

Soil loss: The point of a construction SWPPP is to not only to manage storm water (as we have seen illustrated in the previous equations) but to control erosion on construction projects. How do we know if we are successfully controlling soil particles from becoming detached? Sure, we can visually observe for the effects of erosion as discussed in Chapter 2. But it would be nice to quantify how much eroded. Better yet, it would be hugely beneficial if we could predict how much erosion or soil loss might occur on a project. As it turns out, we can. The USDA has been developing soil loss prediction tools since the days of the Dust Bowl as a part of its soil conservation program. In the 1930s and 1940s, scientists and agronomists working for the USDA started to note factors that played into erosion such as soil type, length and steepness of slopes, location, and the extent that soil was exposed to the elements. This led to the development of several early tools to allow for the mathematical prediction of soil loss based on empirical data (data based on field observations and experience rather than scientific theory or logic). Because of the empirical approach to developing a soil loss prediction tool, the tool has been refined throughout the subsequent decades to what it is today, the **Revised Universal Soil Loss Equation (RUSLE)**.[83]

The mission of the USDA is obviously to assist farmers with soil conservation and productivity, but in the past couple of decades another group has benefited from their efforts—the construction industry. The USEPA and many state agencies, such as the California State Water Resources Control Board, have noticed the practical benefits of RUSLE to projects with soil disturbance and have incorporated it into the storm water NPDES permits in a variety of ways. In California, RUSLE is used to determine the risk level of a construction project, quantify the protective benefits achieved in the utilization vegetative buffers and BMPs, assist

---

83 United States Department of Agriculture, Agriculture Research Service, Agriculture Handbook Number 703, Predicting Soil Erosion by Water: A Guide to Conservation Planning with the Revised Universal Soil Loss Equation (RUSLE), K.G. Renard, G.R Foster, G.A. Weesies, D.K. McCool, and D.C. Yoder, January 1997 https://www3.epa.gov/npdes/pubs/ruslech2.pdf.

with the evaluation of compliance with various TMDLs, and assess whether site stabilization has been adequately achieved.

There are various soil loss prediction tools available today to use in assessing erosion and erosion control efforts. Although we will predominantly focus on RUSLE (or RUSLE 1 as it is sometimes referred to), other tools include RUSLE2[84], which is a computer modeling software based on the RUSLE equation, and the Modified Universal Soil Loss Equation (MUSLE).[85] These tools can be beneficial and sometimes required by regulatory agencies to be utilized for site management. **The Revised Universal Soil Loss Equation (RUSLE)** is as follows:

Equation 7 – Revised Universal Soil Loss Equation $A = (R)(K)(LS)(C)(P)$

Where:

- A = the average amount of soil loss due to raindrop, sheet, and rill erosion expressed in tons/acre/year
- R = the rainfall-runoff erosivity factor
- K = the soil erodibility factor
- LS = the length and steepness of slope factor
- C = the cover factor (Raindrop BMPs)
- P = the soil management practice factor

---

[84] The official USDA Natural Resources Conservation Service RUSLE2 program can be downloaded from: https://fargo.nserl.purdue.edu/rusle2_dataweb/RUSLE2_Index.htm A Caltrans version of RUSLE2 can be downloaded from: https://dot.ca.gov/programs/design/hydraulics-stormwater/bsddd-erosion-prediction-with-rusle2.

[85] Modified Universal Soil Loss Equation: $T=95(V \times Q_p)^{0.56} \times K \times LS \times C \times P$, where the "R" erosivity factor in RUSLE is replaced with "$95(V \times Qp)^{0.56}$", V is volume of runoff in acre-feet as shown in Equation 4, and Q_p is peak flow as shown in Equation 6; for a specified storm size, MUSLE calculates the amount of eroded soil that settles out at a specific point in the watershed that is remote from the origin of the detached particles and includes erosion from slopes, channels, and mass wasting minus (through geometry calculations) any sediment deposited before reaching the point of interest. For more information, see Estimating Watershed Runoff and Sediment Yield Using a GIS Interface to Curve Number and MUSLE Models By Jacek Blaszczynski, Physical Scientist, BLM, National Science and Technology Center, https://www.govinfo.gov/content/pkg/GOVPUB-I53-PURL-gpo129658/pdf/GOVPUB-I53-PURL-gpo129658.pdf

Let's evaluate each one of these variables.

Rainfall Erosivity Factor: According to the USEPA, *"Erosivity is the term used to describe the potential for soil to wash off disturbed, de-vegetated earth during storms. The potential for erosion is in part determined by the soil type and geology of the site. For instance, dense, clay-like soils on a glacial plain will erode less readily when it rains than will sandy soils on the side of a hill. Another important factor is the amount and force of precipitation expected during the time the earth will be exposed."*[86] It has been said that if there were two construction projects where everything is the same (size, soil type, slope, and site activities) except for the location, it would be the erosivity "R" factor that would make the difference in the amount of soil loss experienced at the two sites. To illustrate, if one project is located in Southern California's Orange County, and the other identical project is located in Northern California's Stanislaus County, which project would experience greater soil loss? Southern California would have more soil loss because, in Anaheim, the annual R factor is 40.24, while the Northern California project in Modesto has an annual R factor of 28.68. This is also illustrated by looking at the twenty-four-hour, twenty-five-year storm volumes for these two locations. In Anaheim, it is 4.82 inches, but in Modesto, it is 2.52 inches. Although the two locations receive just about the same amount of annual rainfall (Anaheim, 13.43 inches and Modesto, 13.11 inches), the erosivity is higher in Anaheim because

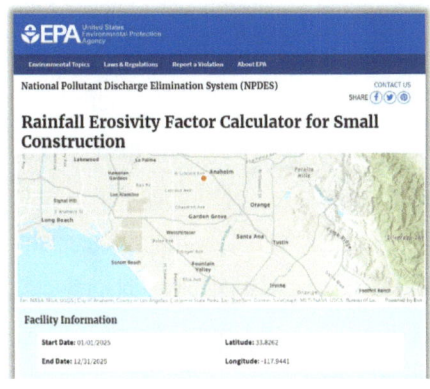

Figure 120 - The USEPA's online Rainfall Erosivity Factor Calculator is a convenient way of determining the "R" factor. To identify R, you only need to know the location and starting and ending dates for the project. https://lew.epa.gov/

---

86 United States Environmental Protection Agency, Office of Water, EPA 833-F-00-014, March 2012, Stormwater Phase II Final Rule, Construction Rainfall Erosivity Waiver; https://www.epa.gov/sites/default/files/2015-10/documents/fact3-1.pdf.

when it rains there it really comes down with lots of energy thanks to the Pacific Ocean's "Pineapple Express" effect. Modesto receives about the same amount of rainfall, but the storms don't pack the same punch as they do down south.

To determine the "R" factor for a construction project, only three pieces of information are needed. The start date of earth disturbing activities, the project's stabilization date, and the location. Using these three pieces of data, the erosivity can be determined either manually following the USEPA's guidelines[87] or by using the USEPA's online calculator.[88] The USEPA and the California Water Board allow smaller construction projects, occurring exclusively during dry periods of the year, to apply for an Erosivity Waiver. In order to qualify for the waiver, the project must have less than five acres of soil disturbance and must occur within a period of time that has an R factor value less than 5. Projects that qualify for the waiver are not required to file for coverage under the CGP or to prepare a construction SWPPP.

A difference in how the USEPA and the California Water Board handle the "R"

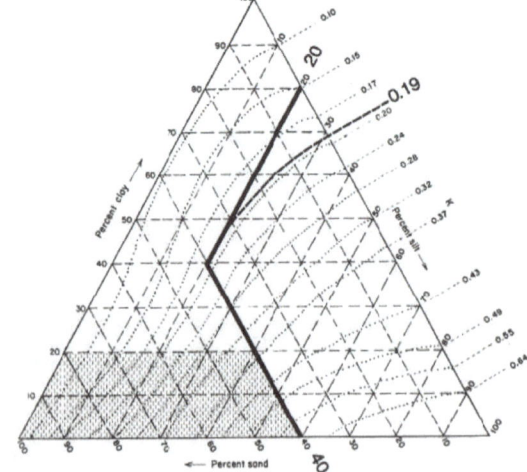

Figure 121 - The Erikson Triangle Nomograph can be used along with site-specific soil texture percentages to determine the K factor. (Source: Attachment D.1 California Construction General Permit Order 2022-0057-DWQ)

---

87   Ibid.
88   USEPA Rainfall Erosivity Factor Calculator for Small Construction, https://lew.epa.gov/.

Connecting the Dots of SWPPP Development

factor is in the time period used to calculate the value. The USEPA states that the maximum period of time for the R factor is one year. In fact, even if you enter a longer period of time into the USEPA's online calculator, it will only give a value for a one-year period of time. However, the California Water Board requires the R factor to be calculated for the entire duration of the project. If the project is exactly three years long, the California R value will be three times the USEPA annual value. If the project is three and a half years long, then it would be three times the USEPA annual value plus the R value for the remaining six-month period.

Soil Erodibility (K) Factor: When discussing wind erosion in Chapter 2, we learned that of the three basic soil textures (sand, silt, and clay), silt is the most erodible. You might recall the reason is that it is a much smaller particle than sand and is the easiest to mobilize and be carried away by water. Clay and sand will certainly erode, but they are less erodible because sand tends to have a bigger, heavier particle size and will generally settle out almost immediately. Clay, although having a smaller particle size than silt, has another property that makes it less erodible: it is cohesive. It wants to stick together when wetted. There are two basic ways to determine the "K" factor for soils. The first is to use the soils report that we discussed previously when we were doing our homework for the SWPPP preparation. The soils report will often provide the percent sand, silt, and clay of site's soil. This site-specific data can then be used with the Erikson Triangle nomograph.[89] As shown in Figure 121, soil that is 40% sand, 40% clay, and 20% silt, per the nomograph, has a K value of 0.19.

---

89 The Erickson Triangle Nomograph is provided in the California Construction General Permit as a means for determining the K factor using site-specific soil texture data. https://www.waterboards.ca.gov/water_issues/programs/stormwater/construction/docs/2022-0057-dwq-with-attachments/cgp2022_att_d1.pdf

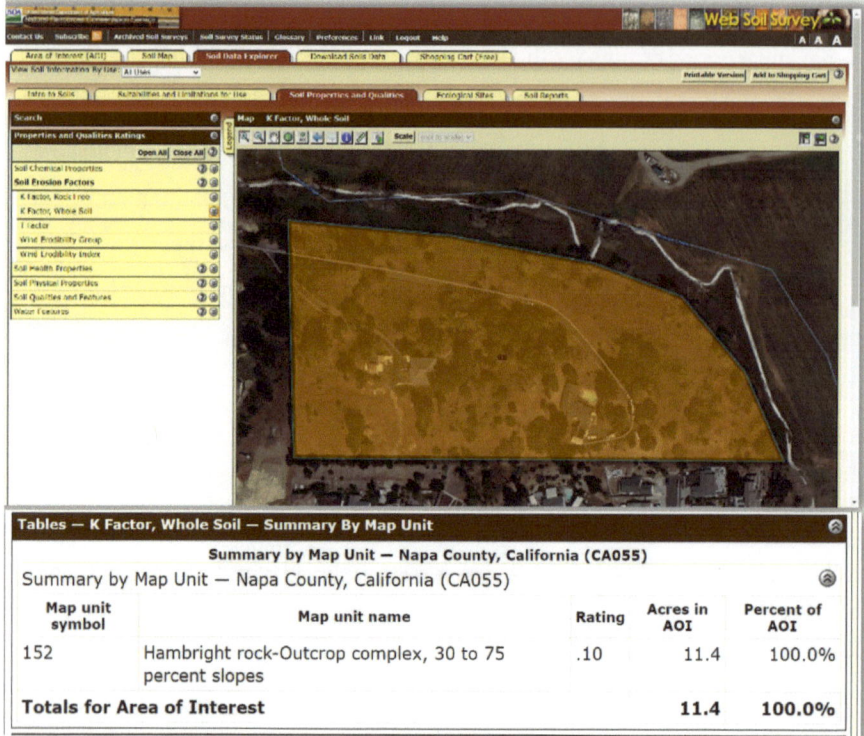

Figure 122 - The USDA NRCS Websoil Survey can also be used to determine the K factor for soil types present on a construction site.

Another way to find the K value for a soil is to utilize the online Web Soil Survey[90]. After defining the area of interest, pull down menus under "Soil Properties and Qualities" and "Erosion Factors" will direct the user to the erodibility K factor for the native soil.

For projects in California, the State Water Board provides one additional way of determining the K factor for a particular location. The Water Board maintains an online, interactive Geographical Information System (GIS) mapping tool[91] to view K factors for locations throughout the state. The data used for this

---

90   USDA NRCS Websoil Survey: https://websoilsurvey.nrcs.usda.gov/app/
91   California Water Board's Soil Erodibility (K) Factor Map Tool, https://gispublic.waterboards.ca.gov/portal/home/item.html?id=59bb6ae7996d415bb43d13420212a823

Connecting the Dots of SWPPP Development

tool is the same used to populate Notice of Intent (NOI) applications on the state's Stormwater Multiple Application and Report Tracking System (SMARTS)[92] website. It is important to note that these three methods do not always produce the same, or even similar, values. The K factor in Figure 122 using the Websoil Survey is 0.10, and the K factor in Figure 123 using the SMARTS GIS mapping tool is 0.32.

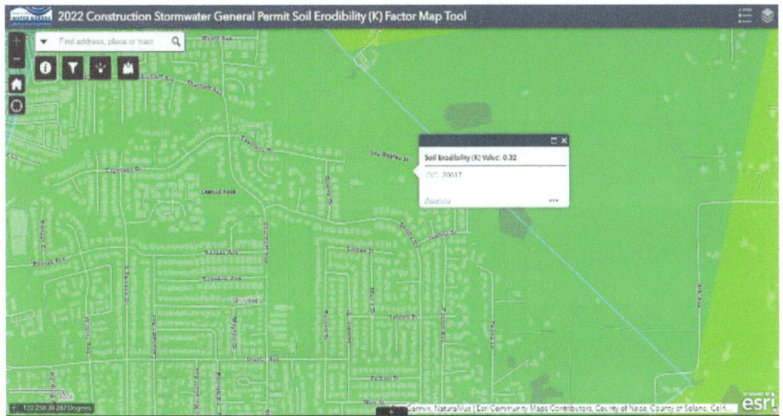

Figure 123 - The California State Water Board has an online interactive GIS mapping tool to be able to find K values for locations throughout the State

Length of Slope and Steepness of Slope (LS) Factor: Most people know intuitively that the longer a slope and the steeper it is, the more erosion will occur. In Chapter 2, we saw the reason for this. Steep, long slopes mean fast moving water, which causes erosion. The "LS" factor is the metric used to take into account in the soil loss prediction the length and steepness of the slope. Also, LS is not two variables but one. It is not L times S, but just one single variable like "X" or "Y." Both letters are used for this variable to remind us of what it represents. There may be multiple slopes on a construction project, therefore, the LS is going to need to be an average of all slopes within the boundary for which we are wanting to predict soil loss. There are two ways in which the LS value can be calculated.

---

92   https://smarts.waterboards.ca.gov/

The first, as we just mentioned, is to take a sitewide average of the sheet flow lengths and the slope percentages. This data is then evaluated with reference tables that were originally produced in the USDA's Agriculture Handbook Number 703.[93] However, a more convenient reference table, based on this same USDA reference, is included in the California Construction General Permit[94] as shown in Figure 124.

Sheet Flow Length (ft)	Average Watershed Slope (percent)										Sheet Flow Length (ft)	Average Watershed Slope (percent)								
	0.2	0.5	1.0	2.0	3.0	4.0	5.0	6.0	8.0	10.0		12.0	14.0	16.0	20.0	25.0	30.0	40.0	50.0	60.0
<3	0.05	0.07	0.09	0.13	0.17	0.20	0.23	0.26	0.32	0.35	<3	0.36	0.38	0.39	0.41	0.45	0.48	0.53	0.58	0.63
6	0.05	0.07	0.09	0.13	0.17	0.20	0.23	0.26	0.32	0.37	6	0.41	0.45	0.49	0.56	0.64	0.72	0.85	0.97	1.07
9	0.05	0.07	0.09	0.13	0.17	0.20	0.23	0.26	0.32	0.38	9	0.45	0.51	0.56	0.67	0.80	0.91	1.13	1.31	1.47
12	0.05	0.07	0.09	0.13	0.17	0.20	0.23	0.26	0.32	0.39	12	0.47	0.55	0.62	0.76	0.93	1.08	1.37	1.62	1.84
15	0.05	0.07	0.09	0.13	0.17	0.20	0.23	0.26	0.32	0.40	15	0.49	0.58	0.67	0.84	1.04	1.24	1.59	1.91	2.19
25	0.05	0.07	0.10	0.16	0.21	0.26	0.31	0.36	0.45	0.57	25	0.71	0.85	0.98	1.24	1.56	1.86	2.41	2.91	3.36
50	0.05	0.08	0.13	0.21	0.30	0.38	0.46	0.54	0.70	0.91	50	1.15	1.40	1.64	2.10	2.67	3.22	4.24	5.16	5.97
75	0.05	0.08	0.14	0.25	0.36	0.47	0.58	0.69	0.91	1.20	75	1.54	1.87	2.21	2.86	3.67	4.44	5.89	7.20	8.37
100	0.05	0.09	0.15	0.28	0.41	0.55	0.68	0.82	1.10	1.46	100	1.88	2.31	2.73	3.57	4.59	5.58	7.44	9.13	10.63
150	0.05	0.09	0.17	0.33	0.50	0.68	0.86	1.05	1.43	1.88	150	2.51	3.09	3.68	4.85	6.30	7.70	10.35	12.75	14.89
200	0.06	0.10	0.18	0.37	0.57	0.79	1.02	1.25	1.72	2.34	200	3.07	3.81	4.56	6.04	7.88	9.67	13.07	16.16	18.92
250	0.06	0.10	0.19	0.40	0.64	0.89	1.16	1.43	1.99	2.72	250	3.60	4.48	5.37	7.16	9.38	11.55	15.67	19.42	22.78
300	0.06	0.10	0.20	0.43	0.69	0.98	1.28	1.60	2.24	3.09	300	4.09	5.11	6.15	8.23	10.81	13.35	18.17	22.57	26.51
400	0.06	0.11	0.22	0.48	0.80	1.14	1.51	1.90	2.70	3.75	400	5.01	6.30	7.60	10.24	13.53	16.77	22.95	28.60	33.67
600	0.06	0.12	0.24	0.56	0.96	1.42	1.91	2.43	3.52	4.95	600	6.67	8.45	10.26	13.94	18.57	23.14	31.89	39.95	47.18
800	0.06	0.12	0.26	0.63	1.10	1.65	2.25	2.89	4.24	6.03	800	8.17	10.40	12.69	17.35	23.24	29.07	40.29	50.63	59.93
1000	0.06	0.13	0.27	0.69	1.23	1.86	2.55	3.30	4.91	7.02	1000	9.57	12.23	14.96	20.57	27.66	34.71	48.29	60.84	72.15

Figure 124 - Length-Slope (LS) Factor Table form Attachment D1 of the California 2022 CGP

Using the table in Figure 124, if a project has an average slope percentage of 2% and an average sheet flow length of 300 feet, the LS value would be 0.43.

Similar to the K factor, the California Water Board also has an online GIS mapping tool for LS.[95] This will provide average LS values for native conditions at locations throughout the state and is the same data that will be auto-populated onto the NOI form in SMARTS.

---

93 United States Department of Agriculture, Agriculture Research Service, Agriculture Handbook Number 703, Predicting Soil Erosion by Water: A Guide to Conservation Planning with the Revised Universal Soil Loss Equation (RUSLE), K.G. Renard, G.R Foster, G.A. Weesies, D.K. McCool, and D.C. Yoder, January 1997 https://www.ars.usda.gov/arsuserfiles/64080530/rusle/ah_703.pdf.
94 Length-Slope (LS) Factor Table for Construction Sites provided in the California Construction General Permit. https://www.waterboards.ca.gov/water_issues/programs/stormwater/construction/docs/2022-0057-dwq-with-attachments/cgp2022_att_d1.pdf.
95 California State Water Board Length-Slope (LS) Factor Map, https://gispublic.waterboards.ca.gov/portal/home/item.html?id=d71546a521ed4829aaa0e6c7b245fd56.

Connecting the Dots of SWPPP Development   305

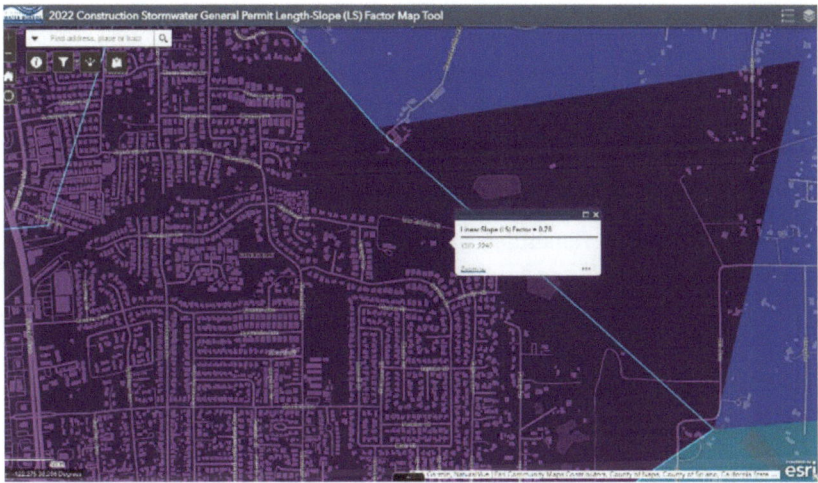

Figure 125 - California Water Board's online LS mapping tool where the LS value for this location is 0.78. But be careful! That might not be representative of the actual LS value.

Care needs to be taken when using data from this online GIS mapping tool because it is based on average native conditions for that region. However, the actual slopes may be considerably different. It may be the project is on a relatively flat parcel within a hilly or mountainous region in California. The LS shown on this mapping tool and auto-generated in SMARTS will be much larger than actual conditions and the value derived from the LS table (Figure 124). Conversely, if the project is within a relatively flat area, such as the California Central Valley, and the project involves constructing a highway overpass, the actual conditions would result in a much higher LS value than shown on the mapping tool or in SMARTS.

Before continuing with the other RUSLE variables, it is worth noting that, up until this point, the variables we have discussed are fairly inherent to the project. They can't be changed, or at least not altered very much or very easily. The R, K, and LS factors are what they are for a particular project occurring during a particular time at a particular location. But that's not true about the last two variables. Project operators can affect these last two variables and, thereby, reduce or increase soil loss. **This is an important dot to connect.** You have control over the outcome of the RUSLE equation, and it has everything to do with concepts we have covered in this book thus far.

Cover (C) factor: In Chapter 4, we discussed Raindrop BMPs, which are essentially things we do or install to keep Jr. Raindrop from making contact with bare soil. Methods to stop raindrop erosion could include maintaining an existing cover, performing soil disturbing activities when it is not likely to rain, installing a temporary effective soil cover, or reestablishing permanent final stabilization such as vegetation, crushed rock, or impervious surfaces. Now as you might imagine, some covers are better and more effective than others. Although they both would keep you relatively dry, you probably would get a little less wet sitting in a house than you would in a canvas tent. That is the idea when it comes to the "C" factor. Some methods are just better than others and, therefore, have a better C rating. Manufacturers of erosion control products such as mats, fabrics, and sprayed on mulches will often have a university or other storm water research organization evaluate the product and derive a C rating for it. However, when it comes to identifying C values for other more natural methods used on construction sites, there are not very many readily available resources for identifying these values. (RUSLE was primarily developed for agricultural soil conservation, and the available C factors tend to be specific to farming practices and certain types of crops.) The primary reference on C factors still remains the USDA's Agriculture Handbook Number 703[96] that we have already referenced several times in this section on the RUSLE equation. But authoritative sources of construction-related C factors are mostly limited to the State of Minnesota in their online Minnesota Stormwater Manual[97] and an online document that was created by the USEPA in

---

96   United States Department of Agriculture, Agriculture Research Service, Agriculture Handbook Number 703, Predicting Soil Erosion by Water: A Guide to Conservation Planning with the Revised Universal Soil Loss Equation (RUSLE), K.G. Renard, G.R Foster, G.A. Weesies, D.K. McCool, and D.C. Yoder, January 1997 https://www.ars.usda.gov/arsuserfiles/64080530/rusle/ah_703.pdf.

97   Minnesota Stormwater Manual, Examples of RUSLE cover management factors for construction sites, https://stormwater.pca.state.mn.us/index.php/Examples_of_RUSLE_cover_management_factors_for_construction_sites.

support of the proposed Construction General Permit.[98] Table 14 is a compilation of "C" factors from these two resources.

Table 14 – C Factors for Selected Construction-Related Cover Methods

Cover Method	C Factor[99]	Percent soil loss reduction
Bare soil (no cover)	1.0	0
Vegetated cover:		
Native vegetation (undisturbed)	0.01	99
Temporary ryegrass, 90% (perennial)	0.05	95
Temporary ryegrass, 90% (annuals)	0.10	90
Permanent seedlings (90%)	0.01	99
Sod (laid immediately)	0.01	99
Mulching (for slopes 2:1 or less)		
Straw (0.5 tons/acre)	0.25	75
Straw (1.0 tons/acre)	0.13	87
Straw (1.5 tons/acre)	0.07	93
Straw (2.0 tons/acre, a 1-2" thick layer)	0.02	98
Wood chips (6 tons/acre)	0.06	94
Wood cellulose (1.75 tons/acre)	0.10	90
Gravel (competent layer of 0.25 to 1.5" crushed stone)	0.05	95
Spray-on Products[100]		
Polyacrylamide (PAM)	0.13-0.65	35-87
Hydraulic mulch	0.1-0.6	40-90

---

98   USEPA, Appendix H – Compliance with the C-Factor Stabilization Criteria, https://www3.epa.gov/npdes/pubs/cgp_appendixh.pdf.
99   C-factors for slopes 5% or less.
100 Actual values will be product and application rate dependent. Refer to the manufacturer's testing literature.

Cover Method	C Factor[99]	Percent soil loss reduction
Rolled Erosion Control Blankets[89]		
Netless biodegradable woven, glued, or bond fibers	0.10	90
Jute or coir open weave mesh	0.10	90
Single-net biodegradable woven fibers	0.10	90
Double-net biodegradable woven fibers	0.10	90

Practice factor (P): There is one more part of the soil loss equation we need to consider: the "P" factor. Soil loss is, in part, dependent on what we do to the site. Over the years, I have had more than a couple of well-meaning contractors tell me how they prepared for the storm season by compacting and smoothing the dirt surface on their project. By now, you have learned why this is a mistake in controlling erosion. Velocity is our enemy when it comes to managing soil loss. The faster the water is moving (like over a compacted and smooth surface), the more particles will become detached and the more erosion the site will experience. That is why we use Slow-the-Flow BMPs to manage erosion and to facilitate sedimentation to occur where we want it to happen.

As was the case with C factors, it is also difficult to find an extensive and authoritative list of P factors for construction sites. The State of New York[101] and the State of Minnesota[102] have both published lists of P factors applicable to construction sites. Table 15 is a compilation of "P" factors from these two sources.

---

101   New York State Standards and Specifications for Erosion and Sediment Control, Department of Environmental Conservation, November 2016, Appendix A, Table A.8 references USDA-NRCS as the source, https://extapps.dec.ny.gov/fs/docs/pdf/erosionsediment_bluebook.pdf

102   Minnesota Stormwater Manual, Examples of RUSLE practice management factors for construction sites (which references the New York State Standards and Specification in the previous footnote), https://stormwater.pca.state.mn.us/index.php/Examples_of_RUSLE_practice_management_factors_for_construction_sites.

Connecting the Dots of SWPPP Development

Table 15 – P Factors for Construction Sites

Cover Method		P Factor	Percent soil loss reduction
Bare soil (no practice in place)		1.0	0
Freshly disked or rough irregular surface		0.9	10
Compacted smooth by equipment uphill and downhill		1.3	-30
Compacted smooth by equipment across the slope		1.2	-20
Contoured furrows (including track walking):			
Percent slope	Max. downslope length (ft.)		
1-2%	350	0.6	40
3-5%	250	0.5	50
6-8%	200	0.5	50
9-12%	125	0.6	40
13-16%	75	0.7	30
18-20%	60	0.8	20
>20%	50	0.8	20

To illustrate how the cover and practice factors will affect soil loss at a construction site, using the project depicted in Figure 122, Figure 123, and Figure 125, and an annual R factor of 75.3 for that location, we can plug in the values for R, K, and LS into the RUSLE equation:

Where:

      R = the rainfall-runoff erosivity factor = 75.3 (obtained for this location at https://lew.epa.gov/)
      K = the soil erodibility factor = 0.1 (Figure 122)
      LS = the length and steepness of slope factor = 0.78 (Figure 125)

Therefore, for an **_unprotected_** site with bare soil (C=1 per Table 14 and P=1 per Table 15):

    A = the average amount of soil loss due to raindrop, sheet, and rill erosion expressed in tons/acre/year

    = (R)(K)(LS)(C)(P) = (75.3)(0.1)(0.78)(1)(1) = 5.87 tons of annual soil loss/acre

But remember, this is soil loss value for an unprotected site based on the RUSLE variables that we have little or no control over. Now, let's do something about the remaining two variables for which we do have some control. Supposing we track walk all of the slopes so that we have an average P factor of 0.5 (Table 15), the predicted soil loss would now be reduced by 50%.

    A = (75.3)(0.1)(0.78)(1)(**0.50**) = 2.94 tons of annual soil loss/acre

Next let's cover the disturbed soil with 2 tons/acre of straw mulch. We would now have a C factor of 0.02 (Table 14) instead of 1, which dramatically changes the predicted soil loss:

    A = (75.3)(0.1)(0.78)(**0.02**)(0.50) = 0.06 tons of annual soil loss/acre

These two erosion control measures result in an overall 99% reduction in soil loss! Not bad results for running some equipment up and down a slope and covering the soil with straw mulch! But someone might ask, does this match up with reality? Yes, in my experience, it certainly does. Remember, the RUSLE formula is an empirical formula, meaning that it was derived from field observations, not theory. I have seen many sites, when track walked and covered with an effective soil cover (such as straw mulch), obtain an immediate improvement in water quality because the amount of soil particles becoming detached was greatly reduced.

Connecting the Dots of SWPPP Development

The California Water Board[103] requires the RUSLE equation to be utilized for one half of the risk determination. But the Water Board requires some differences in how RUSLE is utilized. For determining risk, the C and P factors must each equal 1.0 to simulate bare ground conditions. The state wants to know the risk level for a site where the soil is totally exposed. Second, as previously mentioned when we discussed the R factor, the State Water Board requires the R factor to be calculated for the entire project duration (from the start of construction to the approval of the Notice of Termination). The second half of the risk determination is based on the receiving water risk level. Water bodies impaired for turbidity or sediment or that have been designated with the beneficial uses of spawn, cold, and migratory are considered to be a high receiving water risk. Therefore, a low sediment risk and low receiving water risk would be a Risk Level 1 project. A high sediment risk and a high receiving water risk would elevate it to a Risk Level 3 project. Any other combination of sediment and receiving water risks would result in a Risk Level 2 rating.

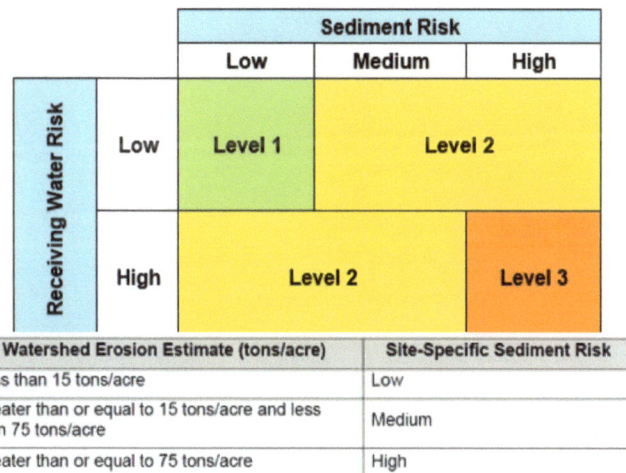

Figure 126 - The California Construction General Permit categorizes projects into one of three risk levels based on the sediment risk of the project and the receiving water risk. Sediment risk is calculated using RUSLE. Solving RUSLE for the "A" value will allow the site-specific sediment risk to be categorized as low, medium, or high. (Source: 2022 CGP, Order2022-0057-DWQ, Attachment D1)

---

103   California Construction General Permit, Order WQ 2022-0057-DWQ, Attachment D.1, https://www.waterboards.ca.gov/water_issues/programs/stormwater/construction/docs/2022-0057-dwq-with-attachments/cgp2022_att_d1.pdf.

DEVELOP SWPPP MAPS THAT TELL THE STORY OF THE PROJECT FROM BEGINNING TO END

I am often asked how many SWPPP maps a project needs to have. The short answer: as many as is necessary to tell the erosion control story of the project from beginning to end. The SWPPP maps should connect the dots from the time of the project's first soil disturbance to final site stabilization, and that might take more than one map. With that said, it is also important to find out what the local CGP or NPDES oversight agency requires. For example, at the beginning of this chapter, we saw that the California CGP requires a minimum of three maps: a vicinity map, a pre-earthwork map, and a map for the construction and earthwork phase. Although the vicinity map is typically just one drawing or aerial photo (and now required to be included with the title sheets), the pre-earthwork and construction and earthwork drawings could certainly include multiple sheets to allow ample detail to be shown and may include drawings for the various phases of the project.

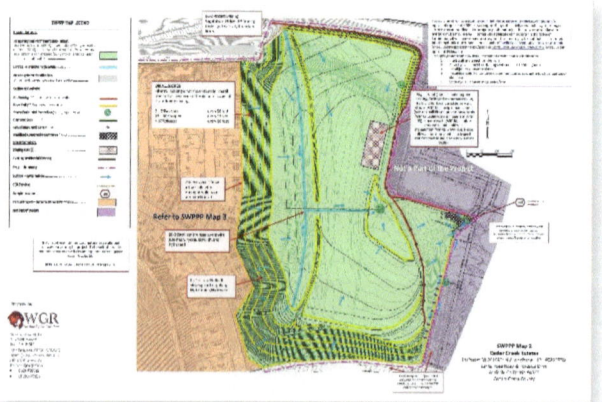

Figure 127 - A good SWPPP map should tell the erosion control story. We like to have them colorful and easy to read. (Source: WGR Southwest, Inc.)

The format of the drawings can vary depending on the tools that a SWPPP preparer may have at his or her disposal. Engineering firms will typically use software like AutoCAD or some other computer automated design tool. Our preference, as a consulting firm, has always been to utilize PDF files of the civil drawings provided by the civil engineering firm, convert them to image files (JPG or PNG), and insert them into a Microsoft Word document on which we can add lines, shading, and text boxes to tell the SWPPP story.

Since a picture is worth a thousand words, and because it may be the only part of a SWPPP some of the on-site personnel will read, try to load up your SWPPP map with as much information as possible so that, if a contractor installs and/or implements everything shown on the map, the site will largely be compliant with the permit requirements.

Before concluding this section on mapmaking, let's review a few details about the various maps that may need to be included in the SWPPP:

> **Vicinity Map:** The vicinity map is more than just something to help a directionally challenged inspector to find their way to the project. It provides the larger context for the project. Take, for example, the project shown in Figure 127, where is it located? It might be in an urbanized area, the coastal foothills, or in the Sierra Nevada. What is immediately downstream of the site? From where does project run-on originate? How big of a watershed flows onto the project? What existing development is surrounding the project? Are there nearby environmentally sensitive areas? The vicinity map will help answer all of these questions and make understanding the SWPPP document a little easier. The vicinity map should include a north arrow and a scale to help orient the user to the project site. I prefer using aerial imagery (such as from Google Earth™) so that regional and surrounding features and terrain are readily perceived. It

is also good to outline or shade the project site with a distinct color to help identify its position and relative size on the vicinity map.

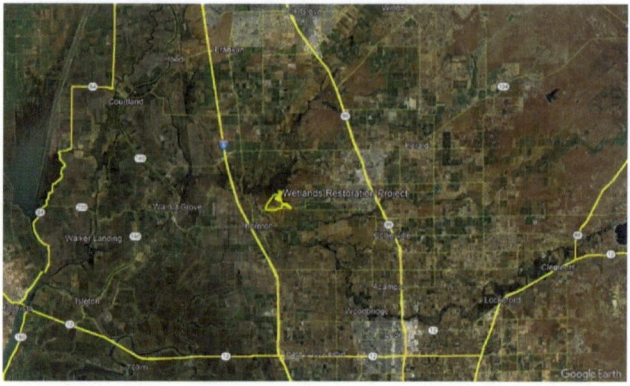

Figure 128 - A good vicinity map will provide context to the project. (Source: Google Earth™)

Demolition phase: Any time there is significant demolition on a project, a separate SWPPP map should be created and dedicated to identifying the pollutants of concern associated with the demolition activities and the proposed BMPs to mitigate the potential pollutants. Perimeter controls, construction site exits, drain inlets, and locations of stockpiles, port-a-potties, and the construction staging area may be very different during this initial phase of construction than during the latter subsequent phases. If an environmental investigation has been conducted that identified potential hazardous pollutants, such as asbestos, leaded paint, or PCBs, the locations of materials containing those pollutants should be identified on the demolition SWPPP map, including their original on-site location and the locations of stockpiling or storage areas of the demolished materials that contain the pollutants. Other demolition activities that should be included on this SWPPP map include concrete crushing activities, sanitary sewer excavations and disconnections, locations where impervious surfaces will be removed, and locations where vegetation will be taken out. Typically, a demolition drawing will be included in the civil drawings packet, which can be used as the base map for this SWPPP map.

Grading phase: When selecting a base map to use for the creation of the SWPPP map, I will typically use the grading map, which often will also contain drainage information. As depicted in Figure 105, the grading drawing will typically show the new darker grading contours overlain on the existing lighter topographic contours and will provide information regarding the planned cut and fill activities. For many projects, this is the only map I will use for creating the SWPPP map. But if the grading is complex or has multiple phases, a SWPPP writer may need to include more than one drawing to be able to adequately tell the erosion control story.

Vertical construction phase: As previously mentioned, the majority of projects can have the BMPs adequately shown on one SWPPP map for both the grading and vertical phases. But there are times when the vertical construction activities are either not adequately shown on the grading drawings or the BMP configuration needed during this phase of work is so dramatically different than during the grading phase that a separate SWPPP map will need to be created for the vertical phase. Some larger projects have various phases of vertical construction, which will necessitate SWPPP maps for each phase of work.

Figure 129 - Before a baseball game, the coach hands the umpire a lineup card that shows not only positions and the batting order but also the names of players. (Artwork credit Kerry Sue Teravskis)

Final stabilized condition: This is where I see quite a few SWPPP maps go wrong. Oftentimes, a SWPPP writer will specify on the SWPPP maps either just the temporary erosion controls or only the method for final site stabilization such as landscaping. To adequately tell the erosion control story, a SWPPP writer needs to specify both. During or right after the grading phase, what will the erosion control look like? Most likely it will not be landscaped until the end of the project, so a temporary effective soil cover or raindrop BMP will need to be specified on the SWPPP map for this phase of work. However, it is equally important to include a SWPPP map that shows how final site stabilization will be achieved. This map oftentimes will also include the post-construction storm water treatment and low impact development project features that we will discuss in Chapter 7.

IDENTIFY THE PLAYERS INVOLVED IN THE PROJECT

As a kid, baseball was my favorite pastime. I not only lived baseball, but I also ate, drank, and breathed it! Because I grew up in Anaheim, California, the Angels was my team of choice. I would listen to their games almost daily on the radio and, whenever I had the opportunity, I would go to the stadium to watch them play. I remember seeing Nolan Ryan get one strikeout after another with his 100 mph fast balls, Rod Carew never missing a throw at first base, and then, of course, Mr. October, Reggie Jackson, doing his postseason magic. In

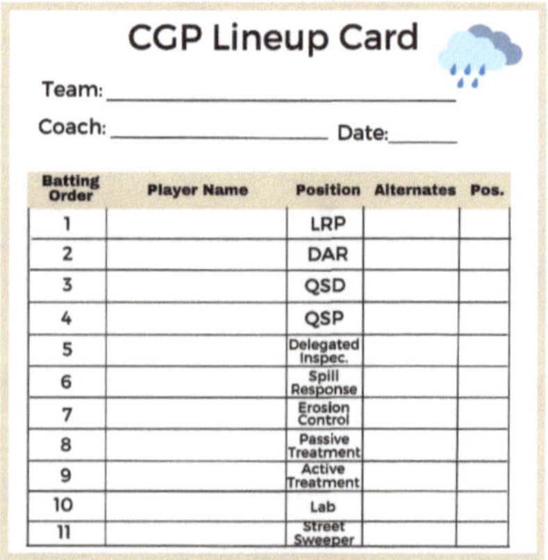
CGP Lineup Card

Team: ____________

Coach: ____________ Date: ______

Batting Order	Player Name	Position	Alternates	Pos.
1		LRP		
2		DAR		
3		QSD		
4		QSP		
5		Delegated Inspec.		
6		Spill Response		
7		Erosion Control		
8		Passive Treatment		
9		Active Treatment		
10		Lab		
11		Street Sweeper		

Figure 130 - A SWPPP should also contain a lineup card with names and contact information for the various positions needed to assure compliance. (Artwork credit Kerry Sue Teravskis)

Connecting the Dots of SWPPP Development

the summer, when I wasn't listening to or watching a game, I would be at the local park playing pickup baseball games. But the problem was...I was just like Charlie Brown. Loved the sport, but could not hit a baseball for the life of me and was never on a winning team. However, I did learn a thing or two about the rules of baseball. One of the first things that needed to happen before a game started was for the coach to give the umpire a lineup card listing not only the positions and batting order but also the player names next to each position.

A properly developed SWPPP should be like a lineup card. It should list the various positions involved in the project's storm water compliance program. Instead of pitcher, catcher, outfielder, and shortstop, SWPPP positions include:

- Legally Responsible Person (LRP)
- Duly Authorized Representatives (DAR) / approved signatories
- Project Managers / Resident Engineers
- Contractor and subcontractors
- Qualified SWPPP Developer (QSD)
- Qualified SWPPP Practitioners (QSP)
- Trained delegate inspectors
- Analytical testing laboratory
- Active treatment / passive treatment contractors

Erosion and sediment control installers

- Street sweeper
- Spill response contractors

The SWPPP template[104] provided with this book contains a SWPPP Roster where the names and contact information can be entered for a particular project. The roster is located up front so that the information for the various team players is readily available should you need to call on that position.

INCORPORATE THE POLLUTANT SOURCE ASSESSMENT AND BMP SELECTION

In connecting the dots of developing an effective SWPPP, we now need to "draw a line" in our document from the pollutant source assessment that we performed in Chapter 3 to the BMPs we selected in Chapter 4. This includes incorporating the following into the written SWPPP document:

- Describe the scope of the project and list the trades involved in the project (Table 2);
- List pollutants associated with each trade (Table 2) and take an inventory of potential pollutant sources present on the jobsite (Table 4);
- Identify BMPs that will be used to address the pollutants associated with each trade, construction activity, and potential sources of pollutants; and
- Identify a schedule for implementation of the BMPs based on when the activities and/or trades will be present.

These steps may seem obvious and somewhat elementary, but this is exactly where many SWPPPs become disconnected. The dots are there. The numbers are there. So is the information and data. But it is not until we draw the lines of logic that we have successfully connected the dots. This is a cause-and-effect

---

104   You can access the template for free with the following link: https://wgr-sw.com/TheRaindropConnection/.

Connecting the Dots of SWPPP Development

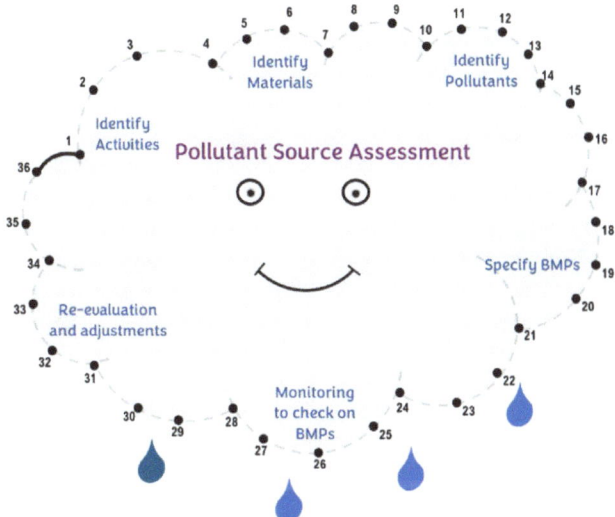

Figure 131 - The raindrop connection involves drawing lines of logic between the activities, materials, pollutants, and BMPs presented in the SWPPP.

relationship. If stucco work is going to be performed at the construction project, there will be an effect. For this type of construction activity, we know that the materials present will be sand, stucco mix, water, paper, plastic, fuel, and oil. Furthermore, the pollutants will be sediment and turbidity, pH altering substances, solid waste (trash), hydrocarbons, and oil & grease. Which, in turn, means we will need to have BMPs in place to prevent stockpiles of sand from spreading and being mobilized by wind and rain. We will need to control non-storm water discharges. Good housekeeping and spill prevention and response measures will also be needed to prevent pH altering substances, lubricants, and fuel from coming into contact with storm water.

There is another dot that needs to be connected and addressed in the SWPPP: the monitoring program. In the next chapter, we will explore the various components of an effective storm water monitoring program and see why it is needed for maintaining adequate control of water quality discharging from a construction site.

CHAPTER 6
Connecting the Dots of an Effective Monitoring Program

Up to this point in the SWPPP, we have attempted to connect the dots of construction activities, materials used on a construction site, pollutants potentially present, and best management practices to control the pollutants. But how do we know if the dots have actually been connected? Was the SWPPP we prepared for the project successful in connecting these dots to the final dot—water quality? You won't know the dots have been connected until it is field verified. That is why a monitoring program is essential to any connected storm water management program. Monitoring can be as simple as visual observations, because turbid water is fairly easy to recognize and to compare with runoff from a site that has stabilized soil. But as we saw in Chapter 3, there are a host of other construction-related pollutants, such as pH-altering substances, that are not visually detectable

For these potential pollutants, it may be necessary to utilize a field analytical instrument or to collect a sample and submit it to an analytical laboratory for analysis to determine their absence or presence. The monitoring program contained in the SWPPP will need to list the run-on and run-off locations at the project site, identify who will be responsible for performing the inspections and sampling activities, describe when visual inspections and sampling should be conducted, identify the tools needed for facilitating the sample collection, and explain how to utilize the visual and analytical data obtained from the field monitoring activities.

IDENTIFY RUN-ON AND RUN-OFF LOCATIONS

In the previous chapter, we discussed how a SWPPP developer should first do their homework. This included using Google Earth, civil drawings, and even a site visit to identify where and how water flows at the project site during the pre-development site conditions but also throughout the construction duration as the project begins to take shape. The results of the homework should have identified the points at which water flows onto the site, where it discharges from the site, and the types of runoff conveyances (sheet flow, pipe, manhole, channel, swale, etc.) that move water across the site.

Figure 132 - Discharge locations (as well as run-on) locations need to be identified not just in the field but also in the SWPPP. (Photo credit: John Teravskis)

Another one of the homework items was for the SWPPP preparer to identify and understand the characteristics of the drainage management areas for each discharge point. This will enable the preparer to answer the question, *"How big*

Connecting the Dots of an Effective Monitoring Program

of an area is draining to the discharge point?" It will also provide clues about how much water will flow to it and how quickly it will flow. These clues can be plugged into Equation 3, Equation 4, Equation 5, and Equation 6 to determine the runoff volume, when to expect runoff to occur, and what the peak flow rate of the discharge will be.

Locations where storm water runs onto the project from off-site also need to be identified. This will help the inspector understand the volume and characteristics of the flow at the downgradient discharge point and it will provide some insight into the types of erosion and sediment control measures needed for effectively controlling the flow as it intersects the project. But it is particularly important to have run-on locations identified and part of the monitoring program if the water quality from any of them is poor and affecting the discharge from the project.

It is important to note that both run-on and run-off (discharge) locations can change through the course of the project. This, of course, is not always the case, but when grading is extensive or a drainage system is being constructed as a part of the project, run-on and discharge locations can be created, eliminated, changed, or moved to another location. The SWPPP and SWPPP maps should show the drainage changes throughout the course of the project, and as such, how the monitoring program will need to morph with it.

The SWPPP should include a list of run-on and discharge locations. In my SWPPPs, I like to include tables containing both a latitude and longitude coordinate and a narrative description of the location, as shown below.

Table 16 – Storm Water Run-on Locations

☑ **Check the box if there is no run-on.**

Identifier on Drawings	Latitude / Longitude	Description of Run-on

Table 17 – Storm Water Pre-Grading Discharge Locations

Identifier on Drawings	Latitude / Longitude	Description of Run-off
Pre-DI 1	38.123815,-121.783636	Existing drain inlet to be demolished south of west driveway along the existing curb.
Pre-DI 2	38.123508,-121.783098	Existing drain inlet to be demolished south of the east driveway at the end of the sweeping curb.
Pre-DI 3	38.123778,-121.783108	Existing drain inlet to be demolished south of the east wing of the existing church.
Pre-DI 4	38.124140,-121.782817	Existing drain inlet to be demolished in the east driveway just south of the Central Avenue exit/entrance.

Table 18 - Storm Water Discharge Locations During Construction

Identifier on Drawings	Latitude / Longitude	Description of Run-off
SP1	38.124342,-121.783408	Before drain inlets are active: sample sheet flow to Central Avenue from the west driveway. After drain inlets are active: sample water entering and passing through the storm drain pipe at CB-1.
SP2	38.124190,-121.782821	Before drain inlets are active: sample sheet flow to Central Avenue from the east driveway. After drain inlets are active: sample water entering and passing through the storm drain pipe at CB-5.
SP3	38.124262,-121.782654	During off-site work, sample downgradient of the project in the Central Avenue south gutter.

It is also good to include the discharge locations on the pre-earthwork and the construction and earthwork SWPPP maps:

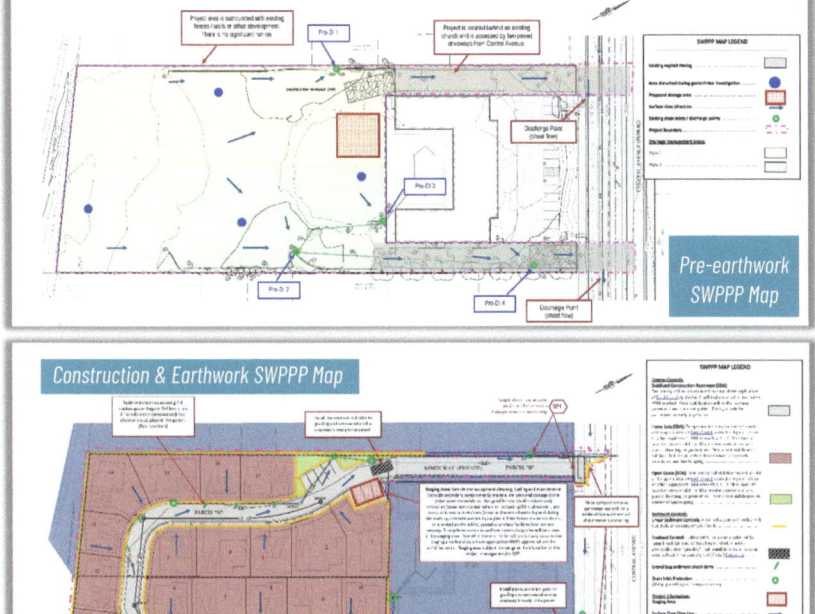

Figure 133 - Discharge locations may be different on the Pre-earthwork SWPPP map and the Construction & Earthwork SWPPP map. (Source: WGR Southwest, Inc.)

Sometimes, there is confusion about what is a construction site discharge. I will occasionally hear someone state, *"Our project's runoff flows to, and remains in, the municipal storm water retention basin and is, therefore, not a regulated discharge."* I have also heard similar statements about runoff to a neighboring property, adjacent agricultural fields, or roadside swales that do not directly connect with a municipal drainage system or Waters of the United States. While there may be legitimate instances where the local NPDES oversight agency may allow for these situations to not require coverage by the Construction General Permit, if a construction SWPPP is being prepared, it is safe to say that it is for a project subject to NPDES permit requirements. Therefore, regardless of its ultimate fate, any water leaving a project site should be depicted on a SWPPP map as a point of discharge.

INSPECTOR QUALIFICATIONS

Who can perform construction site inspections and monitoring activities may largely depend upon the requirements of the local NPDES oversight agency. For example, in California, for CGP projects, a Qualified SWPPP Practitioner (QSP) is required to perform (or in some cases, oversee) the storm water inspections and sampling. The California Water Board also allows for appropriately trained delegate inspectors to perform some of the inspections and sampling tasks under the supervision of a QSP. Previously, we saw that the California requirements for an individual who wants to obtain the QSP certification include:

1. Taking a two-day course from a CASQA Trainer-of-Record[105] and passing the online exam; and
2. Obtaining one of the following underlying prerequisite credentials:
    - A Certified Erosion, Sediment, and Stormwater Inspector (CESSWI)™ registered through Enviro Cert International, Inc.;
    - A certified inspector of sediment and erosion control (CISEC)™ registered through Certified Inspector of Sediment and Erosion Control Inc. (now under Ecopliant™);
    - A Construction Management degree from an accredited four-year institution that includes coursework that covers the

---

[105] For more information about the CASQA QSP / QSD certifications and training programs, go to https://www.casqa.org/resources/training/cgp-training-program/qsd-qsp-qualification.

underlying principles of erosion and sediment control and practices of reducing pollution in storm water; or
- Any prerequisite course approved by the State Water Board's Division of Water Quality Deputy Director.

Storm water inspectors in other states should review their local CGP requirements (as shown on Table 11) to see if there are any specific training or certification requirements for performing inspections at construction sites at their location. Some states have requirements and others do not, but regardless of what regulatory requirements there may be, construction storm water inspectors should be knowledgeable in the following ways:

☑ **Be familiar with construction sites and activities,** including the various trades and materials present, the sequencing and phasing of the work, the chain-of-command, sign-in and sign-out procedures for the project, required personal protective equipment (PPE), emergency alarms, and hazards associated with the planned construction work (i.e., trench and excavation safety, confined spaces, electrical energy hazards, working around heavy equipment, and hazardous materials present on the jobsite.)

Figure 134 - There is some basic information that any storm water inspector needs to be aware of regardless of what certification may be required by the local NPDES agency. (Photo credit: John Teravskis)

- ☑ **Be familiar with the local NPDES and municipal requirements and the site-specific SWPPP.** The inspector should understand the objectives of the SWPPP and how erosion and sediment control measures and pollution prevention practices are to be implemented on-site. The inspector should also be knowledgeable about the local CGP, and in particular, the inspection and monitoring requirements.
- ☑ **Be familiar with the site hydrology,** including where water flows onto the site and off the site, and how water flows across the site.
- ☑ **Be familiar with the monitoring instruments and sample collection kits and containers**. If pH and turbidity is required to be tested, the inspector should know how to calibrate and use the instruments. If samples need to be collected and sent to a laboratory, the inspector should know the protocols for collecting, packaging, and shipping or transporting the samples to the laboratory.
- ☑ **Be familiar with the inspection documentation forms and protocols**. The inspector should have access to electronic or paper forms and know how to complete them and where they should be maintained, uploaded, or posted.
- ☑ **Be familiar with the project's chain of command and communication methods.** Whether it is just for transferring routine inspection reports or to communicate items needing corrective action, the inspector should know to whom the item needs to be communicated and how to transfer such information to them. It may be just a cell phone number to text or call to report issues, or it could be an online documentation system where official communications and requests for information (RFIs) are transmitted and stored. The inspector should also be aware of routine project meetings and tailgate sessions and understand the expectation concerning their presence and involvement at these meetings.

☑ **Be familiar with their scope of work and contractual agreements.** The inspector should know what services have been contracted and where their responsibilities start and stop both in scope and duration.

PERMIT-REQUIRED INSPECTION PROGRAM

Let's face it, even though we might know the importance of a monitoring program is to verify that the dots of erosion and sediment control are being connected, the number one reason construction sites are inspected is because the local CGP requires inspections. These inspections will vary from state to state, but in general, they include baseline inspections and storm event inspections. To illustrate this, we will look at the California CGP requirements.

Weekly Baseline Inspections: Routine storm water inspections are required at construction sites in California year-round, regardless of whether or not rain is in the forecast. These weekly baseline inspections serve to evaluate whether BMPs specified in the SWPPP or required by the CGP are properly installed and effective. The baseline inspections are also for identifying any pollutant sources needing corrective action, such as a spill of oil, open bags of stucco mix, or concrete washout systems that have reached their maximum effective capacity. During

Figure 135 - Remember to not only photo document problems (which is where our cameras usually turn to) but also to document corrected issues. (Photo Credit: John Teravskis and Gretchen Johnson)

the dry season, baseline inspections are monitoring for problems associated with wind erosion or non-storm water discharges. Regular baseline inspections will reveal the project's compliance track record and how quickly project supervisors resolve items needing corrective action. But remember, it is equally important to document the corrected items and not only the items needing correction. An inspector needs to close the documentation loop that was opened when the problem was first observed by recording how it was resolved.

Storm Event Inspections: The real test of how well we have connected the dots in controlling erosion and sedimentation occurs when it is raining. That is when it is most important for the inspector to don rain gear and mud boots and go tramping through the project site. Flowing water will tell the story of whether or not the program is effective. But it is not just any storm that we need to observe; it is necessary to make sure it is a qualifying precipitation event (QPE). Again, this will typically be defined by the local NPDES authority. In California, a QPE is defined by the State Water Board in the glossary of the CGP:

> Qualifying precipitation event is any weather pattern that is forecast to have a 50 percent or greater Probability of Precipitation (PoP) and a Quantitative Precipitation Forecast (QPF) of 0.5 inches or more within a 24-hour period. The event begins with the 24-hour period when 0.5 inches has been forecast and continues on subsequent 24-hour periods when 0.25 inches of precipitation or more is forecast.

Inspectors will want to make sure that they are inspecting any storms that meet the local QPE definition.

Once there is a QPE in the forecast, several types of storm event inspections will be triggered.

Connecting the Dots of an Effective Monitoring Program   333

Pre-storm inspections: These are, perhaps, the most important of the inspections. A pre-storm inspection is typically performed forty-eight to seventy-two hours before the rain arrives. Since the purpose of the inspection is to observe problem areas, you want to allow enough time for on-site personnel to take corrective action. It does no good to beat the storm by several hours and hurriedly produce and distribute a pre-storm inspection report if the contractor

Figure 136 - A pre-storm inspection should identify things that need to be addressed before the rain arrives. How many items in this photo need to be addressed? (Photo credit: John Teravskis)

has no opportunity to take action before the rain begins. Inspectors performing pre-storm inspections should look for the following conditions:

☑ **BMPs that need maintenance, repair, or replacement.** This might be slow-the-flow BMPs that have captured sediment from a previous storm and do not have sufficient capturing capacity for additional sediment expected to be generated in the upcoming storm. It could also be a track-out control measure that has filled up with sediment or a concrete washout collection system that is nearing maximum capacity. It might also include areas of soil disturbance that need an effective soil cover placed on it as a Raindrop BMP.

- ☑ **Pollutants exposed to storm water.** While performing the pre-storm inspection, be on the lookout for materials that might be mobilized by wind or water runoff. These materials might be powders, soluble substances, or liquids used by the trades currently present on the project. Items to look for include stockpiles of soil and landscaping materials, bagged or stockpiled concrete or cementitious products or wastes, paints and solvents, fertilizers, oil and grease, fuel, antifreeze, glues and adhesives, and solid waste. The pre-storm inspection should suggest that such materials be removed or covered with a stormproof covering. Trash and other waste bins should be covered with lids or tarps.

- ☑ **Things that need to be secured.** Some items—such as stockpile and waste bin covers and port-a-potties—can be affected by high winds. If there is a wind warning in the forecast, make sure that these items have been properly secured.

- ☑ **Non-storm water discharges.** Identify any flows of non-storm water and determine whether it is an allowable or unauthorized discharge. If unauthorized, or if authorized but causing erosion or pollutant transport, identify it on the pre-storm inspection report as an item needing to be addressed.

Figure 137 - Go ahead! Stomp in a few puddles while performing during-storm inspections. (Photo credit: John Teravskis)

During-storm inspections: When rain is falling and running off is when we get to observe our BMPs in action. How are they doing? Is everything working as planned? Is water flowing where you thought it would? How are the BMPs holding up? This is where the inspector gets to let his or her inner child out and go stomp in some puddles. It is actually great fun! But just so you appear to be a responsible adult, make sure you are also carefully observing the BMPs and water flow. (It also helps to wipe that silly grin from your face and shake your head while looking at the BMPs with a rather somber face—this helps to put the contractor at ease.) Seriously, you can learn much from during-storm inspections; not only will you see the concepts we talked about in Chapter 2 play out in front of your eyes, but you can learn firsthand what works and what doesn't work when it comes to erosion and sediment control. People often think that, once installed, these control measures are immediately effective. The truth is this is not an exact science, and establishing and maintaining good control over the project site requires the iterative approach—meaning that we try one thing and, if it does not work as planned, we try something else. Getting out in the rain will give the inspector the best insight into how to fine tune the BMPs in order to establish effective control of erosion and sedimentation.

Post-storm inspections: There is always going to be a certain amount of "collateral damage" after a storm event passes through. The elements will take their toll on even the best installations of BMPs, and things will need to be repaired or cleaned out, which brings us to the purpose of the post-storm inspections. With the pre-storm inspection, you created a punch list of items needing attention before the rain began. Now, with the post-storm inspection, you are creating a punch list of items needing maintenance or repair as a result of the storm. Usually, most of the BMPs needing attention will fall in the [Slow-the-Flow category,](Slow-the-Flow category) because they were probably doing their job and collecting sediment. This sediment will need to be cleaned out in order to assure that there is adequate sediment capturing capacity for the next storm event. Sediment control devices also seem to get the most abuse from wind and rain during storm events because they are placed in areas that receive flow and are often wind exposed. While performing a post-storm inspection, look for sediment upgradient of control devices that needs to be cleaned out, linear controls that need to be resecured, or those items that should be replaced altogether.

Figure 138 - In large open areas like this, silt fence can take a beating from the wind. A post-storm inspection should note such situations. (Photo credit: John Teravskis)

Documentation: An inspection without documentation never happened, at least in the mind of a NPDES compliance inspector. Therefore, it is absolutely essential to document all weekly and storm event inspections. The Clean Water Act and many state NPDES permits require that all compliance documentation, including but not limited to inspection reports, be maintained by the Legally Responsible Person

(LRP) for a minimum of three years. Therefore, a system needs to be utilized by the inspector to not only generate the inspection reports but to also make them accessible during the project and to transfer them to the LRP after the project has been completed. In the earlier days of my career as an inspector, inspection reports were always completed on paper forms. On the one hand, it was somewhat convenient because all you needed was a form and a pen. But there were also challenges in using paper, such as getting copies of the completed inspection reports to everyone who needed or wanted them (remember, we also didn't have smart phones to take pictures of the forms to text or email to everyone). Another challenge was having a secure document retention system. I had a jobsite in Oakland, California where—not once, but twice—the job trailer containing the SWPPP and paper inspection forms was burned to the ground. Another challenge was needing to get all of the paper records from the contractor to the LRP after the end of the job. Because I was seldom involved in the handoff, I really don't know how often this actually occurred, but I suspect quite often there was no handoff and the records just ended up in a warehouse somewhere or in a landfill. That is why I am so thankful for the electronic digital age. We no longer need to worry about such things. NPDES agencies allow for inspection records to be created and stored electronically as long as they can be produced upon demand. Now, once an inspection report is created in the field, it is automatically emailed to anyone specified, a PDF of the report is generated, and the inspection report and data are automatically uploaded to a cloud server to which the LRP has access. At the end of the project, all we need to remember to do is to remind the LRP to download all of the inspection reports. Today's inspection apps also provide and record weather forecasts, contain mapping tools to help you find the site, imbed photos in the reports, send out corrective action due date and follow-up inspection reminders, have built-in report templates, and have many other useful features. Who says you can't teach an old dog a new trick? I love these inspection apps!

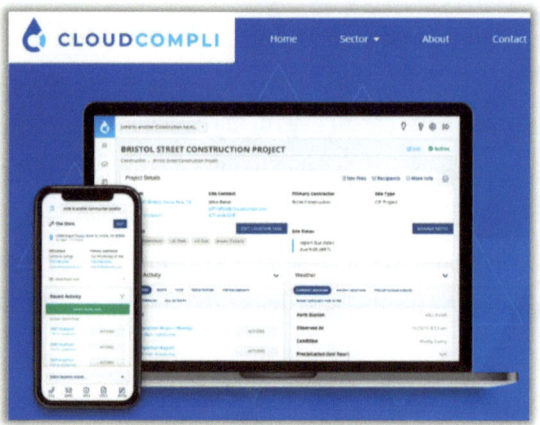

Figure 139 - Software and apps like CloudCompli provide innovative inspection documentation tools. This makes the documentation responsibilities of an inspector so much easier. For more information go to https://www.cloudcompli.com/.

PERMIT-REQUIRED MONITORING PROGRAM

While an inspection program may give us a good qualitative indication of the effectiveness of the storm water management program, it may be desirable or necessary to have a quantitative measure of its effectiveness. This is accomplished through sampling and analysis of storm water discharges. Although it is not unheard of having a project proponent voluntarily test its runoff water, usually there is an NPDES permit that is requiring runoff to be sampled and tested. Therefore, it is necessary to identify what the permit requires regarding the parameters being tested, the location of samples, and the frequency of sampling.

Connecting the Dots of an Effective Monitoring Program

Analyses: The CGP will tell the project proponent if sampling is required and, if so, what analyses need to be performed. In California, as we learned during the RUSLE equation discussion, there are three possible risk levels for permitted construction projects—Risk Levels 1, 2, and 3. Risk Level 1 projects are not required to perform analytical testing; however, Risk Levels 2 and 3 are required to monitor discharges of QPEs for pH and turbidity. The California CGP also requires other analyses to be conducted if there was a discharge of a pollutant to the ground or a failed BMP that caused the release of a pollutant source at the jobsite. Applicable TMDLs may be another cause for additional monitoring parameters. The following is a summary of the typical analyses performed for runoff from construction sites.

pH:

Technically speaking, pH is the measure of hydronium ions ($H3O+$) in a solution. The more hydronium ions present, the more acidic is the solution. That is because when an acid (such as hydrochloric acid, HCl) combines with water it forms hydronium ions. When hydroxide ions ($OH-$) are more prevalent than hydronium ions, the solution will be more basic or sometimes referred to as caustic or alkaline. This is because a base (such as sodium hydroxide, NaOH) when combined with water forms hydroxide ions. A perfect balance of hydronium and hydroxide ions would be a neutral solution and is assigned a pH value of 7.0 (measured in pH units or standard units, S.U., but often the units are omitted). As the hydronium ions increase, the pH values lower. As the hydroxide ions increase, the pH increases. The pH scale is logarithmic, meaning that with each change from one whole integer to another (i.e., a value of 7 to 8, or 8 to 9), the acidity or alkalinity changes by an order of magnitude. In other words, compared to a value of 7, a pH of 8 is 10 times more caustic, and 9 is 100 times more caustic, and 10 is 1,000 times more caustic. Same with values below 7: a pH of 6 is 10 times more acidic than 7, 5 is 100 times more acidic, and 4 is 1,000 times more acidic. As we discussed in Chapter 3, there are a variety of pollutants present at most construction sites that can alter the pH of storm water runoff. These commonly include concrete and other cementitious products, lime treating of soils, and acids used for preparing surfaces.

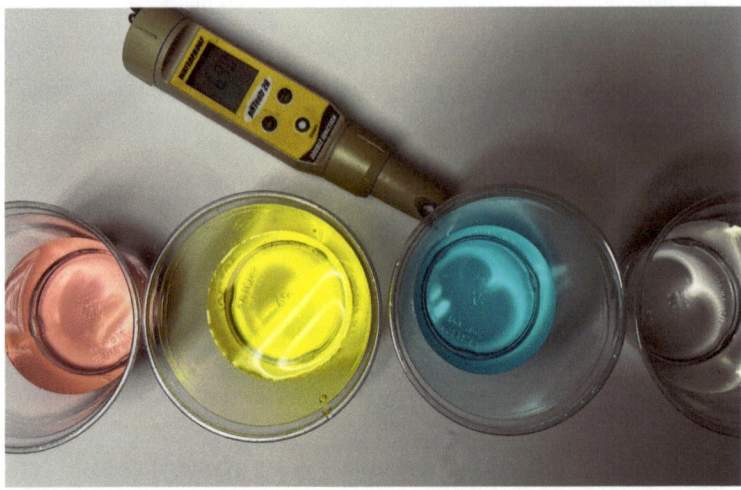

Figure 140 - pH is the measure of acidity or alkalinity of a solution. At construction sites, we measure pH to test for the impact of pH altering substances on storm water runoff. Field pH instruments should be calibrated at the beginning of each day of use following a 3-point calibration protocol with the 4.0 (red), 7.0 (yellow), and 10.0 (blue) buffer standards. (Photo credit: John Teravskis)

Because the pH of storm water runoff can quickly degrade or change due to other internal and external factors, it should be tested on location with a field instrument within fifteen minutes[106] of the sample collection. Prior to performing field measurements with the pH instrument, it should be calibrated per the manufacturer's instruction manual. It is common for manufacturers to specify an initial calibration of the instrument on each day of use and to use a three-point calibration method with buffer standards of 4, 7, and 10. Although different manufacturers and instrument

---

106   Code of Federal Regulations 40 CFR Part 136; https://www.ecfr.gov/current/title-40/chapter-I/subchapter-D/part-136

users have differing approaches to how a three-point calibration is performed, I was taught as a chemistry major to always calibrate with the low value first (4.0), and then with the high value (10.0) buffer, which sets the "zero and span" values. If the instrument is working correctly, when it is placed in the 7.0 buffer, the reading should be pretty close to 7.0; but, of course, you do this third point of calibration to fine-tune the instrument. It is also recommended to have deionized water for rinsing the instrument probe between and after dipping into each standard. For confirmation of the calibration, you can then take a pH measurement (not using the calibration mode) of the calibration buffer that is closest to the expected value of the storm water you will be testing. If it differs from the standard by +- 0.2 or more, then the instrument should be recalibrated or not used. Other than at the beginning of each day of use, pH field instruments should be recalibrated if they are dropped, experience a significant temperature change, or have had the batteries changed. The calibration buffer standards can be reused several times but should be replaced when they start to look cloudy or when there are problems with calibrating the instrument. The calibration buffers have expiration dates and should not be used after expiration.[107]

Documentation of pH testing should include the make, model, and serial or other identification number of the instrument, the calibration date and time, the values obtained during calibration, the initials of the person performing the calibration, and the values obtained during the field use of the instrument along with the date and time of each measurement.

---

107 For additional information about field pH measurements, refer to the USEPA Operation Procedure for Field pH Measurement, ID: LSASDPROC-100-R6, April 22, 2023, https://www.epa.gov/sites/default/files/2017-07/documents/field_ph_measurement100_af.r4.pdf.

Turbidity:

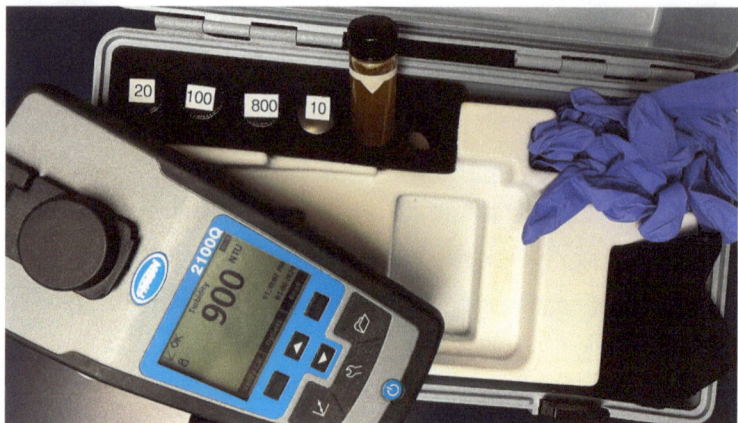

Figure 141 - Turbidity meters pass light through a glass sample vial to indirectly measure the amount of suspended particles in the water sample. (Photo credit: John Teravskis)

Turbidity is the measurement of the cloudiness or, conversely, the clarity of water. Suspended particles in the water cause turbidity. The color of a liquid does not necessarily affect its turbidity. For example, coffee or tea may have a dark hue but have relatively low turbidity. Analytical instruments that measure turbidity do so by passing a light beam through a clear vial filled with the water sample. If there are significant suspended particles present, not as much light will pass through the sample as it would in a sample not containing suspended particles. The amount of light passing through the sample (or reflecting back) is proportional to the amount of solids present. On construction sites, turbidity values are quantified and reported in Nephelometric Turbidity Units (NTU) by a calibrated field instrument. Similar to the pH calibration, several vials of a standard of known turbidity values (typically, 20, 100, and 800 NTU) are used to calibrate the instrument. Also like the pH instrument calibration, the turbidity meter should be calibrated per the manufacturer's instructions at the beginning of each day of use and again if the instrument has been jarred, experienced a significant temperature change, has had the batteries changed, or is producing unexpected results.[108] It is best to test for turbidity as soon as possible after the sample is collected so that suspended particles do not settle out. You should also know what the upper range of the turbidity meter is and how it reports an out-of-range value.

Figure 142 - The vial on the left is 170 NTU and the one on the right is 900 NTU. (Photo credit: John Teravskis)

Non-visible pollutants:

As we discovered in Chapter 3, beside sediment, there are many other potential pollutants on a construction site. These pollutants can find their way into storm water runoff by a variety of methods including mismanagement, spills, leaks, and the use of the pollutant-containing materials during storm events. Typically, these pollutants are not visible in storm water. In California, if any of these non-visible pollutants are exposed to storm water due to a breach, leak, spill, or BMP failure, additional samples will need to be collected and analyzed. The State Water Board requires that a sample be collected from downgradient of the pollutant release incident and tested

---

108   For more information about the use of field turbidity meters refer to the USEPA Operating Procedure: Field Turbidity Measurement, ID: LSASDPROC-103-R6, April 22, 2023, https://www.epa.gov/sites/default/files/2017-07/documents/field_turbidity_measurement103_af.r4.pdf.

for an indicator analysis. For example, if a port-a-potty were blown over during a high wind event and "blue stuff" was spilled on the ground, during the next storm event (after the blue stuff was cleaned up) a sample would need to be collected at the discharge point hydrologically downgradient of the incident and tested for an indicator pollutant (such as fecal coliform). Since there are a myriad of pollutants and potential release scenarios, it may be difficult to predict what might be spilled and need to be tested. The SWPPP preparer can assist the inspector by including in the SWPPP some common non-visible pollutants and release scenarios. The inspector can then work with the local analytical laboratory to assure that they have an ample collection of sample containers for common release scenarios.

Figure 143 - This type of an incident very well could trigger a non-visible pollutant sampling event. Besides generating more field monitoring activities, it is also extremely gross! Make sure you have your gloves on! (Photo credit: Steven Bender)

TMDLs:

In Chapter 3, we learned that certain pollutants identified as impairments in a receiving water may be issued a total maximum daily load (TMDL) by the State Water Board and USEPA, which can come in the form of a narrative restriction, a numeric action level (NAL), or a numeric effluent limitation (NEL). If these pollutants are associated with construction activities, it is very possible that discharges from the construction site will need to be monitored for their presence. The California CGP provides an attachment [109] which lists the applicable construction-related TMDLs for various locations around the state. However, that does not mean that these pollutants will automatically need to be included in the monitoring program. Two other precursors need to have happened first: 1) the listed TMDL pollutant needs to have been identified in the pollutant source assessment that was performed for the project; and 2) there has to have been a mishap involving that pollutant—triggering the non-visible pollutant sampling requirement that we discussed in the previous section. Of course, each state may have their own take on how and when TMDLs are to be monitored at construction sites, so you will want to review the CGP requirements for your particular location.

Locations: Not surprisingly, the CGP requires that discharges of storm water be tested. After all, that is the point of the permit—to control and monitor the water quality leaving the project. But sometimes identifying the sampling location for a given discharge point is not as obvious as it might first seem. Take, for example, a 500-foot run of silt fence at the toe of a slope on the edge of the project. The entire length of silt fence would be considered a single discharge point, especially if runoff were, more or less, uniformly passing through the silt fence and there were no breaches along this

Figure 144 - Where would the sampling point be along 500 linear feet of silt fence on the edge of your project? The Golden Rule of Sampling will help to identify it. (Photo credit: John Teravskis)

---

109   California Construction General Permit Order 2022-0057-DWQ, Attachment H https://www.waterboards.ca.gov/water_issues/programs/stormwater/construction/docs/2022-0057-dwq-with-attachments/cgp2022_att_h.pdf.

linear sediment control. So, where does the sample need to be obtained? The storm water inspector will need to rely on the **Golden Rule of Sampling**.

> The Golden Rule of Sampling
> Samples must be representative of the overall discharge.
> Not cleaner than average and not dirtier than average.

Now, I have met some very well-meaning individuals who would look for the location along the stretch of silt fence that has the highest turbidity and sample there, even if they had to walk past a lot of clean water to find it. Does this comply with the Golden Rule of Sampling? No, of course not! But neither does looking for the absolute cleanest and clearest water meet the Golden Rule of Sampling. The sampler will want to evaluate the entire length of the discharge point and identify a location that appears to be average. The sample needs to be representative of the overall discharge. There are also other considerations when selecting a sampling location which include safety, logistics, outside influencers, and the likelihood of having sufficient flow to obtain a sample. When given options for sampling locations, the sampler will want to make sure that he or she is in a safe environment—protected from vehicular traffic, inundation, entrapment, or steep banks. The sampler will also want to plan for logistics in obtaining the sample, which might include stabilizing the approach to the sample location or the actual sampling location itself so that they are not artificially muddying up the runoff as they approach the location and attempt to grab a sample. In line with the Golden Rule of Sampling, the sampler will want to make sure that outside influencers are avoided. These might include vehicles operating near the sample collection point, runoff from areas outside of the project boundary combining with the project's discharge (such as multiple pipes entering a manhole from which a sample is to be collected), and utilizing sample collection equipment or containers that are contaminated or were previously used and not adequately decontaminated. The sampler will also want to identify locations that are likely to flow. In reality, a 500 linear foot silt fence will rarely, if ever, have uniform flow over the entire length of the installation. In SWPPPs that I prepare with such a situation, I will identify the entire length of silt fence as a potential sampling location, but I will also typically include a note that the actual field sampling location is to be field verified by the sampler. Keeping the Golden Rule in mind, the sampler will need to identify where runoff actually occurs in a sufficient way to facilitate the collection of a sample.

Other sampling locations that could be required by the CGP may include points of run-on and in an adjacent receiving water. It is typically a good idea to sample run-on, whether it is required by the permit or not, especially if the water quality appears to be turbid or poor. This data can be used to show why the quality of the project's discharge is also less than desirable and may help to provide some regulatory relief. In California, for Risk Level 3 projects (the highest risk level), the Water Board may require monitoring of the receiving water for pH and turbidity if a project has a direct discharge to a receiving water and if the project's discharge monitoring has elevated pH and/or turbidity.[110]

A Construction General Permit will typically not require samples to be collected within the construction project upstream of the discharge point (internal sampling) except for unique situations such as the use of an active treatment system. However, construction operators may find it useful to obtain and test some internal samples to evaluate BMP performance and to help determine the source of pollutants (especially for pH-altering substances, which are not usually visible).

---

110 Risk Level 3 projects are required to sample upstream and downstream in a receiving waterbody to which there is a direct discharge if the discharge monitoring results show that turbidity is 500 NTUs or greater and/or pH is 6.0 or less or 9.0 or greater.

Frequency and Number of Samples: The sampler will need to be familiar with the CGP requirements to determine the required frequency for sampling. In California, for Risk Level 2 and 3 projects, the CGP requires that discharges of runoff from all Qualifying Precipitation Events [111](QPE) be sampled. California requires that one sample from each discharge location be collected from each twenty-four-hour period

Figure 145 - A sampler needs to be familiar with the requirements of the Construction General Permit to understand when and how often samples need to be collected and tested. (Photo credit: John Teravskis)

of the QPE. Some projects have only one discharge point, but other projects, such as roadway projects, may have dozens of discharge points. In California, within each twenty-four-hour period, there is no timing requirement for the sampling to occur—it just needs to happen during discharge and within site operating hours.[112] However, for discharges of impounded water (such as from a retention pond or pumped from an excavated trench), the California Water Board requires a sample to be collected and tested for pH and turbidity within the first hour of discharge and daily for continuous de-watering discharges.[113]

---

111 Per Attachment B of the California Construction General Permit, Order 2022-0057-DWQ, a Qualifying Precipitation Event is "any weather pattern that is forecast to have a 50 percent or greater Probability of Precipitation (PoP) and a Quantitative Precipitation Forecast (QPF) of 0.5 inches or more within a 24-hour period. The event begins with the 24-hour period when 0.5 inches has been forecast and continues on subsequent 24-hour periods when 0.25 inches of precipitation or more is forecast.", https://www.waterboards.ca.gov/water_issues/programs/stormwater/construction/docs/2022-0057-dwq-with-attachments/cgp2022_att_b.pdf
112 California Construction General Permit, Order 2022-0057-DWQ, Attachment D, Section III.D.1, https://www.waterboards.ca.gov/water_issues/programs/stormwater/construction/docs/2022-0057-dwq-with-attachments/cgp2022_att_d.pdf
113 California Construction General Permit, Order 2022-0057-DWQ, Attachment J, Section C, https://www.waterboards.ca.gov/water_issues/programs/stormwater/construction/docs/2022-0057-dwq-with-attachments/cgp2022_att_j.pdf

Monitoring exceptions: No one expects a sampler to risk life or limb to collect a sample. We have already touched on some exceptions to the monitoring requirements, but let's review. The first and, perhaps, most obvious exception is for nonqualifying precipitation events. If the permit does not require a rain event to be sampled, under normal conditions, you would not want to collect and analyze samples. The second exception is for safety concerns: snow (yes, it snows in California!), icy conditions, high winds, downed powerlines and trees,

Figure 146 - You don't have to risk life or limb to collect a sample. If it is unsafe to do so, such as for road flooding, turn around! (Photo credit: Mel Todd)

and flooding are all legitimate reasons for staying at home or turning around and going home. The first priority is to stay safe! After you have completed that first priority, be sure to document the reason why it is unsafe to sample and inspect the job, and submit the inspection report to the project team for their records. The other exception for performing inspections or sampling is for storm events that occur during nonworking hours. It might be at night, on weekends, or paid holidays, but, if there is no work normally scheduled at the project, you do not need to sample or inspect. However, that does not mean you do not need to inspect or sample if the construction crews have gone home because of rain (as they often will do). The CGP requirement to perform during-storm inspections and storm water sampling implies being there when it is raining. You just don't have to get out of bed or show up on a weekend to do it if the project is normally active Monday–Friday from 7:00 a.m. to 3:30 p.m. For some projects, especially roadway projects, normal working hours are at night or on the weekends. In those cases, at least in California, the project will need to be inspected and storm water sampled during night hours or on weekends. Whatever the case may be, the project's operating days and hours should be clearly defined in the SWPPP.

TOOLS OF THE TRADE

Before heading out to "play" in the rain, you will want to make sure you have the necessary tools of the trade to keep you safe, dry, and able to collect the required samples. It is always best to assemble your sampling kit well ahead of time so there is no last-minute scramble that causes you to either miss the rain event or leave something important behind—like your rain jacket! What you take with you to the project will depend largely on the site logistics and requirements. Are you sampling sheet flow or in a manhole? Are you needing a telescoping pole for a far reach? Do samples need to be collected for laboratory analysis of TMDL or non-visible pollutants? What are the project's personal protective equipment (PPE) requirements?

Figure 147 - What's in your sampling kit? Pictured are some of the items in my kit. But don't forget the snacks—cookies are a must on a cold, rainy day! (Photo credit: John Teravskis)

Here is a list of items you might consider including in your sampling kit:

- ☑ Turbidity meter and calibration standards
- ☑ pH meter and calibration buffers
- ☑ Clean, disposable cups for calibration and sample testing
- ☑ Spare batteries for the meters and a spare pH probe assembly
- ☑ Deionized or distilled water for rinsing and decontaminating equipment
- ☑ Terry cloths, microfiber cloths, paper towels, and sanitizing wipes
- ☑ Hand sanitizer (always good to have after visiting the port-a-potty)

- ☑ Permanent marker, grease pen, pens, and pencils
- ☑ Notebook
- ☑ A new dust pan for sheet flow sampling (buy them at a dollar store)
- ☑ Clean buckets
- ☑ New nylon twine and a clean rope with a carabiner at each end
- ☑ Knife or scissors
- ☑ Telescoping boom sampler or bilge pump sampler with new hose or a dedicated hose for each sample location
- ☑ Sample containers and ice chest from the laboratory
- ☑ Chain-of-custody document and sample container labels
- ☑ Ice (purchase on the way to the project)
- ☑ Spare rain gauges (to replace missing or damaged ones)
- ☑ Manhole cover hook
- ☑ Rain gear (jacket and pants)
- ☑ Mud boots (possibly steel toed if the job requires it)
- ☑ Nitrile gloves (plenty of them)
- ☑ Hearing protection (if around loud noises)
- ☑ Safety glasses (most jobs require it)
- ☑ Hard hat
- ☑ Smart phone with camera
- ☑ First aid kit
- ☑ A head lamp
- ☑ Hiking sticks for traversing steep terrain
- ☑ An extra change of dry clothes and socks (samplers have been known to get wet, and it is a long drive home in wet clothes)
- ☑ Drinking water and snacks

USING THE DATA FOR CONNECTING THE DOTS

I know I am stating the obvious, but if you go to all the trouble to perform the inspections and collect and analyze the samples, you should actually use the information! You might be surprised by how often collected information and data is ignored or not looked at in a timely manner. The name "numeric action level" suggests that action needs to be taken if and when it is exceeded. The California Water Board requires that all NAL exceedances or other items requiring corrective action be addressed by beginning to take the necessary corrective action within seventy-two hours of identifying the issue and completing the changes as soon as possible, prior to the next forecasted precipitation event. This means there is a time clock, so it is important to look at the data as soon as possible, not just when the annual report is due. In California, both pH and turbidity[114], and some TMDLs[115], have action levels against which monitoring data will need to be compared.

> California Construction General Permit Action Levels
> pH <6.5 or >8.5 S.U.
> Turbidity >250 NTU
> TMDLs (as specified in Attachment H of the CGP)

Other times when collected data needs to be used is to make comparisons for non-visible pollutant sampling and receiving water monitoring. For both of these

---

114 California Construction General Permit, Order 2022-0057-DWQ, Attachment D, Section III.G., https://www.waterboards.ca.gov/water_issues/programs/stormwater/construction/docs/2022-0057-dwq-with-attachments/cgp2022_att_d.pdf.

115 California Construction General Permit, Order 2022-0057-DWQ, Attachment H, https://www.waterboards.ca.gov/water_issues/programs/stormwater/construction/docs/2022-0057-dwq-with-attachments/cgp2022_att_h.pdf.

sampling scenarios, there is an upstream "unaffected" sample and a downstream "affected" sample that were collected and analyzed for one or more constituents. If the downstream sample is significantly higher in concentration, it can be assumed that the construction activities have had an impact on the discharge or receiving water. Interpretation of this data may lead the project proponent to take further mitigation steps for the pollutant of concern or to make some changes in its practices or BMP configurations.

Ultimately, field analytical data will be reported in the annual report, which in California is due on September 1 of each year for active projects or prior to submitting a Notice of Termination for projects that have been completed. Keep in mind that even if the discharger is not looking at the data, there may very well be others who are. Since the CGP is an NPDES Permit under the auspices of the Federal Clean Water Act, as allowed by the Clean Water Act[116], *"any citizen can file a suit against any violator of the Clean Water Act, only after the 60th day of the period of notification of Intent to sue and if the following two actions occurred during the 60-day period: (1) the regulatory agency failed to require a violator's compliance with the Clean Water Act's effluent standards or limitations or with an Order requiring compliance with these standards or limitations, and (2) the regulatory agency did not begin, and did not continue, to diligently prosecute a civil or criminal action against the violator."*[117]
A discharger permitted under the CGP will want to know what kind of data is being posted on publicly accessible platforms (such as the California State Water Board's SMARTS System) [118]and take timely and effective measures to mitigate issues causing less than desirable data.

---

116   United States Code, Title 33, Section 1365, https://www.govinfo.gov/content/pkg/USCODE-2022-title33/html/USCODE-2022-title33-chap26-subchapV-sec1365.htm.
117   Citizen Suit Enforcement Under the Clean Water Act, A Snapshot of the California Experience Based on Notices of Intent to Sue March 2009 through June 2010; Reed Sato, Director Office of Enforcement, May 2011, https://www.waterboards.ca.gov/water_issues/programs/enforcement/docs/citizen_suits/citzn_suit_rpt.pdf.
118   California Water Boards Stormwater Multiple Application and Report Tracking System (SMARTS); https://smarts.waterboards.ca.gov/smarts/.

The purpose of this book has been to guide us through the process of connecting the dots of erosion and sediment control, and that is where the real use of the field data generated from inspecting and monitoring construction sites comes to play in making connections. Installing BMPs without having—and using—the data from a monitoring program keeps the dots disconnected. When this happens, we fail to see and understand the cause-and-effect relationship between the construction activities and pollutant sources, the control measures we implement, and the quality of the water that flows off the construction site. Without analyzing and using this data, all of these elements will just remain isolated dots.

There is one last dot that now needs to be connected: project completion. How do we bring the project and soil disturbance to a happy ending from an erosion and sediment control perspective? This final dot is called "stabilization."

CHAPTER 7
Connecting the Dots of Final Site Stabilization

The point of construction is to actually construct (or sometimes deconstruct) something. The planned project will eventually reach its intended state of completion. Ultimate erosion and sediment control is achieved by bringing the project to a stabilized state, which is free of the accelerators we discussed in Chapter 2 (or at least has permanent mitigators in place to offset any ongoing accelerators). This is where we bring the dot-to-dot exercise full circle, connecting the last dot to the first one. As far as water quality is concerned, we want the result to be as if our project never occurred at this location. We do this by implementing the following:

FULL SWPPP IMPLEMENTATION

Nothing illustrates the need to "connect the dots" as much the requirement by NPDES regulatory agencies for a project to have obtained full SWPPP implementation as a prerequisite for terminating permit coverage. This means that a project needs to be verifiably complete. A question posed to me often by contractors is, "*Hey, I'm done with the outside work, can we file the Notice of Termination and get out of the permit?*"

The answer is generally, "No." But it can be a bit of a tricky question to answer. The California Water Board states the following concerning closing out permit coverage.[119]

The Regional Water Board will consider a site, parcel, or individual lot complete **only when all** portions of the site comply with all the following conditions:

  a. The discharger has completed all construction activity;
  b. There is no greater potential for construction-related storm water pollutants to be discharged into site runoff than prior to the construction activity;
  c. Construction-related equipment and temporary BMPs have been removed from the site;
  d. Construction materials and wastes have been disposed of properly;
  e. Soils disturbed by construction activities have been permanently stabilized (final stabilization), using materials that:
      i. Have a product life that support the full and continued stabilization of the site;
      ii. Achieve stabilization without becoming trash or debris; and
      iii. Minimize the risk of wildlife entrapment;

Figure 148 - Ready to submit the Notice of Termination? You might have a hard time convincing the Water Board that the port-a-potty is a permanent feature and not construction related. (Photo credit: Dan Baumbach)

---

119 California Construction General Permit, Order 2022-0057-DWQ, Order, Section III.H.4., https://www.waterboards.ca.gov/water_issues/programs/stormwater/construction/docs/2022-0057-dwq-with-attachments/cgp2022_order.pdf

Connecting the Dots of Final Site Stabilization

Figure 149 - Temporary BMPs, after they have served their purpose, can become trash and an entrapment danger for wildlife. (Photo credit: John Teravskis)

When asked this type of a question, I will point to this section of the CGP and go down the list. Usually we have a hard time getting past the first point: all construction activity has been completed. Now, I suppose there could be a project that still has interior work going on but, from the outside, there is no indication that construction is occurring. There are no longer any dumpsters, port-a-potties, temporary storage bins, or construction-related equipment on the project site, and all areas of soil disturbance have been stabilized with permanent landscaping. For such a project, the NPDES oversight agency might possibly agree that construction is complete. But in my experience, this would be an exception, not the norm.

Temporary erosion and sediment control devices that are not intended by design to remain at the site or be incorporated into the permanent site features need to be removed prior to filing a Notice of Termination (NOT) for ending the permit coverage. In some instances, the control measure is biodegradable, such as burlap wrapped fiber rolls or jute mesh, and can be left in place without becoming a construction-related solid waste. But fiber rolls or erosion control mats having monofilament netting and silt fence should be removed once final stabilization is achieved. Monofilament netting is of a particular concern, because when it is degraded it will break down into microplastics and will also become an entrapment danger for wildlife.

A well-connected SWPPP will describe what a project site should look like starting with the pre-construction conditions, through the grading and earthwork phase, during the vertical construction phase, and all the way to the final stabilization phase. A fully implemented SWPPP will result in a site where the actual conditions match the final stabilization conditions specified in the SWPPP. This means that not only are all of the construction activities completed and construction materials, equipment, and wastes demobilized, but any areas where soil disturbance occurred now have a permanent, effective soil cover in place.

FINAL STABILIZATION

When it comes to obtaining final stabilization, the main objective is to place a permanent effective cover on soils that were disturbed during construction. This, of course, would include impervious surfaces, such as constructed structures, and paved surfaces, such as roadways, parking lots, and sidewalks. Permeable surfaces may be effectively stabilized with vegetation, mulch, or crushed aggregate. On [Table 7 in Chapter 4](), we identified several soil covers that can be utilized to provide stabilization, some of which are permanent control measures. When selecting an effective soil cover (or Raindrop BMP), as site conditions allow, it is often preferable to choose one that may also serve as the ultimate permanent control. This will help minimize the project cost by avoiding the need for a temporary control measure.

Occasionally, we have a project where the contractor or project owner argues that the site was bare soil before construction and, therefore, they should be allowed to leave it as bare soil. That argument will typically not be accepted by the NPDES oversight agency. Usually, they will still require that the disturbed soil be stabilized. However, over the years, we have seen a few exceptions granted. One is for earth disturbing work where, under normal post-project conditions, the site will be inundated or remain under water. We have had river restoration and water reservoir projects where the Water Board did not require stabilization of surfaces for the portion of the project that would be inundated. Another exception to stabilization that we have seen granted is for work that was performed in an agricultural field, such as a pipeline installation project in an agricultural field where the field will continue to be cultivated after the pipeline has been installed and backfilled. Keep in mind that final stabilization does not mean that all nonbuilt areas need to be lush and green. When construction is performed in an arid region, such as the California Mojave Desert, natural conditions are considered when determining adequate final stabilization.

Figure 150 - For locations like this desert terrain, final stabilization will be based on the regional pre-construction conditions. RUSLE2 may also be a resource for demonstrating stabilization for projects in these types of climates and terrain. (Photo credit: John Teravskis)

When it comes to determining what meets the final stabilization, the California Water Board, similar to other NPDES agencies, will accept the following methods:[120]

Seventy percent final cover method. No computational proof is required for this method, but it does require a demonstration that permanent vegetative cover has been evenly established over 70 percent of all disturbed and exposed areas of soil (nonpaved or nonbuilt). In areas that naturally have low vegetative coverage (e.g., deserts), 70 percent of the natural conditions of local undisturbed areas is acceptable. In other words, if the regional natural vegetation is only at 50 percent coverage, calculating 70 percent of 50 percent would mean that the project would need to achieve at least 35 percent vegetative coverage to qualify as

---

120   Ibid.

a sufficiently stabilized site. Photos of all site areas are required to be submitted to verify compliance with the 70 percent final cover requirement.

Or the project proponent may utilize the RUSLE equation (Equation 7) or the RUSLE2 computer modeling tool.

Revised Universal Soil Loss Equation (RUSLE or RUSLE2) method. With this method, computational proof is required. Site conditions need to match values used for the assumptions and values utilized in the method computations. California requires the submission of photos of all site areas to verify pre-construction and post-construction conditions used in the computations. In Chapter 4, we looked at how to use the RUSLE equation to predict soil loss. In order to demonstrate final stabilization, it is necessary to use the equation or the computer modeling tool to show the soil loss for a one-year period for the pre-construction conditions and for a one-year period for the post-construction conditions.

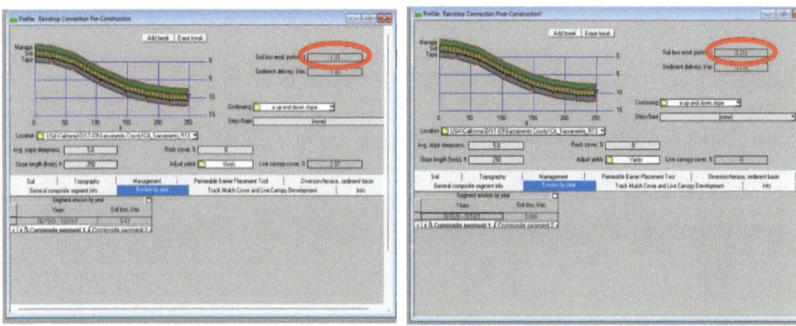

Figure 151 - RUSLE2 can be used to calculate the soil loss for a one-year period before the project started based on pre-project conditions and for a one-year period after the project based on the type of stabilization utilized. If the post-project soil loss is less than that of the pre-project, the site is considered to be stabilized. In the case illustrated here, the pre-project soil loss was 1.33 tons/acre/year and it was reduced to 0.216 tons/acre/year.

POST-CONSTRUCTION STORM WATER CONTROL MEASURES

Managing construction-related storm water runoff quality does not end with the completion of the project. The USEPA and State NPDES agencies implementing the Clean Water Act are concerned about the continuing impact storm water from developed projects has on water bodies and watersheds. According to the California Water Board, urban storm water runoff is listed as the primary source of impairment for ten percent of all rivers, lakes and reservoirs, and seventeen percent of all estuaries in California.[121] While these numbers may not seem significantly large, considering that urban areas cover only six percent of the land mass of California,[122] the impact that runoff from urban areas have on California's surface waters is disproportionally large. When the Water Board uses the term "urbanization," it is referring to the development of land through which the imperviousness percentage increases; meaning that buildings and hardscapes prevent water from infiltrating into the ground, thereby, causing it to flow off of the property.

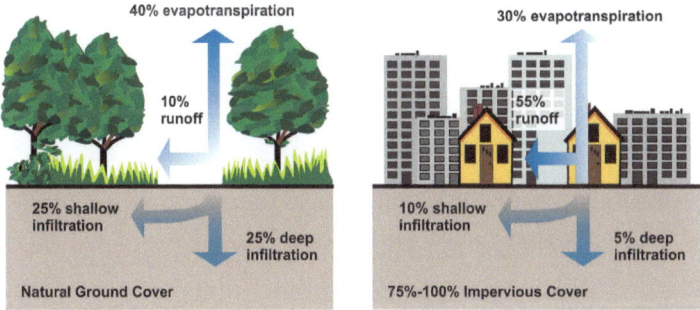

Figure 152 - As development increases in a watershed, the hydrology also changes. With urbanization, runoff is increased and infiltration is decreased. (Source: USEPA)

---

121 Fact Sheet of the Phase II MS4 Permit, Order No. 2013-0001-DWQ, p. 33–34
122 .S. Department of Agriculture, 2009

Increased urbanization through new development and redevelopment has been shown to cause more frequent storm water discharge events, higher peak flow velocities, and larger volumes of storm water runoff. These conditions, if not properly managed, can affect water quality by mobilizing greater and more frequent loads of pollutants, such as sediment, organic material, trash, nutrients, pathogens, heavy metals, and other toxic substances. These conditions also overtax existing natural and man-made drainage systems, causing accelerated erosion of channels and deposition of sediment and pollutants in estuaries, deltas, and basins.

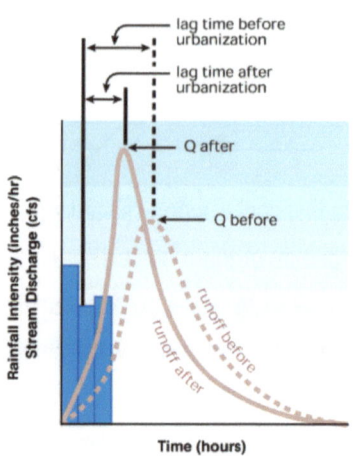

Figure 153 - Increases of impervious surfaces and runoff coefficients in a watershed can have an impact on the streams and waterways downgradient of the watershed. They will see more frequent and larger flows. (Source: USEPA Watershed Academy Web, Stream Corridor Structure)

Conditions such as these could cause flooding and deterioration of waterways that, at one time, may have been adequate to handle expected runoff. This has a direct impact on municipalities by causing them to perform more maintenance on existing systems and to develop new drainage systems with higher capacities. Urbanization and the resulting runoff can also impact the state's ability to realize the full potential of the beneficial uses of its surface waters. Through both the CGP and the municipal NPDES permits, the California Water Board requires project designers to mitigate the negative impact of increases in storm water runoff caused by new development and redevelopment. This is accomplished through the incorporation of Low Impact Development standards and hydromodification management techniques. Low Impact Development (LID) is a method of design that mitigates excessive runoff by the use of evapotranspiration, infiltration, capture and reuse, and/or biotreatment to mimic the runoff characteristics of a natural environment.

Connecting the Dots of Final Site Stabilization

> **Low Impact Development:** A sustainable practice that benefits water supply and contributes to water quality protection. Unlike traditional storm water management, which collects and conveys storm water runoff through storm drains, pipes, or other conveyances to a centralized storm water facility, Low Impact Development (LID) takes a different approach by using site design and storm water management to maintain the site's pre-development runoff rates and volumes. The goal of LID is to mimic a site's predevelopment hydrology by using design techniques that infiltrate, filter, store, evaporate, and detain runoff close to the source of rainfall. LID has been a proven approach in other parts of the country and is seen in California as an alternative to conventional storm water management.
> *Source: California Phase II MS4 NPDES Permit Glossary*

Hydromodification techniques are also incorporated into the design of development sites so that post-construction runoff flow rates do not exceed those of the pre-construction conditions usually for a two-year, twenty-four-hour rain event.

Collectively, the LID and hydromodification techniques are often referred to as post-construction storm water control measures. However, I have always felt that this term is a bit of a misnomer. It is true that these measures are left at the project site after construction is completed, hence the name "post-construction." But what we refer to as post-construction measures actually has far more to do with the pre-construction activities; namely, engineering and design. The design team, including civil engineers, structural architects, and landscape architects, develop a plan to manage water on-site as much as possible. The overall goal of this team is to reduce the quantity of storm water discharged by utilizing site design measures that rely on infiltration, evapotranspiration, bioretention, and capture and reuse techniques. The following are some examples of site design measures used to accomplish this goal at new development or redevelopment projects.

Stream Setbacks and Buffers are vegetated areas (including trees, shrubs, riparian habitat, or natural vegetation) that exist or are established to protect a stream system, lake, reservoir, or estuary. These areas provide a buffer between the development and the waterbody to filter out pollutants carried by storm water, provide stabilization of erodible banks and opportunities to infiltrate water prior to discharging, and help to slow peak flow rates.

Figure 154 - Providing a permanent setback or buffer from a stream is required by the California Construction General Permit during construction but will also have a lasting impact on protecting water quality. (Photo credit: Mike Lewis)

Soil Quality Improvement and Maintenance is accomplished through the addition of soil amendments and the creation of a healthy microbial community. Soils with higher organic content are less likely to erode and also provide nutrients needed to maintain healthy plants. This, in turn, means that landscaping will require less fertilizers and pesticides. Soils with more organic content or covered with a compost layer will retain moisture, requiring them to be irrigated less often. Engineered soils (typically a mixture of composted organic material and sand) provide a growing media for vegetation while still allowing water to infiltrate quickly to be stored below grade in an underlying gravel layer. This provides both LID and hydromodification benefits. The USDA's Natural Resources Conservation Service (NRCS) has a publication titled *Urban Soil Primer* which is an excellent resource in helping developers understand how healthy soils improve water quality. [123]

---

123 Scheyer, J.M., and K.W. Hipple. 2005. Urban Soil Primer. United States Department of Agriculture, Natural Resources Conservation Service, National Soil Survey Center, Lincoln, Nebraska (https://www.nrcs.usda.gov/sites/default/files/2023-01/Urban-Soil-Primer-Homeowners-and-Renters.pdf).

Figure 155 - An excellent way to improve the infiltration and filtering of storm water is to amend soils and to not overcompact areas to be landscaped. (Photo credit: John Teravskis)

Tree Planting and Preservation includes the preservation of existing trees and the establishment of new ones. Both evergreens and deciduous (broad leaf) trees are beneficial to water quality in many ways. Their roots and leaf litter help stabilize and cover erodible soil. The tree canopy intercepts raindrops and dissipates the energy of the falling rain. Roots uptake water and transpire water vapor through the leaves. A study performed by the Center for Watershed Protection[124] found that urban trees play a significant role in reducing runoff. The study showed that, in California, a large deciduous tree could reduce storm water runoff by up to 555 gallons per year and, for a large coniferous evergreen tree, by up to 383 gallons per year. Based on this study and other studies like it, the Water Balance Calculator utilized by the California Water Board on SMARTS and

Figure 156 - Trees play a significant role in reducing and slowing runoff. (Photo credit: John Teravskis)

---

124 Hynicka, J. and D. Caraco. 2017. Relative and Absolute Reductions in Annual Water Yield and Non-Point Source Pollutant Loads of Urban Trees. Crediting Framework Product #2 for the project Making Urban Trees Count: A Project to Demonstrate the Role of Urban Trees in Achieving Regulatory Compliance for Clean Water. Center for Watershed Protection, Ellicott City, MD. https://owl.cwp.org/mdocs-posts/relative-and-absolute-reductions-in-annual-water-yield-and-non-point-source-pollutant-loads-of-urban-trees/?_gl=1*12zi7mw*_ga*MTkyNjc4NDI4MS4xNzEwODYyMzUx*_ga_B5ZWOO3LE3*MTcxMDg2MjM1MS4xLjAuMTcxMDg2MjM1MS4wLjAuMA..

many other municipal post-construction sizing tools provide water quantity reduction credits for new and existing trees planted within the development.

Rooftop and Impervious Area Disconnection is where roof drains and hardscapes do not discharge directly to a storm drain inlet but are directed to permeable areas or rain water collection and harvesting mechanisms. Water, in excess of the permeable area's infiltration and storage capacity or the capacity of the collection/harvesting system, can then be directed to a drainage system. Typically, the disconnected impervious areas are directed to a bioretention cell or storm water garden that has aboveground ponding capacity and a below ground high-infiltration growing media layer placed on a gravel layer for water storage. Often landscaping can serve as storm water treatment devices. In soils having lower infiltration rates (HSG C and D soils), roof drains and impervious area drainage can still be directed to an infiltration device but may also need to have an underdrain to convey water away once the underground storage is saturated.

Figure 157 - By utilizing landscaping, roof drains can be effectively disconnected from drainage systems even in densely developed areas, such as this student housing area at the University of California, Davis. (Photo credit: John Teravskis)

Porous Pavement is pavement that allows runoff to pass through it and infiltrate into the underlying soils. Porous pavement systems are typically designed with a subsurface drainage and storage system that consists of a bed of rock and piped collection system below the porous pavement. Where soils have high infiltration rates, water is allowed to dissipate directly into the native soil. Where infiltration rates are less than desirable, a sub-grade gravity collection system (underdrain) conveys excess water to a storm water outfall or storm water sewer system. Porous pavement includes porous asphalt and concrete, porous pavers and bricks, cobbles, reinforced grass pavement, and gravel covered surfaces.

Figure 158 - Porous pavement, such as this example from Stanford University, is an effective way to manage water by infiltrating it into subterranean gravel layers used for storage and infiltration into native soil. (Photo credit: John Teravskis)

Green Roof is an engineered vegetative layer grown on a roof that allows a certain amount of runoff reduction by infiltration, storage, and evapotranspiration. Green roofs are beautiful to look at and can be an effective way to reduce, slow down, and improve runoff from large impervious surfaces. However, they need to be carefully planned for the region where they will be utilized and maintained for long-term longevity. In 2010, the USEPA published a document titled *Design Guidelines and Maintenance Manual for Green Roofs in the Semi-Arid and Arid West*. [125]

Figure 159 - Shasta County incorporated a green roof on part of a new library complex that was built in Redding, California (a very warm part of the state). After nearly two decades, the green roof is still thriving but has required several maintenance overhauls. (Photo credit: John Teravskis)

---

[125] Design Guidelines and Maintenance Manual for Green Roofs in the Semi-Arid and Arid West by Leila Tolderlund, In collaboration with Green Roofs for Healthy Cities City and County of Denver Environmental Protection Agency Region 8 Urban Drainage and Flood Control District Colorado State University; https://www.epa.gov/sites/default/files/2019-08/documents/greenroofssemiaridaridwest_508.pdf.

Bioretention Cells, Bio Swales, and Vegetated Swales are vegetated open conveyances or storm water retention areas that have been designed specifically to treat and reduce storm water runoff through infiltration, biotreatment, and evapotranspiration. This type of treatment often includes a certain amount of aboveground ponding capacity with belowground storage and infiltration capabilities. Planting media should consist of engineered soils with a significant percentage of organic material and sandy soil to allow rapid flow through of water from the surface to the subgrade gravel storage zone. These devices may be utilized where native soil has low infiltration rates as long as an underdrain is placed at the top of the subgrade gravel layer.

Figure 160 - Bioretention cells and swales come in all sizes and shapes that can range from this small parking lot island version to large retention basin-sized cells. (Photo credit: John Teravskis)

Infiltration Trenches are underground storage and infiltration devices. They work well where soils have moderate to high infiltration rates. Excavations filled with rock or oversized pipe can provide subgrade storage of runoff and the infiltration interface with native soils. Many times these systems are used in lieu of a connection to a municipal drainage system or where there are no available municipal systems to tie into. They can range in size from small trenches along borders of sidewalks or landscaping to very large systems that can accommodate runoff from the entire site.

Figure 161 - When aboveground real estate is needed for other purposes, storm water runoff can be dissipated belowground using an infiltration trench or vault. (Photo credit: John Teravskis)

Rain Barrels and Cisterns are a vital part of a system that collects and stores storm water runoff from a roof or other impervious surfaces. Collected water is saved and reused for irrigation or other purposes. According to the USEPA,[126] rainwater reuse offers a number of benefits.

- Provides inexpensive supply of water;
- Augments drinking water supplies;
- Reduces storm water runoff and pollution;
- Reduces erosion in urban environments;
- *Provides water that needs little treatment for irrigation or non-potable indoor uses; and*
- Helps reduce peak summer demands.

Rainwater collection systems usually capture runoff from roofs since this water is generally cleaner than water from other impervious surfaces. The captured water is then stored in an aboveground or belowground tank or cistern until it is needed for the site's water demands. Without an additional purification system,

---

126   Kloss, Christopher, United States Environmental Protection Agency, EPA-833-F-08-010, Managing Wet Weather with Green Infrastructure Municipal Handbook – Rainwater Harvesting Policies, December 2008; https://nepis.epa.gov/

the stored water can only be used where non-potable water is tolerated (such as landscape irrigation).

Figure 162 - A storm water collection and reuse demonstration project at the U.C. Davis Robert Mondavi Institute for Wine and Food Science. (Photo credit: John Teravskis)

Retention Basins are perhaps the most common form of LID and hydromodification storm water control and treatment. They are particularly common in locations where a municipal drainage system is not present, such as in unincorporated county areas. Municipalities will condition such projects with a retention basin for flood control. Usually the basin sizing criteria for flood control (a 100-year+ storm event) far exceeds the storm water LID treatment criteria (typically a 2-year storm event). Because of vector control concerns, the municipality will typically require that the volume from the design storm be dissipated via infiltration and evaporation within 72 hours. One drawback to retention basins is they can require a significant amount of real estate that is utilized only for storm water storage and infiltration.

Figure 163 - Retention basins serve dual purposes: flood control and storm water treatment. (Photo credit: Mike Lewis)

Connecting the Dots of Final Site Stabilization

New development and redevelopment projects are typically conditioned with post-construction measures by the local municipality during the plan check and building permitting process. However, in California, some projects will occur outside of the municipality's permitted boundary for their municipal NPDES permit. These projects, not being conditioned by the municipality for post-construction measures, will need to comply with the California State Water Board's post-construction requirements if the project is subject to the Construction General Permit. This means that the project will need to utilize control measures to replicate the pre-construction water balance for the smallest storms up to and including the 85th percentile, 24-hour precipitation event.[127] An 85th percentile, 24-hour precipitation event is a statistical rainfall volume that is defined as a value where 85% of all of the observed historic 24-hour rainfall totals are less than that volume. Included on the Water Board's SMARTS[128] online CGP permitting website is a Water Balance Calculator that the project proponent will need to populate to demonstrate they have replicated the pre-construction water balance. In addition to this requirement, to address hydromodification, the Water Board requires that projects having a disturbed area exceeding two acres must be designed so that the post-project runoff time of concentration is equal to or greater than the pre-project time of concentration. You might review Equation 5 in Chapter 5 where we learned how to calculate the time of concentration.

Just as erosion and sediment control BMPs require maintenance to keep them effective, so do the permanent post-construction storm water treatment control measures. The State Water Board or the permitting municipal agencies require the project owner to submit a long-term operation and maintenance plan and signed agreement. This is to ensure that the installed treatment devices (i.e., bioretention

---

127   California CGP, Order 2022-0057-DWQ, Section IV.N., https://www.waterboards.ca.gov/water_issues/programs/stormwater/construction/docs/2022-0057-dwq-with-attachments/cgp2022_order.pdf

128   lifornia Water Boards Stormwater Multiple Application and Report Tracking System (SMARTS); https://smarts.waterboards.ca.gov/smarts/

cell or permeable pavement) will be periodically inspected to assure they are functioning as designed and that the routine preventative maintenance is being performed. If it is found that a treatment device is not functioning as designed, the owner is then obligated by the signed agreement to repair and restore the system to an operable condition. These agreements are to be transferred to subsequent property owners, and often the municipality requires the signed agreement to be recorded with the property deed by the County Clerk.

PERMIT TERMINATION

In the State of California, the Notice of Termination (NOT) process begins with a site visit by the QSP to assure that the project is indeed completed. The QSP then prepares and uploads onto SMARTS a report that, through maps and photographs, shows construction to be completed, construction materials and wastes demobilized, areas of soil disturbance sufficiently stabilized, and post-construction storm water treatment measures installed. The Water Board will also require a long-term maintenance plan for the post-construction measures to be uploaded onto SMARTS. Before the NOT can be certified on SMARTS by the Legally Responsible Person (LRP), if it has been more than three months since the last reported project period, another annual report will need to be prepared on SMARTS and certified by the LRP. The local Regional Water Quality Control Board will review the submitted NOT documentation and, quite often, will also inspect the site before taking action on the NOT. The NOT will then be either returned (rejected)

Figure 164 - Photographs will be required to demonstrate that construction is completed and areas of soil disturbance are stabilized. (Photo credit: John Teravskis)

or accepted. If it is returned, there will be an explanation as to why it was not accepted, which will usually require the submission of additional documentation or for the site to achieve a greater level of permanent stabilization.

Then comes the day when the closure requirements have all been met and you finally receive an email as shown in Figure 165. What an amazing day! Congratulations are in order, because you have connected the last dots of erosion and sediment control for the project and have brought the raindrop connection to a successful ending. You can now relax and take in the scene for a job well done in achieving a stabilized and protected project site—at least, until the dots need to be connected on the next project.

Figure 165 - Nothing makes your day quite like receiving an email like this! Congratulations! You are done with the project and have connected the last dots of the raindrop connection.

CHAPTER 8
Closing Summary

We opened this book by asking the question, "Why does it matter that we connect the dots of erosion and sediment, as well as pollutant control?" The answer is water! In particular, water quality. You did not need to read this book to know that we all depend upon water for life itself. From what we drink, to what we use to grow food, bathe, wash and clean, and provide a sanitary and healthy environment, clean water is absolutely essential.

Figure 166 - To help keep all of the state and federal storm water regulations in perspective, I have this photo hanging up in my office with the words "What happens to countries with no environmental regulations." This photo is of the Urubamba River and was taken in 2019 by a friend who was traveling through Aguas Calientes, Peru. (Photo credit: Brandon Alexander)

We are all sometimes guilty of just going through the motions. After all, the cookbook approach to life is the easiest. Do this, do that, and do this, and voila! Success! As we have pointed out in this book, many have taken this approach to storm water quality and have, perhaps inadvertently, fallen into a formulaic approach to controlling erosion, sedimentation, and pollutants in storm water runoff. While this is certainly (in most cases) better than no approach at all, it can lead the storm water professional to frustrating and ineffectual outcomes on a construction project.

It is our hope that this book challenged you to consciously think through the various dots to be connected and provided the tools needed to devise a systematic and concerted plan for a project site. Our goal is for you to now be able to make the connection between theory and practice. The connection of permit compliance to sound best management practices. The computer screen to the subdivision lot. Budget line items to what is actually installed and maintained. The actions we do to the water quality we observe. And the connection of the start of the project to its final completion by:

- Connecting the dots of erosion and sediment theory;
- Connecting the dots of pollutant source assessment;
- Connecting the dots of best management practices;
- Connecting the dots of SWPPP development;
- Connecting the dots of an effective monitoring program; and
- Connecting the dots of final site stabilization.

Closing Summary

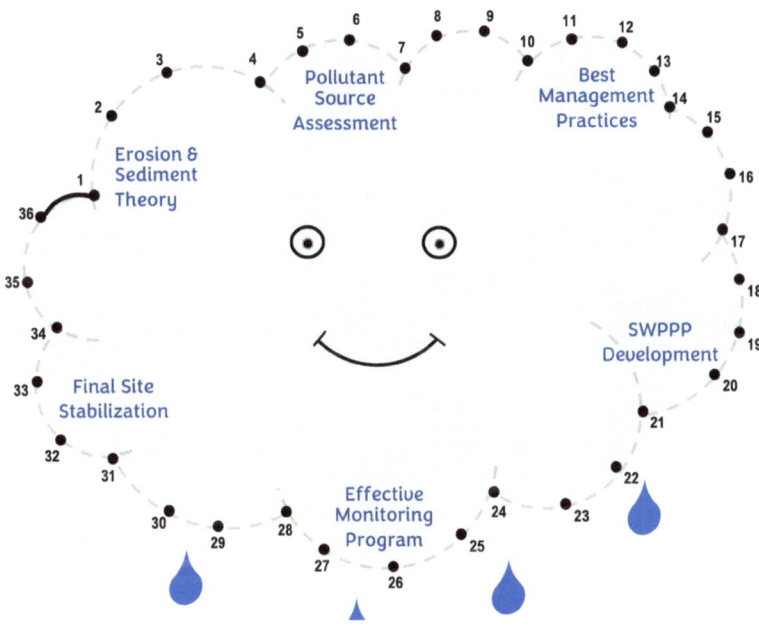

Figure 167: The raindrop connection involves drawing lines of logic between theory and practice, between the conceptual and practical, and between the start of the project and final site stabilization.

List of Acronyms [129]

ASBS	Area of Special Biological Significance
AST	Aboveground Storage Tank
ATS	Active Treatment System
BAT	Best Available Technology Economically Achievable
BCT	Best Conventional Pollutant Control Technology
BFM	Bonded Fiber Matrix
BMP	Best Management Practice
BOD	Biological Oxygen Demand
Cal/OSHA	State of California Division of Occupational Safety and Health (DOSH)
CASQA	California Stormwater Quality Association
CBPELSG	California Board of Professional Engineers, Land Surveyors and Geologists
CEQA	California Environmental Quality Act
CESSWI	Certified Erosion, Sediment, and Storm Water Inspector
CFR	Code of Federal Regulations
CFS	Cubic Feet Per Second
CGP	Construction General Permit
CISEC	Certified Inspector of Sediment and Erosion Control
COD	Chemical Oxygen Demand
COI	Change-of-Information
CPESC	Certified Professional in Erosion and Sediment Control
CTR	California Toxics Rule

---

[129] Adapted from the California Construction General Permit, Order WQ 2022-0057-DWQ, Attachment A.

CWA	Clean Water Act
DAR	Duly Authorized Representative
DI	Drain Inlet
DMA	Drainage Management Area
DO	Dissolved Oxygen
ECTC	Erosion Control Technology Council
ESA	Environmentally Sensitive Area
ESCP	Erosion and Sediment Control Plan
FGM	Flexible Growth Media
GPM	Gallons Per Minute
HECP	Hydraulic Erosion Control Product
HSG	Hydrologic Soil Group
HUC	Hydrologic Unit Code
HVAC	Heating, Venting, and Air Conditioning
LID	Low Impact Development
LRP	Legally Responsible Person
LUP	Linear Underground and Overhead Projects
MDL	Method Detection Limit
MS4	Municipal Separate Storm Water Sewer System
MUSLE	Modified Universal Soil Loss Equation
NAL	Numeric Action Level
NEL	Numeric Effluent Level
NEPA	National Environmental Policy Act
NOAA	National Oceanic and Atmospheric Administration
NOI	Notice of Intent
NONA	Notice of Non-Applicability
NOT	Notice of Termination
NPDES	National Pollutant Discharge Elimination System
NRCS	Natural Resources Conservation Services, a division of the USDA

Closing Summary

NTU	Nephelometric Turbidity Units
O&M	Operation and Maintenance
PAM	Polyacrylamide
PCB	Polychlorinated Biphenyl
PE	Professional Engineer
PG	Professional Geologist
PoP	Probability of Precipitation
POTW	Publicly Owned Treatment Works
PPE	Personal Protective Equipment
PRD	Permit Registration Document
QA/QC	Quality Assurance / Quality Control
QPE	Qualifying Precipitation Event
QSD	Qualified SWPPP Developer
QSP	Qualified SWPPP Practitioner
RECP	Rolled Erosion Control Product
RWQCB	State of California Regional Water Quality Control Board
RUSLE	Revised Universal Soil Loss Equation
SC	Specific Conductivity
SDS	Safety Data Sheet
SMARTS	State of California Storm Water Multiple Application and Report Tracking System
SOP	Standard Operation Procedure
SVOC	Semi-Volatile Organic Compound
SWPPP	Storm Water Pollution Prevention Plan
TDS	Total Dissolved Solids
TMDL	Total Maximum Daily Load
ToR	California QSP/QSD Trainer of Record
TSS	Total Suspended Solids
USACE	United States Army Corps of Engineers

USDA	United States Department of Agriculture
USEPA	United States Environmental Protection Agency
VOC	Volatile Organic Compound
WDID	Waste Discharge Identification (California NPDES Permit Coverage Number)
WEQ	Wind Erosion Equation
WET	Whole Effluent Toxicity
WOTUS	Waters of the United States
WPCM	Water Pollution Control Manager
WPCP	Water Pollution Control Plan

Index

A

accelerators *12, 32, 47*
agents *12, 32, 42*

B

BMP (Best Management Practice) *73, 78, 79, 81, 82, 83, 84, 87, 88, 104, 105, 106, 108, 110, 114, 116, 117, 142, 143, 144, 146, 147, 149, 150, 151, 154, 156, 160, 164, 166, 171, 172, 190, 204, 207, 208, 217, 218, 223, 225, 226, 227, 257, 267, 269, 280, 315, 316, 318, 334, 339, 343, 347, 353, 358*
    active Treatment *10, 32, 138, 139, 140, 141, 162, 163, 165, 169, 171, 172, 173, 175, 180, 183*
    active treatment system *186*
    bioretention *10, 32, 138, 139, 140, 141, 162, 163, 165, 169, 171, 172, 173, 175, 180, 183*
    check dams *10, 32, 138, 139, 140, 141, 162, 163, 165, 169, 171, 172, 173, 175, 180, 183*
    compost blanket *10, 32, 138, 139, 140, 141, 162, 163, 165, 169, 171, 172, 173, 175, 180, 183*
    compost socks *85, 141, 142, 144, 145, 150, 154, 166, 167, 168, 169, 180, 181, 182, 183, 188, 193, 194, 195, 196, 197, 198*
    curb cutback *142, 143, 151*
    detention pond *175, 176*
    DI protection *164, 165, 168*
    drain inlet protection *11, 77, 82, 169, 180, 182*
    erosion control blankets *82, 118*
    fat spot *204*
    fiber roll *3, 4, 11, 19, 51, 78, 82, 85, 106, 140, 141, 142, 143, 144, 146, 147, 148, 149, 150, 151, 152, 154, 162, 167, 207, 261, 262, 269*
    geotextile fabric *178, 187*
    gravel bag berms *145*
    gravel bags *77, 87, 124, 166, 167, 168, 169*
    hydraulic mulch *19, 82, 85, 87, 122, 135, 144, 199, 203, 226, 280*
    hydroseed *19, 226*
    jute mesh *78, 202, 357*
    linear sediment controls *19, 85*

PAM (polyacrylamide) *126, 128, 195, 197, 201, 202, 203, 307*
passive treatment *195, 200, 201, 203, 204, 205, 317*
perimeter controls *143, 144, 162*
pine duff *130, 135, 197*
riprap *124, 160, 169, 178*
sandbags *124, 156, 197*
silt fence *4, 10, 11, 28, 51, 86, 141, 144, 145, 146, 150, 162, 166, 262, 269, 336, 345, 346, 347, 357*
slow the flow *10, 32, 138, 139, 140, 141, 162, 163, 165, 169, 171, 172, 173, 175, 180, 183*
soil binder *126, 137, 203*
speed bump *156, 163, 164, 172*
straw *4, 122, 126, 128, 140, 142, 147, 152, 280, 310*
street sweeping *187, 189, 192*
track-out control *81, 82, 185, 186, 187, 188, 192, 334*
track walking *30, 170, 171, 172, 309*
treatment train *193, 194, 195, 196, 197, 204, 205*
velocity dissipators *205*
wood mulch *38, 130, 154, 194, 195, 196*

C

Caltrans *73, 78, 79, 80, 81, 87, 143, 147, 150, 187, 190, 216, 218, 219, 220, 221, 223, 256, 297*
CASQA (California Stormwater Quality Association) *73, 81, 216, 217, 218, 223, 224, 254, 255, 256, 328*
CGP (California General Permit) *5, 8, 76, 77, 212, 214, 215, 216, 217, 220, 221, 222, 223, 226, 227, 228, 234, 240, 242, 244, 248, 255, 266, 279, 300, 304, 311, 312, 328, 329, 330, 331, 332, 339, 345, 347, 348, 349, 352, 353, 357, 362, 371*
climate *88, 93*

D

detached *286, 308*
de-watering *199, 204, 205, 206, 224, 227, 348*
DI (drain inlet) *164, 165, 166, 167, 168, 325*
discharge *32, 100, 151, 156, 164, 166, 232, 234, 238, 240, 242, 244, 246, 252, 289, 290, 322, 325, 326*
dissolved oxygen *49, 59*
disturbed soil *118, 310, 358*
DMA (Drainage Management Area) *271, 272, 273, 284*
Dust Bowl *94*

Index

E

equipment
heavy *13, 35*
erodibility *93*
erosion *12, 31, 32, 33, 47, 92, 94, 98, 104, 122, 124, 126, 128, 130, 132, 152, 156, 158, 160, 164, 227, 230, 232, 236, 240, 242, 246, 252, 305, 308, 323*
    channel *21, 22, 156, 173, 178, 322*
    gully *20, 21, 162*
    movement *9, 14, 29, 31, 162, 197, 200, 275*
    raindrop *15, 16, 17, 18, 19, 23, 47, 115, 116, 117, 118, 119, 120, 126, 130, 132, 137, 139, 171, 173, 200, 298, 305, 310, 316, 319, 373*
    rill *18, 19, 139, 145, 146, 152, 162, 298, 310*
    sheet *17, 18, 19, 57, 139, 143, 146, 147, 150, 156, 162, 171, 214, 259, 264, 266, 269, 272, 298, 303, 304, 310, 322, 326, 350, 351*
    temporary erosion control *94, 117, 132, 186*
    wind erosion *22, 23, 24, 25, 26, 27, 29, 92, 94, 98, 102, 116, 118, 137, 189, 300, 332*
        saltation *22, 23, 24, 27, 28, 93*
        soil creep *22, 24, 27, 93*
        suspension *22, 25, 27, 30, 51, 52, 93, 100, 141, 186, 194, 198, 203*
erosion control measures *29, 31, 98, 117, 118, 120, 126, 128, 132, 158, 172, 186, 232, 305, 310*

G

groundwater *49, 50, 53, 69, 74, 89, 204, 205, 206, 276*

J

Junior Raindrop *14*

L

LRP (Legally Responsible Person) *209, 317, 337, 372*

M

Microplastics *43, 124, 189*
municipal *v, 2, 68, 76, 77, 137, 184, 205, 223, 226, 327, 330, 362, 366, 368, 370, 371*

N

non-storm water *13, 29, 31, 32, 44, 89, 104, 204, 227, 319, 332, 334*
NOT (Notice of Termination) *166, 357, 372, 380*
NPDES (National Pollutant Discharge Elimination System) *v, xiv, 3, 6, 75, 76, 77, 81, 199, 200, 204, 205, 206, 211, 212, 216, 227, 228, 229, 234, 236, 238, 240, 242, 244, 248, 297, 312, 327, 328, 329, 330, 332, 336, 337, 338, 353, 355, 357, 358, 359, 361, 362, 363, 371*

P

particles *8, 9, 10, 11, 14, 17, 18, 20, 23, 24, 25, 27, 29, 30, 31, 35, 36, 37, 38, 39, 40, 41, 42, 45, 50, 51, 53, 66, 92, 93, 96, 98, 100, 115, 126, 134, 137, 138, 139, 140, 141, 142, 164, 168, 175, 180, 189, 190, 191, 194, 195, 198, 200, 201, 202, 203, 205, 273, 296, 297, 308, 310, 342, 343*
pH *5, 35, 36, 37, 38, 39, 41, 44, 49, 52, 53, 57, 58, 59, 62, 64, 69, 75, 126, 130, 132, 193, 194, 196, 205, 206, 319, 321, 330, 339, 340, 341, 342, 347, 348, 350, 352*
phases of construction *61*
pollutant *6, 32, 33, 43, 44, 45, 47, 48, 55, 56, 57, 60, 61, 66, 67, 68, 69, 71, 72, 73, 74, 77, 82, 88, 98, 126, 154, 160, 189, 190, 210, 211, 262, 318, 331, 334, 339, 343, 344, 345, 352, 353, 354, 365, 375, 376*
post-construction *30, 124, 227, 266, 269, 270, 271, 272, 284, 288, 316, 360, 363, 366, 371, 372*
POTW (publicaly owned treatment works) *205, 206*

Q

QSD (Qualified SWPPP Developer) *iii, 4, 5, 232, 254, 255, 256, 281, 317, 328*
QSP (Qualified Stormwater Professional) *iii, 4, 5, 8, 108, 254, 255, 256, 317, 328, 372*

R

raindrop *15, 16, 17, 18, 19, 23, 47, 115, 116, 117, 118, 119, 120, 126, 130, 132, 137, 139, 171, 173, 200, 298, 305, 310, 316, 319, 373*
rain event *46, 60, 86, 87, 89, 124, 138, 184, 349, 350, 363*
Regional Water Quality Control Board *4, 71, 206, 226, 372*
runoff *3, 9, 20, 43, 44, 47, 48, 50, 53, 67, 68, 69, 71, 74, 78, 83, 87, 100, 115, 124, 126, 128, 130, 132, 134, 136, 138, 142, 144, 145, 146, 154, 156, 158, 160, 162, 163, 164, 169, 170, 174, 175, 176, 180, 181, 184, 188, 194, 197, 200, 209, 258, 270, 271, 272, 274, 275, 284, 285, 288, 289, 290, 291, 292, 293, 295, 297, 298, 309, 321, 322, 323, 327, 334, 338, 339, 340, 343, 345, 346, 347, 348, 356, 361, 362, 363, 365, 366, 367, 368, 369, 371, 376*
run-on *13, 18, 189, 260, 313, 321, 322, 323, 324, 347*

Index

RUSLE (Revised Universal Soil Loss Equation) *134, 297, 298, 303, 305, 306, 308, 309, 310, 311, 339, 360*

S

sediment *2, 4, 6, 7, 9, 10, 11, 17, 18, 19, 20, 22, 30, 31, 32, 33, 45, 49, 50, 51, 52, 54, 74, 75, 77, 82, 83, 84, 85, 87, 92, 104, 111, 115, 116, 124, 132, 135, 138, 139, 140, 141, 145, 146, 147, 149, 150, 151, 152, 154, 156, 160, 164, 165, 168, 169, 171, 172, 173, 174, 175, 176, 180, 182, 183, 184, 185, 186, 187, 188, 189, 190, 191, 192, 194, 195, 196, 199, 200, 201, 202, 203, 204, 205, 206, 207, 210, 218, 224, 226, 230, 232, 236, 242, 246, 252, 255, 260, 261, 262, 271, 272, 273, 297, 311, 317, 319, 323, 328, 329, 330, 331, 333, 334, 335, 336, 343, 346, 354, 355, 357, 362, 371, 373, 375, 376*
sedimentation *2, 4, 7, 8, 9, 10, 11, 45, 52, 54, 73, 109, 115, 138, 139, 141, 162, 163, 169, 172, 173, 174, 175, 203, 204, 207, 209, 219, 254, 270, 308, 332, 335, 375*
sediment load *146, 152, 164, 172, 174, 195, 200, 262*
slope *17, 18, 19, 20, 50, 122, 124, 126, 128, 130, 132, 134, 135, 139, 143, 144, 145, 146, 147, 152, 154, 156, 158, 162, 169, 170, 171, 172, 173, 188, 195, 259, 269, 284, 285, 288, 289, 290, 292, 298, 303, 304, 307, 309, 310, 345*
slow the flow *10, 32, 138, 139, 140, 141, 162, 163, 165, 169, 171, 172, 173, 175, 180, 183*
soil disturbance *13, 41, 45, 117, 122, 124, 126, 128, 137, 139, 154, 192, 221, 257, 279, 284, 297, 299, 312, 334, 354, 357, 358, 372*
soil loss *1, 2, 18, 20, 24, 25, 26, 29, 92, 134, 137, 146, 160, 176, 177, 211, 259, 296, 297, 298, 299, 303, 305, 307, 308, 309, 310, 360*
speed bumps *164*
stabilization *6, 41, 61, 79, 87, 120, 122, 124, 126, 130, 132, 137, 156, 172, 224, 227, 297, 299, 305, 312, 316, 354, 356, 357, 358, 359, 360, 364, 373, 376*
stockpile *11, 13, 38, 39, 62, 91, 94, 111, 124, 130, 334*
storm event *10, 11, 113, 114, 189, 200, 294, 331, 332, 335, 336, 344, 370*
storm water *v, xiii, xiv, 3, 5, 7, 10, 13, 29, 30, 31, 32, 33, 43, 44, 45, 47, 48, 51, 52, 53, 56, 57, 58, 59, 60, 61, 66, 67, 68, 69, 71, 72, 74, 76, 77, 78, 84, 88, 89, 90, 91, 96, 100, 103, 104, 105, 106, 109, 110, 111, 112, 113, 114, 116, 117, 124, 126, 128, 130, 132, 139, 140, 146, 151, 152, 160, 163, 168, 169, 172, 174, 175, 176, 178, 180, 181, 184, 188, 192, 193, 194, 195, 199, 200, 202, 204, 205, 209, 210, 217, 218, 223, 226, 227, 230, 240, 242, 254, 255, 256, 258, 266, 270, 271, 272, 284, 288, 289, 296, 297, 305, 316, 317, 319, 321, 323, 327, 328, 329, 331, 332, 334, 338, 340, 341, 343, 345, 346, 349, 356, 361, 362, 363, 364, 365, 366, 367, 368, 369, 370, 371, 372, 375, 376, 377*
SWPPP (Storm Water Pollution Prevention Plan) *xi, 3, 4, 6, 7, 8, 14, 30, 33, 61, 67, 68, 73, 74, 78, 79, 81, 82, 84, 85, 86, 88, 103, 104, 105, 108, 109, 110, 111, 112, 113, 114, 141, 145, 209, 210, 211, 212, 214, 215, 216, 217, 218, 219, 220, 221, 222, 223, 224, 225, 226, 227, 228, 229, 230, 232, 238, 242, 248, 250, 254, 256, 257, 258, 263, 264, 265, 266, 267, 268, 269, 270, 271, 272, 273, 276, 277, 279, 280, 281, 282, 283, 284, 285, 289, 296, 300, 301, 312, 313, 314, 315, 316, 317, 318, 319, 321, 322, 323, 327, 328, 330, 331, 337, 344, 350, 355, 358, 376,*

T

TMDL (Total Maximum Daily Load) *70, 71, 72, 262, 344, 345, 350*
topsoil *13, 17, 136*
total suspended solids *189*
track-out *11, 31, 45, 81, 82, 185, 186, 187, 188, 189, 192, 334*
turbidity *5, 54, 68, 100, 132, 141, 149, 183, 193, 194, 196, 199, 311, 319, 330, 339, 342, 343, 346, 347, 348, 352*

U

USEPA (United States Environmental Protection Agency) *1, 3, 6, 53, 55, 71, 75, 76, 77, 154, 205, 216, 293, 297, 298, 299, 300, 306, 341, 344, 361, 362, 367, 369*

V

velocity *9, 15, 29, 50, 124, 138, 140, 141, 156, 163, 169, 171, 173, 176, 177, 178, 195, 199, 204, 205, 206*

The Raindrop Connection Resources

To access updated tables and to download a copy of WGR's construction SWPPP template go to WGR's Raindrop Connection Resource Webpage at:

https://wgr-sw.com/TheRaindropConnection/

 The author, **John Teravskis**, has more than 30 years of experience in the environmental field and specializes in storm water regulatory compliance and erosion and sediment control. He holds the certifications of a Qualified SWPPP Practitioner (QSP) and Qualified SWPPP Developer (QSD), a Certified Professional in Erosion and Sediment Control (CPESC), a Certified Erosion, Sediment, and Storm Water Inspector (CESSWI), a Qualified Industrial SWPPP Practitioner (QISP), and a Caltrans approved Water Pollution Control Manager. He has prepared Storm Water Pollution Prevention Plans (SWPPPs) for dozens of residential, commercial, industrial, roadway, and utility projects. In addition, John has provided the State of California, local counties and municipalities, farmers, and the National Parks Service support with erosion and sediment control for post-wildfire response, restoration projects, and sustainable management of soils and other natural resources.

WGR Southwest, Inc. (WGR), with John Teravskis as their Director of Storm Water Services program, has been an authorized Trainer of Record (ToR) for both industrial and construction storm water certifications in California since 2010. As such, WGR has successfully trained over 1,500 applicants for the State's QSP, QSD, and QISP certifica-tions.

WGR with John Teravskis as the Editor-in-Chief, publishes a monthly newsletter, called *The Monthly Dirt*, which focuses on helping people better understand and comply with the California Construction General Permit. It has a circulation of over 20,000 people.

WGR Southwest, Inc. was also previously hired by the California Office of Water Programs to develop the training platform and assist in the development of curriculum for the State Water Board's QISP certification program.

www.ingramcontent.com/pod-product-compliance
Lightning Source LLC
Chambersburg PA
CBHW040933030426
42337CB00001B/1